HISTORY OF THE

RAF

HISTORY OF THE RAF

RAF

Chaz Bowyer

Hamlyn

London · New York · Sydney · Toronto

A Bison Book

To My Son Jeff

This book was designed and produced by
Bison Books Limited
4 Cromwell Place, London SW7

Published by
The Hamlyn Publishing Group Limited
London · New York · Sydney · Toronto
Astronaut House, Hounslow Road
Feltham, Middlesex

ISBN: 0-600-37588-9

Printed in Hong Kong by
Leefung-Asco Printers Limited

Contents

Introduction

The Royal Air Force was 'born' on April 1, 1918 by an amalgamation of the Royal Flying Corps and the Royal Naval Air Service. On that date its members were embroiled in a critical stage of the greatest war in man's long history; and, indeed, since its inception, the RAF has rarely been able to claim an entirely non-operational period of service. Thus it will be patently obvious to any student of aviation history that to attempt to describe almost 60 years of virtually constant operational employment of the RAF within the necessary confines of a single volume is an impossible task. Instead I have set out to describe the roots, birth, and general progress of Britain's Third Service from 1912 to the present day in broad terms, a panoramic account which might be considered useful as a skeletal frame on which might be added the flesh and sinews of historical detail already available in a host of published works, the cream of which is in the bibliographical appendix.

The history of the RAF is essentially a record of men and machines, but predominantly it is a saga of men and the unconquerable human spirit. Even the most advanced aircraft design remains a superbly sophisticated concoction of computerised metallurgy until a human being presses the first button, or flips the first switch. Accordingly, this history is mainly one of men, of their deeds, their courage, their foresight, and – above all – their sacrifices. It is also, though incidentally, a record of triumph over many obstacles, not the least of which are those imposed by faceless bureaucrats and politicians attempting to balance safety of the realm with an auditor's neat columns. It is essentially a story of youth, as indeed any Service history must be, just as long as the human race continues to countenance each generation's splendid youth sacrificing its birthright to preserve old men's shallow pride and nationalistic arrogance. It is a well-worn cliché but nevertheless wholly true that 'Old men make wars – young men fight them'. Age cannot necessarily be equated with greater wisdom, only greater experience. That every generation refuses to learn from the bitter experience of its predecessor is

Right: Aerial view of the awesome destruction of Cologne, Apr 1945 – a microcosm of the devastation wrought by the Allied bomber crews across Germany. Below: The Fairey Swordfish was an antiquated plane, but she served with distinction throughout World War II.

Hawker Fury I

Engine: Rolls-Royce Kestrel IIS,
525hp
Max Speed: 207mph at 14,000ft
Range: 305 miles
Service Ceiling: 28,000ft
Armament: Two fixed, synchronised
.303 Vickers mg
Weights: Empty 2623lb; Loaded
3490lb

Bristol F2b

Engine: 280hp Rolls-Royce Falcon III
Max Speed: 125mph at sea level
108mph at 13,000ft
Service Ceiling: 20,000ft
Endurance: 3 hrs
Armament: One fixed .303 Vickers
mg forward
One Scarff Ring mounted .303 Lewis
mg rear (often two)
Two 112lb bombs under wings
Weights: Empty 1745lb; Loaded
2590lb

Sopwith F.1 Camel

Engine: 130hp Clerget rotary or,
110hp Le Rhone rotary.
Max Speed: 105mph at 10,000ft
Endurance: $2\frac{1}{2}$ hrs
Service Ceiling: 18,500ft
Armament: Two fixed, synchronised
.303 Vickers mg forward
Could be fitted with four—25lb Hales
bombs under fuselage
Weights: Empty 962lb; Loaded 1482lb
Cost: Airframe (less engine, guns,
instruments), £874.10.0d
Engine, £907.10.0d

a tragedy in human affairs; but that old men in positions of power and authority refuse to benefit from their own experience and deliberately commit young men and women to paying with their lives for such folly, is little short of criminal.

One thing this book is *not* is any form of glorification of war. Rather it is intended to record in broad terms the background, actions and circumstances in which a particular section of Britain's defences served its country over a period of six decades. Like his brothers-in-arms in the Army and Navy, the professional airman of the RAF has tended to be taken for granted by his paymaster, the ordinary British tax-paying citizen except in times of national emergency. Then, like Kipling's Tommy Atkins, '. . . it's "Thin red line of 'eroes" when

the drums begin to roll . . .' The regular-serving airman accepts his status (or lack of it) philosophically and quietly, patiently continues to give of his best, and when war comes, as it is hoped this account will illustrate, exemplifies the hackneyed military phrase 'Devotion to Duty' in superlative manner. In the British national characteristic made of deliberate understatement, such men are the first to deny any outstanding qualities; burying a deep, genuine embarrassment when showered with fulsome praise in an outward armour of nonchalance and quick humour.

Now, on the eve of celebrating its Diamond Jubilee, the Royal Air Force remains Britain's premier line of defence and offence should any would-be aggressor choose to pick up the traces of past candidates for world domination. In

keeping with an ever-changing world situation, it is no longer simply an esoteric national safeguard, but an integral section of the western powers' armoury against any threat to national freedom. Despite such partnership status, the Royal Air Force remains the only air service in the world not to include its country's name in its title – perhaps a legacy of the national conceit which prevailed at the moment of its inauguration, or possibly in deference to the fact that it was the first independent (of army or navy) air service in the world. It is a mark of its international status that few people even today are in any doubt as to its country of origin when reference is made to 'the Royal Air Force' . . .

Chaz Bowyer
Norwich, 1977

*Above: Cap badges of the RFC (left),
RNAS (centre) and the RAF.
Below: Spitfire F.21's of 600 Sqn,
based at Biggin Hill, circa 1948*

Genesis

'In the case of a European war, between two countries, both sides would be equipped with large corps of aeroplanes, each trying to obtain information of the other, and to hide his own movements. The efforts which each would exert in order to hinder or prevent the enemy from obtaining information . . . would lead to the inevitable result of a war in the air, for the supremacy of the air, by armed aeroplanes against each other. This fight for supremacy of the air in future wars will be of the first and greatest importance, and when it has been won the land and sea forces of the loser will be at such a disadvantage that the war will certainly have to terminate at a much smaller loss in men and money to both sides.' This unambiguous prophecy of the future of the aeroplane was made in February 1912 by a Royal Field Artillery officer, Captain Bertram Dickson, in a memorandum submitted to a sub-committee of the Imperial Defence Committee. Dickson, who had learned to fly privately at Châlons-sur-Marne in

1909, first tried to impress the military value of aeroplanes on his superiors when he appeared flying a Bristol aircraft over the British Army annual manoeuvres in 1910; only to be reprimanded for 'unnecessarily frightening the cavalry's horses'. Shortly afterwards Dickson was gravely injured in a flying accident but continued to press for recognition of the importance of the aeroplane until his premature death on September 28, 1913.

His memorandum was one of several individual papers given to the Imperial Defence Committee which had been charged in November 1911 with the task of considering the future development of 'aerial navigation for naval and military purposes' and to suggest measures to secure an efficient aerial Service for the country. The urgent need for such a Service in the British armed forces was emphasised by the comparative development of aerial services in virtually all major European countries by that time. France, the first pioneer of military

aircraft, had at least 200 aeroplanes in military use by 1911; while Germany, though less advanced in the design of heavier-than-air machines, had developed the lighter-than-air rigid airship to a reasonably efficient state and had at least 30 such airships in service, most of which were capable of reconnoitring the whole of the North Sea and of carrying a small bomb load for offensive operations. By comparison, the British services could only point to a very small number of aeroplanes, of motley designs, and two small army airships. While it was true that the British Army had utilised a few free and tethered balloons in various campaigns of the late 19th century, it was not until 1911 that aeroplanes were incorporated in a true Service formation. On February 28, 1911 a special army order created the Air Battalion of the Royal Engineers, comprised of No. 1 (Airship) Company located at South Farnborough, and No. 2 (Aeroplane) Company, based at Larkhill. This formation came into effect officially from April 1, 1911. This marked the No. 2 Company as the first British military unit comprised entirely of heavier-than-air aircraft.

The Air Battalion's career was short-lived, however. Official procrastination in deciding whether to concentrate on development of the airship or the aeroplane led to a lack of practical training in either type of aircraft. The situation was resolved in late 1911 by the setting up of the Imperial Defence Committee's sub-committee to consider the whole question of a national aerial service. With Lord Haldane as its chairman, the sub-committee came to its conclusions in remarkably quick time. Recommending urgency of action, it proposed the creation of a British Aeronautical Service, to

Top: The Short S.45 at Portsmouth during the Jul 1912 Naval Review flown by Lt Spenser D A Grey, RN.
Above: The first military trials for the RFC in Aug 1912. Monsieur Prevost lands his 100hp Gnome Deperdussin during the 'ploughed field' trial. He went on to win the £2000 second prize – the first prize, £5000 was won by Colonel Cody's 'Cathedral' machine.
Right: The Royal Aero Club Certificate issued Apr 25, 1911 to Arthur M Longmore, one of the first four Naval officers to officially qualify as a pilot.
Below: Henry Farmans of 3 Sqn, RFC on display in Abbey Field, Colchester in Jun 1913 – the object of rapt attention by the local populace.

'Unnecessarily frightening the cavalry's horses'.

Above: Maurice Farman, No. 95 (130hp Canton-Unne engine) in Aug 1914.

be designated 'The Flying Corps', in its own right as a separate entity from the existing military formations. The Corps was to consist of a Military Wing, a Naval Wing, and a Central Flying School for training pilots for both Wings. In addition there was to be a Royal Aircraft Factory at Farnborough for experiment and research on all aspects of aeronautics likely to affect the Corps and its vehicles. To administer the new formation, a permanent consultative committee, to be called 'The Air Committee', would be appointed to deal with all aeronautical matters affecting both the Admiralty and the War Office. Preparation of a detailed scheme to implement these proposals was undertaken by yet another sub-committee, with Colonel J E B Seely as its chairman, and again the deliberations were remarkable for swift agreement and result. Seely's sub-committee's report was ready by February 27, 1912, passed through with virtually no amendments, and was approved by the Committee of Imperial Defence on April 25.

Royal approval of the title 'Royal Flying Corps' was given in March 1912, and a Royal Warrant dated April 13, 1912 gave constitution to the new force. Two days later a special Army Order set out the necessary regulations and, on May 13, the old Air Battalion of the Royal Engineers was officially absorbed into the new formation. Initial recommendations for the establishment of the Royal Flying Corps included provision for seven squadrons, each comprising 12 aeroplanes, with two pilots for each machine and an additional reserve of pilots. Total establishment was to be 364 pilots of whom, it was originally intended, about half were to be non-commissioned officers, though in practice the great majority were commissioned ranks. The establishment for the Central Flying School was set out initially as 12 officers and 66 non-commissioned ranks, who were expected to pass out approximately 180 pupil pilots each year. Of these, it was estimated that 40 would join the Naval Wing, while the remainder would go to the Military Wing. The CFS was located at Upavon, near Salisbury on the bald Wiltshire plains, and erection of build-

ings for accommodation of men and machines began in April 1912. Officially declared 'open' on June 19, the CFS began its first course of instruction on August 17, 1912. Overall command of the RFC was given to Captain (temporary Major) Frederick H Sykes of the 15th (The King's) Hussars.

Undoubtedly the most significant aspect of the Haldane sub-committee's recommendations was the establishment of the new aerial service as a single entity, thereby unifying the nation's aeronautical resources. Unfortunately, and in virtual defiance of governmental wishes, the Admiralty never fully implemented this intention. With centuries of naval precedence in defence matters, the Naval authorities resented Army intrusion on what they considered to be purely naval matters. Accordingly, and almost from the very start, the RFC Naval Wing regarded itself as a separate force from the military elements of the corps. Its official title, 'Royal Flying Corps, Naval Wing', was used officially for only a few months and was soon replaced, even on official documents, by 'The Royal Naval Air Service' – a title without official approval until two years later when Admiralty Weekly Orders, dated June 26, 1914, gave the official seal to this designation. Even before the creation of the RFC, the Admiralty had decided to go its own way in matters of aviation. On March 2, 1911 four Naval officers began a course of flying instruction at the Royal Aero Club's flying ground at Eastchurch on the Isle of Sheppey; and in December of the same year the first naval flying school was established at Eastchurch, after the Admiralty had purchased ten acres of ground adjacent to the existing airfield. From then until the end of World War I, Eastchurch remained a solely naval instructional establishment, despite the intended purpose of the newly-created Central Flying School at Upavon.

Beyond taking the normal esoteric pride in their own particular branch of the armed Services, individual co-operation between members of the RFC and so-termed RNAS was always of the best. Only in the higher echelons of command and administration did controversy and acrimony exist, exemplified particularly in the war years by the often selfish attitudes of senior Admiralty officers in matters of equipment and aeroplane supplies. This deliberate divergence of effort by the Admiralty was to become a crucial factor in the post-1918 wrangling over the future of the infant Royal Air Force and a bone of contention for many years thereafter in British Service aviation. At the first-line operational level, however, such intense rivalry only existed in the context of healthy inter-Service competition. In the pre-1914 years, the flying community was small in numbers and a spirit of

'comradeship of the air' existed between all pilots, of all nations, which transcended the intrigues and machinations of their chair-borne superiors. Naval flying officers participated willingly in Army manoeuvres, while RFC crews witnessed naval bomb-dropping and airborne wireless experiments with avid interest, leaving the crusty senior officers at Admiralty and War Offices to sulk or argue amongst themselves.

In one respect naval aviators envied

Above: Lt G I Carmichael of 3 Sqn, RFC, taxiing out in Henry Farman, No. 284, Colchester, Jun 1913.
Below: The BE2a, designed and renowned for its stability in flight. Throughout the early years of the war many hundreds of BEs saw active service in progressively modified forms. This machine, No. 272, saw service with 2 Sqn.

their RFC counterparts. Whereas the War Office had a direct aim for the future development of its flying corps, the Admiralty appeared to have no defined policy or eventual aim in mind for naval aviation. Individual naval pilots pursued various facets of possible 'Fleet' use of aeroplanes, notably the bearded Charles Rumney Samson and Robert Clark-Hall, whose indefatigable experiments in airborne armament and trials with ship-borne aeroplanes pointed the way to the future. Their untiring efforts, though ostensibly approved by naval officialdom, found little real favour with the sea-going pundits in Whitehall whose vision was encrusted and blinkered by lifetimes spent in traditional naval service. The general feeling of despair and abandonment among the rank and file of naval aviators could be adequately summed up in this fragment of poetic doggerel published (anonymously . . .) in that period:

'The Navy is our Father (in the strictly
  legal sense
That binds an obligation just of
  shillings, pounds, and pence)
A parent so neglectful of us children of
  the Air
That had not Hope maintained us we'd
  have died of sheer despair
For Father didn't want us, and he
  didn't want to know
Just what it was we wanted, or the why
  or wherefore, so
When lurid lights of warfare first came
  flashing through the sky,
Our Father quite forgot us and the fact
  that we could fly.
Till someone chanced to tell him, in a
  non-committal way
That if he cared to notice there was
  Purpose in our Play.
Then Father grew uneasy, for he
  found he had to own
That he was going reaping where he
  knew he hadn't sown.'

Within the RFC Military Wing little time was lost in implementing the recommendations of its charter, and the first two squadrons, Nos. 1 and 3, were quickly established. No. 1 Squadron, which in May 1912 was No. 1 (Airship) Company Air Battalion, RE, based at Farnborough, ceased to exist under that nomenclature and was retitled No. 1 Airship and Kite Squadron. Its equipment consisted of dirigible airships (*Beta*, *Gamma*, and by February 1913, *Delta*, *Zeta*, and *Eta*), some free spherical balloons, several man-lifting kites, but no heavier-than-air machines. It remained a lighter-than-air unit until January 1, 1914, when all its equipment was transferred to the RNAS, and in May 1914 the squadron commenced reorganisation as an aeroplane unit.

On the declaration of war with Germany in August that year, however, only the nucleus of the 'new' squadron existed, which prevented the unit going to

Right: The staff of Central Flying School, Upavon, on Jul 24, 1914. Standing, l-r: Sub-Lt Pierce, RN; Lt E L Conran; Capt A G Board; Asst-Paymaster J H Lidderdale, RN; Capt E G R Lithgow, RAMC; Mr G Dobson, MA; Lt F H Kirby, VC; Eng-Lt C D Breeze, RN. Sitting, l-r: Lt-Cdr P A Shepherd, RN; Capt A C H MacLean; Capt G M Paine, CB, MVO, RN (Commandant); Maj H M Trenchard, CB, DSO (Asst Commandant); Maj E L Gerrard; Capt T I Webb-Bowen.

Below: Informal group at CFS, Upavon just prior to the outbreak of war. At right is Maj Frederick Sykes, cdr of the RFC, talking to Maj-Gen Sefton Brancker. Third from right, facing camera, is Lt T O'B Hubbard. The aircraft is a Maurice Farman.

France with the initial air squadrons accompanying the British Expeditionary Force (BEF). No. 3 Squadron was formed at the same time as No. 1, and its 'parent' was No. 2 Company of the old Air Battalion, RE, stationed on the Salisbury Plains at Larkhill, which was suitably retitled when the RFC came into being. No. 3's initial equipment comprised five assorted designs of aeroplane, but by September 1912 the strength had been enlarged to 18 aeroplanes, 14 of which were monoplanes of varying types. In that same month, however, the RFC Military Wing was forbidden – at least, temporarily – to fly monoplanes owing to several fatal accidents in machines of that configuration; consequently, No. 3 Squadron was forced to meet its increasing commitments with its remaining four aircraft. In June 1913 the squadron moved from Larkhill to nearby Netheravon, where it remained until the outbreak of war. Thus, No. 3 Squadron's claim to be the first *aeroplane* squadron to be formed in the British flying services (a claim reflected in its official motto, 'The Third shall be First') is justifiable; though for the pedantically-minded it was the second *squadron* to be formed.

The third unit to form, 2 Squadron, came into existence at Farnborough in May 1912 equipped with a mixture of

Below: Upavon scene, 1914. Aircraft, r–l, are BE2a's Nos. 468; 470; 441; BE8, No. 423; and BE8, 416. Note petrol fuelling cans under fuselage of No. 468.

BE2, Maurice Farman and Breguet machines. In February 1913 the squadron moved en bloc to Montrose in Scotland, where several of its pilots achieved a variety of long-distance flights, including a successful crossing of the Irish Sea by six aircraft in September 1913 to participate in Irish Command manoeuvres. It remained there until war broke out. A nucleus of men from 2 Squadron formed the original No. 4 Squadron at Farnborough in September 1912. On completion of its formation, 4 Squadron moved to Netheravon which it shared with 3 Squadron, again having a variety of aircraft types, including BE2's, Breguets and Maurice Farmans. Farnborough also provided the 'birthplace' for the remaining trio of squadrons envisaged in the RFC's original terms of reference. No. 5 Squadron was formed there in July 1913 from a Flight detached by 3 Squadron, and was soon equipped with Maurice Farmans and the early Avro biplanes. In July 1914, 5 Squadron became based at Fort Grange, Gosport. No. 6 Squadron originated in January 1914 at Farnborough from personnel posted from the first four squadrons, and its initial equipment comprised two BE2's and two Maurice Farmans. No. 7 Squadron only began its formation in May 1914, and was still a skeleton unit by August of that year. The general efficiency of these original formation processes within the RFC Military Wing was such that on July 31, 1914, No. 4 Squadron was in a position to detach two

complete Flights (eight aircraft) to the RNAS at Eastchurch to assist the Navy in their responsibility for the defence of Britain; these Flights eventually flew from Eastchurch to France after the outbreak of war to rejoin their squadron's main formation. In June 1914 the complete strength of the Royal Flying Corps was assembled at Netheravon for a month's combined training, under the military title of a 'Concentration Camp' – a literal description of the bringing together of Nos. 2, 3, 4, 5 and 6 Squadrons, the RFC Headquarters Flight, Aircraft Park, and a detachment of the Kite Section. In all, over 700 officers and men of the Army's air arm were assembled, and during the period of this camp's existence extensive trials were made of every aspect of the military usage of aeroplanes. On July 2 all units returned to their individual base airfields to continue training in anticipation of the imminent annual Army manoeuvres. Within a month, however, all were placed on a war footing, and were hastily making last-minute preparations to fly to France.

For the Naval air service, 1913 was a fruitful year in many respects. In October 1912 the Admiralty had decided to establish a chain of seaplane and airship stations along the east and south coasts of Britain. After Eastchurch, already well established, the first such station to be commissioned was a seaplane base on the Isle of Grain, in December 1912. This was quickly followed in early 1913 by

'*Useless for the purposes of war*'.

Above: A Henry Farman gives full throttle prior to a training flight.

further stations at Calshot, Hampshire; Felixstowe, Norfolk; and Cromarty, Scotland. Headquarters of the Naval Wing was transferred from HMS *Actaeon* to HMS *Hermes* on May 7, 1913, and her commanding officer, Captain G W Vivian, was given overall command of all coastal air stations. In addition airship stations were established at various locations, the first large airship sheds being constructed at Hoo, on the Medway. The station was named Kingsnorth and completed in April 1914. Unlike the Military Wing, the Admiralty did not form individual aeroplane squadrons, preferring to merely base aircraft at the various stations – a legacy of naval think-

ing restricted to 'ships' rather than mobile striking units for offensive or defensive purposes. Nevertheless, a host of individual aspects of naval air requirements was pursued. Experiments in bomb-dropping, torpedo-launching, airborne wireless communication, anti-submarine and anti-ship devices, fitting machine guns to aeroplanes – all were diligently tried and retried with increasing success by individual naval crews. Their efforts remained principally uncoordinated by any mainstream policy from the Admiralty, but at least gave experience and practice which, much later, was to prove invaluable in war. The RNAS's equivalent to the RFC's 1914 'Concentration Camp' occurred between July 18 and 24, 1914 when HM King George V reviewed the British Fleet at Spithead. Most available aircraft were flown or brought to Calshot Station at the mouth of the Solent, and on July 20 a mass formation of 17 seaplanes, two Flights of aeroplanes in formation led by the indomitable Charles Samson, and four naval airships flew and manoeuvred over the long lines of Fleet vessels assembled for the regal inspection. Ironically, this show of 'strength' failed to impress many regular naval officers below, whose general consensus of opinion still regarded the aeroplane as 'useless for purposes of war'.

When Britain declared war on Germany on August 4, 1914, its air services were still in a state of expansion and formation. On July 29 instructions had been issued to the RNAS that the duties of its aircraft were confined to home defence and protection of vulnerable points from possible attack by enemy aircraft or airships, thereby leaving the RFC to fulfil its logical duties of direct support of the army. The original British Expeditionary Force (BEF) began to embark for France on August 9, and two days later RFC Headquarters left Farnborough for Southampton and reached Amiens early on the 13th. Nos. 2 and 3 Squadrons flew across the Channel from Dover on August 13, followed the same

day by the two detached Flights of 4 Squadron based with the RNAS at Eastchurch. No. 5 Squadron followed on August 15. All were concentrated at Amiens, with RFC Headquarters now commanded by Brigadier-General Sir David Henderson, KCB, DSO, whose chief staff officer was the Corps' first commandant, Lieutenant-Colonel F H Sykes. On reaching France No. 2 Squadron was equipped with BE2's; 3 Squadron with Bleriot monoplanes and Henry Farman biplanes; 4 Squadron with BE2's; and 5 Squadron with a mixture of Henry Farmans, Avros, and BE8's. The total strength of this first RFC force consisted of 105 officers, 63 aeroplanes, and 95 mechanical transport vehicles. No aeroplane carried any form of gun, except individual pilots' private revolvers or an occasional rifle; none were fitted to carry a bomb load. The primary function expected of the force was reconnaissance – aerial cavalry for the Army. It was a pitifully small force, yet from it was to come a mighty armada of aircraft which, by the end of the war – little more than four years later – comprised the world's largest air service, honed by war and sacrifice into the first-ever independent air force to be created by any nation, the Royal Air Force. Its official motto, *Per Ardua ad Astra*, regally approved on March 15, 1913, and promulgated in Army Order No. 3 in the following April, had no official translation. It had been the motto of the Irish family of Mulvany for hundreds of years, and was quoted in Sir Henry Rider Haggard's book, *The People of the Mist*. This last reference was remembered by Lieutenant J S Yule, RE (later, Colonel, OBE) as he strolled across Laffan's Plain, Farnborough with Lieutenant J N Fletcher, RE (later, Wing Commander, AFC) one evening in May 1912. The two subalterns were discussing their commanding officer's (Sykes') suggestion that the newly-created RFC needed an official motto, when Yule recalled the passage in Haggard's novel. Its literal translation has never been accurately established, even today, but the Mulvany family had always understood the motto to mean 'Through Difficulties to the Skies'; while Rider Haggard's personal translation had been 'Through Struggle to the Stars'. Untranslatable, with no known origin, it was nevertheless the proud motto with which Britain's pioneer air servicemen prepared for their part in the world's first aerial conflict. That the spirit of the motto was thoroughly understood by each airmen is witnessed by the traditions of courage and devotion to duty established during the years 1914–18, which were to be proudly inherited and superbly embellished by the successors of the tiny group of airmen assembled at Amiens in August 1914.

Aces and Kings

The prime task facing the first RFC squadrons in France in August 1914 was reconnaissance in direct tactical support of the relatively small BEF, and if at first the various Army commanders were highly sceptical of the value of air observation reports, they were quick to appreciate such reports as the German Army juggernaut swept all before it advancing on France through Belgium. The first war reconnaissance by the RFC was flown on August 19, by Captain P B Joubert de la Ferté of 3 Squadron in a Bleriot monoplane, accompanied by Lieutenant G W Mapplebeck of 4 Squadron in a BE2a. This sortie intended to establish the immediate positions of the tiny Belgian Army attempting to halt the German advance. For the following two weeks aeroplanes and crews were constantly in the air, seeking

Below: Anonymous batch of RFC mechanics, fully 'booted & spurred', just prior to embarking for France and active service. All ranks were issued with revolvers as personal side-arms.

out and swiftly reporting the growing danger to the BEF as the opposing armies started to encircle the British and French troops. Based to a large extent on these air reports, the BEF commander, Sir John French, ordered his forces to withdraw in a controlled retreat to more tenable positions. Reconnaissance reports were partially responsible for saving the original BEF from destruction or capture as Sir John acknowledged in his first war dispatch, dated September 7: 'I wish particularly to bring to your Lordships' notice the admirable work done by the Royal Flying Corps under Sir David Henderson. Their skill, energy, and perseverance have been beyond all praise. They have furnished me with the most complete and accurate information, which has been of incalculable value in the conduct of operations. Fired at constantly by both friend and foe, and not hesitating to fly in every kind of weather, they have remained undaunted throughout. Further, by actually fighting in the air, they have succeeded in destroying five of the enemy machines.'

Far left: Bristol Scout C of 5 Sqn RFC, 1914, with Lee Enfield rifle, minus stock, lashed to a centre-section strut; Mauser pistol in holster; and hand grenades with rag 'tails' in homemade rack alongside cockpit.
Left: Officers of 5 Sqn, RFC take a hasty meal during the 1914 Mons retreat of the British Army. Facing camera is J F A Higgins.
Below: Lt (later Maj) H D Harvey-Kelly (at r) with BE2a, No. 347 of 2 Sqn, RFC. He flew this BE to France on Aug 13, 1914, taking off from Dover at 0625 hrs, and landing at Amiens at 0820 hrs – the first RFC machine to land in France.

'I wish particularly to bring to your Lordships' notice the admirable work done by the Royal Flying Corps under Sir David Henderson ... Fired at constantly by both friend and foe, and not hesitating to fly in every kind of weather they have remained undaunted throughout'.
Sir John French.

These comments were significant. By virtue of the constant barrage of small-arms fire which greeted every pilot, from both enemy and 'friendly' infantry – to whom every aeroplane was a novelty to be 'greeted' appropriately – the RFC began painting a small Union Jack on the under-wings of its machines. This marking was soon after replaced by the concentric red, white, and blue roundels now so familiar on all Service aircraft. Of deeper significance was the claim that five German aircraft had been brought down by fighting in the air. Despite a complete lack of armament apart from privately-owned hand guns, the RFC crews displayed an instinctive offensive spirit from the very start of their operations, an eagerness to close in combat with any enemy machine to come within range. It was this aggressive attitude to the air war which was to become the hallmark of British fliers throughout the war, the solid foundation on which the later commander of the RFC and RAF, Hugh Trenchard, was to base his own philosophy of the offensive role of air power. Throughout the many bloody land battles fought by the BEF during the closing months of 1914, the relatively few RFC crews remained a constant sight above the fighting; observing, reporting, occasionally fighting and bomb-

ing, but ever-present despite the innumerable difficulties concerning equipment, lack of facilities for maintenance, and, by no means least, the bitter winter weather conditions. The strength of the force was slightly improved on October 7 when eight aeroplanes of 6 Squadron joined it in France; but wild windstorms alone were responsible for nearly decimating the RFC's aircraft. One such overnight gale struck the RFC's aircraft – unhangared and necessarily pegged down in open fields – on September 12, wreaking extensive destruction which left the force with about ten serviceable aeroplanes by morning. On December 28 a total of 30 aircraft were wrecked (16 beyond repair) by another sudden storm. Such natural hazards, in addition to the complete lack of suitable accommodation for men or machines, were taken as an everyday routine of war by the crews, who cheerfully endured all events and continued to play their full part in air operations.

In the air an increasing number of crews gave considerable attention to the question of armament for their aircraft. The low-powered, lightly loaded types of machine in use then gave little margin for any additional weight to be carried, yet this did not prevent many men from attaching automatic weapons, including

the heavy infantry Lewis machine gun, by means of some privately-designed 'lash-up' fitting. With one such unofficial item – a Lewis gun, rope-tackled, and against orders – Lieutenants Louis Strange and his Observer, F G Small, in an 80hp-engined Avro of 5 Squadron, met a new German Albatros two-seater on November 22. Fastening underneath the German, the British crew emptied two complete drums of ammunition into their opponent. The German NCO pilot's nerve broke and he immediately dived and landed in Allied lines – where his officer-observer promptly knocked him down and kicked him! Other forms of armament carried included hand grenades, dispensed by hand, crude petrol 'bombs', and even canisters filled with up to 250 'flechettes' – steel darts nearly six inches in length which were principally aimed at troops and horses. Proper bomb-carrying equipment had yet to be fitted to any RFC machine, and such explosive stores were literally thrown at a target below. Other facets of the aerial war also had their small beginnings during the early months of the war. Artillery observation from the air commenced in embryo during December 1914, when successful experiments with electric lamps gave a readable signal from as high as 6500

Above: William Barnard Rhodes Moorhouse, RFC, who as a pilot of 2 Sqn, RFC, bombed Courtrai on Apr 26, 1915, receiving mortal wounds, in a gallant solo sortie. He was awarded a posthumous Victoria Cross – the first-ever air VC. Below: The never-to-be-forgotten moment when an embryo pilot first took to the air alone. Avro 500, No. 939 (50hp Gnome) at RNAS Redcar, early 1916.

feet. The use of wireless transmitters soon proved practicable in relaying coded messages from air to ground. One particularly important facet – air photography of enemy ground positions – was in its infancy. On September 15 Lieutenant George Pretyman managed to obtain five exposures of some German troop positions, and when these were developed later, two gave some promise of the future for the airborne camera. Within less than a year complete operational orders for an Army were to be issued prior to a land assault, including accurate maps of German trench developments based entirely on photographic coverage. Such pre-intelligence of the opposing forces immediately became a daily requisite by all ground commanders, and continued to be so for the rest of the war. One novel experience for the RFC crews during the Aisne battle of September was being fired upon by heavy anti-aircraft guns behind the German lines. With a light-heartedness wholly typical of the period, such fire was promptly nicknamed 'Archie' – an allusion to a contemporary British music hall catch-phrase, 'Archibald – certainly not!'

The first months of the war in the air, though predominantly a story of the work of the RFC, was not exclusively confined to the army's air component. The Royal Navy Air Service had assumed responsibility for the aerial defence of Britain in September 1914, due to the entire serviceable strength of the RFC being despatched to France in August. It was more a paper responsibility than any semblance of practical ability to fulfil such a role. In terms of aeroplane 'defence', the protection of the capital city, London, was afforded by a solitary 70hp Gnome-engined Caudron machine, with its pilot who flew it from Eastchurch to Hendon on August 7, 1914. The much-feared Zeppelin raids against England were, fortuitously for the Admiralty, delayed seriously by the shortage of airships in Germany, coupled with several disastrous accidents among the available gas-filled giants of the air. Nevertheless, in the premier tradition of the Royal Navy, the Admiralty immediately pursued an aerial offensive and claimed it to be the finest form of defence. A detachment of the RNAS, based near Antwerp, included a single-seater Sopwith Tabloid biplane, which was piloted by Flight Lieutenant R L G Marix on October 8 when it bombed an airship shed at Düsseldorf, accompanied by Squadron Commander Spenser Grey in another Sopwith. Marix's tiny 20lb Hales bombs

Left: Capt (later Maj) Lanoe George Hawker, VC, DSO, seated centre, with the personnel of A Flt, 6 Sqn, 1915. On Nov 23, 1916, with OC 24 Sqn, Hawker was killed in a classic duel with Leutnant Manfred von Richthofen of Jagdstaffel 2 – the 11th of the 'Red Baron's' claimed 80 victories.

Centre left: The Vickers FB5 two-seater, usually armed with a Lewis machine gun in the forward (observer's) cockpit formed the equipment of 11 Sqn RFC – the first unit formed specifically for 'fighting duties' 11 Sqn arrived in France on Jul 25, 1915.

Below left: HM Queen Mary inspects the RFC Depot at St Omer, France on Jul 5, 1917. On her right is Maj-Gen Hugh Trenchard, GOC RFC. In background are a captured Albatros D III (1) and an Armstrong Whitworth FK8.

found their mark, and one shed erupted in flames which destroyed an airship housed inside. An even more daring venture occurred on November 21, when three Avros, piloted by Squadron Commander E F Briggs and Flight Commanders John Babington and S V Sippe (a fourth Avro failed to take-off) flew from Belfort and followed the Rhine for approximately 120 miles to bomb the Friedrichshafen airship works on the shores of Lake Constance. Their actual attack damaged the huge airship sheds, one airship, and gutted the local gas works. Briggs was forced down and became a prisoner of war, but the other two pilots returned ·safely. These were isolated, though prodigious sorties.

Their effect was to alarm greatly the German authorities who promptly expended much energy, material and personnel in expanding the defences of such apparently vulnerable targets.

The principal RNAS formation to see action during 1914, however, was the Eastchurch Squadron, commanded by the indomitable Charles Samson, which crossed to France on August 26, 1914. With 17 officers, 80 ratings, a widely varying collection of ten aircraft and (initially) the *Astra Torres* airship, Samson's unit was meant to assist a force of Royal Marines. In the event this squadron based mainly at Dunkirk combined air sorties with a number of highly unorthodox ventures with its complement of armoured vehicles on the ground. The outstanding character of its leader, combined with the many individual exploits of its members, soon earned the unit the soubriquet 'Samson's Pirates'. One other notable RNAS achievement before the end of the year came on Christmas Day, when a combined force of two light cruisers and three seaplane carriers (*Engadine*, *Riviera* and *Empress*), each carrying three seaplanes, sailed from Harwich for the Heligoland Bight on December 24. Their objective was the destruction of airship sheds at Cuxhaven, with a secondary, purely naval ploy of obtaining information on the German shipping in the adjacent waters. Early on Christmas morning all nine seaplanes were hoisted onto the sea, but only seven managed to get away. Very low fog banks and clouds effectively prevented the seaplanes from

achieving their purpose, though much valuable intelligence of the nearby German Fleet dispositions was reported.

Thus, the first five months of the war had not only blooded the RFC and RNAS, but had seen the crude beginnings of virtually every facet of aerial warfare, due principally to the cheerful endurance and splendid courage of its individual members. Such men laid the elementary foundations upon which the future of air power was to be constructed, and it is significant that many of the 1914 RFC subalterns and RNAS junior officers were later to rise to distinguished rank and direct the fortunes of the Royal Air Force in 1939–45. The year 1915 was to see the lessons so hard-

Above: Four pilots of the RNAS distinguished for their successes against Zeppelin airships. L-r: Flt Sub-Lt J S Mills; Flt Cdr A W Bigsworth, DSO; Flt Cdr J P Wilson; and Flt Sub-Lt R A Warneford, VC.

ily won by those pioneers, developed and elaborated, becoming a framework for succeeding crews to shape and polish. Possibly the greatest single advancement was in the matter of airborne armament. At the turn of the year only individual examples existed of aircraft fitted with elementary gun fittings, but by the close of 1915 few aircraft were without a machine gun as a normal accoutrement to operations. The other factor was the

Left: Lt Herman W von Poellnitz of 32 Sqn taking off from Vert Galand airfield in his De Havilland 2 Scout, Jul 1916. Note Flt Cdr's streamers attached to outer struts.

Left: Flying instruction in a Maurice Farman 'Shorthorn' trainer, a typical scene in the UK during 1915–17.

evolution of single-purpose squadrons within the RFC. During the 1914 RFC 'Concentration Camp', Sefton Brancker (later, Air Vice-Marshal Sir Sefton) had expounded his belief that '. . . we must have different types of squadrons and aircraft for fighting, long-range reconnaissance, and for artillery observation'. It was to be a further year before his words were to be translated into practice. On July 25, 1915, No. 11 Squadron arrived in France, equipped throughout with Vickers FB5 two-seat 'pusher' aircraft, with terms of reference stated as 'Fighting duties'. Until this time all units had been conglomerates of widely varying designs of aeroplane, with duties which encompassed every aspect of aerial warfare. The advantages of having homogeneous units not only defined specific roles in combat, but con-

Left: The King of Montenegro inspects units of the 9th Wg, RFC at Fienvillers, 1916. Nearest camera is Lt-Col Hugh Dowding, then OC 9th Wing, and later to command RAF Fighter Command during the air defence of the UK in 1940. At left is Maj Sidney Smith, DSO, commander of 27 Sqn RFC, two of whose Martinsyde G.100 'Elephants' can be seen.

siderably eased the problems of maintenance and equipment supply and replacement. Nevertheless the changeover to such an ideal establishment was still tardy. By September 25, 1915 the RFC in France had just 12 squadrons, with a total of 161 aeroplanes, of 14 distinctly different designs. Not until the spring of 1916 were there to be any further single-role units in the frontline ranks of the RFC.

One characteristic of the men of the aerial services never changed from the standards set by the first combatants – sublime courage. Exemplifying the spirit of determination and devotion to duty so prevalent amongst all ranks of the service, Lieutenant William B Rhodes Moorhouse of 2 Squadron, flying BE2b, 687 loaded with a single 100lb bomb, attacked a troop concentration at Courtrai on April 26, 1915. Receiving mortal wounds from the intensive groundfire, he flew 35 miles back to base rather than land immediately, and on his return insisted on giving his report before permitting any attention being given to his wounds. He died the following day, and on May 22 the *London Gazette* announced the posthumous award of a Victoria Cross to this gallant pilot. His was the first of 19 such awards to be made to members of the RFC, RNAS and infant RAF; and if rarity is a criterion of quality, it might be noted

Above: Flt Lt Lloyd Breadner in his Sopwith Pup at Walmer, Kent, 1917. In WWII, Breadner commanded the RCAF.

that an overall total of 633 Victoria Crosses were awarded to servicemen during the years 1914–18. Five more airmen were awarded the supreme honour during 1915, two of them members of the RNAS, Reginald Warneford and Richard Bell-Davies. One recipient was Captain (later Major) Lanoe Hawker, already holder of a DSO for his prowess. Hawker's VC award was the first to be given for air *fighting* – recognition not only of his unceasing gallantry but also of his claims to have brought down at least five enemy aircraft in aerial combat. In the popular phrasing, he had become the first British 'fighter ace' unwittingly inaugurating the layman's image of the so-termed 'ace' fighter pilot.

The era of air-to-air individual combat, and the 'birth' of the fighter aeroplane – an aircraft designed purely for fighting duties – began in 1915. On July 1, Lieutenant Kurt Wintgens of the German air service piloted a Fokker M5K monoplane, single-seat aircraft, fitted with a machine gun synchronised to fire directly through the propeller arc, and destroyed a French Morane two-seater. In doing so he introduced a new, deadly phase of the air war. In the ensuing months more Fokker *Eindeckers* (monoplanes) appeared in the skies over the Western Front. Their prey was the lumbering and less agile two-seater reconnaissance aircraft of the Allied air formations. It was the period when names such as Max Immelmann, Oswald Boelcke, Otto Parschau, Max von Mulzer, and others became nationally revered throughout Germany. They were the scourge of the Allied two-seater crews. Throughout the winter of 1915–16 the *Eindecker* pilots virtually reigned supreme in the air, though their numbers were relatively few. Casualties among the Allied crews rose alarmingly, but at no time was the Allied air effort diminished, despite this additional hazard. In England the need for an aeroplane specifically designed for fighting duties had been recognised early in the war, and by the summer of 1915 the prototype of the De Havilland 2 single-seat biplane

'... we must have different types of squadrons for fighting, long range reconnaissance and for artillery observation'. Sefton Brancker.

Above: Sopwith 1½ Strutters of 5 Wg, RNAS setting out from Coudekerque aerodrome in Feb 1917.

Above: Avro 504, No. 1487, at Redcar, 1916. Though seen here modified to RNAS requirements, the Avro 504 was probably the most-used two-seater trainer by the RFC, RNAS and, later, RAF in the years 1914 to the early 1930s.

Above right: The first Handley Page 0/100, No. 3116, to land at Coudekerque, on Mar 4, 1917, piloted by Sqn Cdr Spenser D A Grey, DSO, RN. The machine's massive proportions are 'scaled' by the attendant Sopwith Triplane (l) and Nieuport Scout.

Right: Fixed and hand-held aerial cameras aboard an Armstrong Whitworth FK3 trainer – illustrating the methods of obtaining air photographs on RFC machines.

Below: An FE2b of 100 Sqn, RFC about to set out on a bombing sortie. Despite its ungainly appearance, the FE proved to be a stalwart war-horse, and saw much active service in many roles during 1916–18. The precarious position of the observer-gunner during any air combat can be appreciated by this view; parachutes were not issued to aircraft crews of the RFC/RNAS throughout WWI.

was finished. A 'pusher' design, thereby circumventing the need for any gun synchronisation gear, the DH2 mounted a forward-firing Lewis gun. Although a few isolated examples of the type were flying in France before the end of 1915, the first unit to be solely equipped with DH2's was 24 Squadron. Formed initially on September 1, 1915 under the command of Lanoe Hawker, VC, DSO, it received its first DH2 on January 10, 1916, and eventually flew to France as a fully-equipped unit on February 10. Two more DH2 units arrived in the fighting zone soon after: 29 Squadron on March 25, and 32 Squadron on May 28. Other fresh designs to become first-line fighting aircraft included the Martinsyde G.100 'Elephant', which 27 Squadron introduced to France on March 1, 1916 and the curiously efficient FE2b two-seat 'pusher', examples of which reached France in the autumn of 1915; but the first complete unit to be FE2b-equipped, 20 Squadron, did not reach the fighting until January 23, 1916.

The combined effect of all these new aircraft was to regain, if only temporarily, a modicum of air supremacy over the Western Front. The Fokker 'Scourge' (as it had been described overdramatically in British Parliament) was quickly abated, permitting the bulk of Allied reconnaissance and bombing operations to be undertaken relatively free from interference. Fresh impetus to the RFC had also come in 1915 when, on August 19, command of the corps in France passed from Sir David Henderson into the capable hands of Hugh Montague Trenchard – a man who was destined to guide the fortunes of the RFC through its remaining existence, and later to become revered as the 'Father of the Royal Air Force.' Born at Taunton on February 3, 1873, Trenchard had served in India and the Boer War before transferring, at the age of 39, to the RFC. After a spell at the Central Flying School, he had commanded a Wing of the RFC in France before succeeding Henderson. Gruff in manner, firmly of the belief that men could not be inspired or commanded at a distance, Trenchard's unorthodox personality made a direct, unforgettable impact on all with whom he came into contact. His unconventional passion for detail, however trivial, and uncompromising determination to increase the efficiency of the RFC in its operational role often led to clashes with his superiors. To the men of the squadrons, however, Trenchard soon became something of an heroic figure – a stern parental symbol who demanded the utmost from them, yet was

equally fierce in securing everything and anything which would enable them to best accomplish their tasks. Above all, perhaps, was his unwavering honesty. Trenchard never once shrank from telling his crews that he was about to place their lives in jeopardy, but if their deaths achieved the purpose they would not have died in vain. Such blunt explanations were entirely contrary to what the young air crews had usually experienced when addressed by generals, whose usual pattern of jingoistic clichés – 'hot air', to use the RFC vernacular – simply insulted their intelligence. This general was different, and the increasingly familiar sight of his tall frame, blue-grey unwavering eyes, and resonant voice – from which his universal nickname 'Boom' was derived – trudging daily around the airfields, hangars and messes, questioning men from commanders to air mechanics with equal verve, soon provided the crews with on-the-spot inspiration and trust in their commander. Perhaps the greatest point in common between Trenchard and his flying crews was his implacable policy of maintaining the offensive role in air operations. It was a philosophy which precisely matched the individual crews' own attitude to their role in the war, and one which was to become the underlying strategic policy of the British flying services for six decades thereafter.

Trenchard's immediate needs for the RFC were men and equipment, particularly of greater quantity and better

quality. In this he quickly found himself at odds with the Admiralty's air chiefs who, consistently, pursued the policy of separatism and unilaterally cornered the products of private aircraft manufacturers, including the engine firms, for their own needs. A special governmental committee, chaired by Lord Derby, was set up with the aim of ending the rivalry for equipment between the two air services, but after only six weeks he resigned his appointment in disgust, remarking, 'It appears to me quite impossible to bring the two Wings closer together . . . unless and until the whole system of the Air Service is changed and they are amalgamated into one service, as personally I consider they must be.' Derby's disillusionment had come simply from his experience with the committee in which the naval representative, Vaughan-Lee, proved utterly obstructive by refusing to commit the Admiralty to any changes in the existing system, however small. By this time, early 1916, Trenchard was absorbed in preparing the RFC for the forthcoming Battle of the Somme. Its strength on July 1, 1916, the opening day of the assault, was 27 squadrons, totalling 421 aircraft, with 216 more machines immediately available at the aircraft depots as replacements for casualties each day. In the battle area itself were 167 aeroplanes, and these were facing a German strength of 129 machines. This gave the RFC a numerical edge at the start. By November 17, as the Somme holocaust petered out, the overall RFC statistics showed a total of 35 Squadrons, but also listed 499 pilots or observers killed, wounded or missing, with a further 268 pilots struck off strength from causes other than battle reasons. Such horrifying casualty figures, proportional to the air service's strength, amplify the chief concern of its commander in seeking urgently an adequate supply of new crews, aircraft and units.

To add to his problems, the German air command was virtually reorganised in the summer of that year. The most immediate evident change was the evolution of new *Jagdstaffeln* – solely fighting units, equipped with the very latest single-seat aircraft types. The most important of these were the Albatros D.I and D.II fighters, each armed with twin synchronised machine guns, and having a performance range superior to any RFC fighter in use. To counter these fresh opponents, the RFC had only the now-obsolete DH2, Martinsyde 'Elephant' and a relative few of the early models of French Nieuport Scouts for fighter offensive operations. An almost unique exponent of the latter type of fighter aircraft was a 19-year old boy from Nottingham, Albert Ball, serving

with 11 Squadron at the start of the Somme offensive. The archetype of the lone fighter, Ball flew alone, fought alone, but tackled all odds on every possible occasion. His tactical instincts, outstanding courage, and personal modesty gave his fellow pilots inspiration and example at a period when RFC casualties and the generally low ebb of the Allied fortunes might have produced a reduction in morale. In a fighting spell of only five months, Ball was credited with more than 30 air victories, and awarded a triple DSO and MC, before returning to England on October 4. The most vital, if unglamorous, aspect of the RFC's part in the autumn battles concerned the invaluable aid afforded to the artillery guns, and in tactical contact patrols. In slow, unwieldy two-seaters, crews were responsible for guiding the guns in the destruction of over 500 German gun emplacements, apart from silencing nearly

Below: Capt H Wilkins of 27 Sqn, RFC (bandaged head & back to camera) surveys the wreckage of his Martinsyde G.102, A3986, in which he crash-landed on Jul 28, 1917 after combat with a two-seater German crew of Flieger Abteilung 45.

300 others. The contact patrol crews, flying at heights well below 1000 feet over the actual fighting zones, through a constant barrage of shells and groundfire, kept in constant touch with the fluctuations of the infantry positions and relayed such information directly to the commanders behind the lines.

Although the major effort of the RFC throughout the war was made along the Western European battle zones in France and Belgium, in Britain an ever-enlarging organisation was necessary to provide training for embryo air crews and skilled maintenance personnel. In addition both the RFC and RNAS provided a steadily widening network of aerial defences to combat the German airship, and later aeroplane raids on England. Providing the bedrock for all these services was a rapidly mushrooming industrial complex for the manufacture of aeroplanes and the myriad of components necessary for such products. The problems of defence of the United Kingdom were basically due to a lack of suitable aircraft able to tackle airborne raiders on anything like equal terms. The ever-open maw of the battle fronts consumed virtually all newly-manufactured aircraft and components

as the attrition rate of combat inevitably rose. Such aeroplanes and equipment as could be spared for defending the homeland were mainly obsolete or unsuited for first-line operational duties. Cumbersome BE2's, hastily armed, but woefully under-powered constituted the main type of defender by 1916, though a few isolated successes against marauding Zeppelins were achieved in late 1916 by pilots flying modified BE's with 39 Squadron, including Captain William Robinson, who was awarded an immediate VC for his destruction of the German airship SL11 on the night of September 2.

Around the coast of Britain the RNAS maintained a more traditional role by providing oversea patrols with flying boats and floatplanes, protecting inshore shipping convoys and deterring the growing submarine menace. As with the later Coastal Command of the RAF in

1939–45, a great majority of naval crews spent many hundreds of hours 'watching water' without ever seeing an enemy, but their constant presence undoubtedly did much to contain the undersea threat to the country's vital ocean lifelines. A great deal of energy was expended by the RNAS in experimental work with anti-Zeppelin devices, including the dual-purpose trials of aircraft flight decks on sea-going vessels, aircraft slung under airships, 'pick-a-back' composite aircraft, and especially in the airborne armament field. Though mostly successful in intention and elementary practice, few of these were actually employed on an operational basis; though many provided a starting point for more widespread usage in the immediate post-1918 years of the RAF. Apart from the relatively few naval flying units in France, much operational work by the RNAS was concentrated in the Mediterranean

Above: Picture of an airman sending a telegram . . . De Havilland 6 two-seat trainer calls in at the camp post office. Appropriately, the DH6 was usually dubbed 'The Clutching Hand'.
Right: De Havilland 4, N6000 of 5 Sqn, RNAS at Petite Synthe airfield, Dunkirk, late 1917, usually piloted by Flt Cdr C P O Bartlett, DSC. RNAS aircraft often carried tail span markings of red/white/blue, as here, in addition to more usual rudder striping.

Above: Sopwith Triplane Scouts of No. 1 Sqn, RNAS at Bailleul, Oct 28, 1917. Aircraft identifiable from nearest: N5454 ('1'); N5475 ('18'); N5472 ('17'); N5387 ('15'); N5449 ('13').

area throughout the war years. These 'side-shows' achieved little publicity but exemplified the naval tradition of individual adaptability.

By the time a watery Spring began to infiltrate the tail of the bitter 1916–17 winter, the general pattern of aerial warfare above the Western Front was all but settled. General standardisations of equipment and role among the squadrons of all nations had been accomplished; broadly segregated into units for reconnaissance, artillery observation and co-operation, bombing, and – latest in concept – fighting. It was the real beginning of the popular lay conception of dogfights and fighting 'aces', where squadron fought squadron, and individual fought individual – to the death. New designs of aircraft were almost ready for production and issue to the RFC, including the Factory-designed SE5 fighter, Bristol F2a two-seat fighter, and Sopwith Camel, three aircraft types which were to dominate the tide of aerial fighting for the remaining years of the conflict. While awaiting such badly-needed replacements, the RFC had to suffer the attentions of the greatly strengthened German fighter units, who were flying Albatros and Halberstadt single-seaters which were definitely superior to the British contemporaries. Supremacy in the air had mainly passed to the new German *Jagdstaffeln* during the closing months of 1916. In December over half the RFC casualties had

been brought down *behind* British lines. Supplies of fresh aircraft from Britain had fallen well below expectation, and the RFC's immediate prospects for the new year were so bad that Trenchard, wrote angrily to London, 'You are asking me to fight the battle this year with the same machines as I fought it last year. We shall be hopelessly outclassed, and something must be done . . .' His plea was unanswered in practical terms until the early summer, and in the interim the RFC, still stoically implementing their commander's policy of constant offensive, incurred its highest casualty rates of the whole war. The first three months' losses in men totalled 249 killed or missing; but April 1917 – 'Bloody April', as it thereafter became known – alone cost 316 men. Yet throughout this period – and, indeed, the remainder of the war – the morale of the squadrons remained extraordinarily high. The pre-1914 RFC unwritten code of 'Flying as usual' in the face of a death of a crew still held. Trenchard's personal edict that all casualties must be replaced immediately by fresh men from the RFC 'Pool' in France maintained the tradition of 'No empty seats' in Mess dining rooms among the front-line units.

The long-standing bitter rivalry between the Admiralty and the War Office continued to blight the supply question, and even the most optimistic adherents to the hope of a unified air effort had become despondent. The spur to such a unification came from the most unexpected source – the enemy. On June 13, 1917, fourteen of an originally despatched total of 30 German Gotha twin-engined bombers appeared over London just before noon, and proceeded

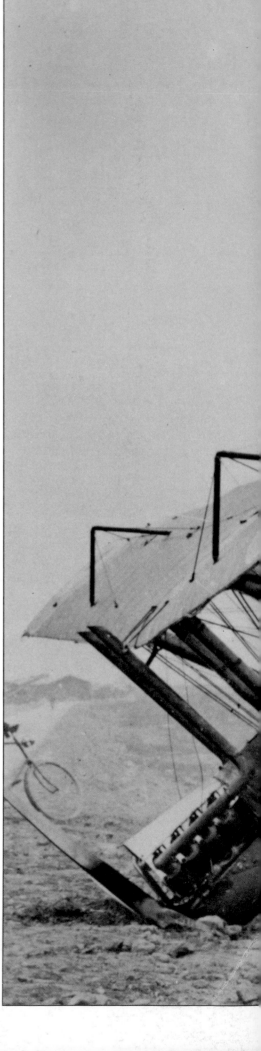

'You are asking me to fight the battle this year with the same machines as I fought it last year. We shall be hopelessly outclassed, and something must be done . . .' Trenchard.

Below: BE2e – a single-bay variation of the standard BE2c type – after a landing accident, Wyton, 1917. The aircraft belonged to 51 (Training) Sqn.

Left: A Short 184 (Improved) seaplane, built by Short Bros. of Rochester, Kent. Below Left: Airship C.21 hit a hut roof as it ascended at Folkstone (Capel) on Jun 1, 1918, gashing the gas envelope and resulting in one bent 'blimp'. (The latter soubriquet was universally applied to all non-rigid types of airship.)

calmly to bomb the dockland area. Four tons of high explosive caused 162 deaths and injuries to a further 432 people. The effect of this raid, where an enemy bomber formation, unmolested and in broad daylight, had coolly attacked the capital, was to create a near-panic among members of the public. Vociferous demands for immediate retaliation against German cities – a wholly impracticable task for the contemporary air services – forced the government to set up an immediate inquiry into the whole question of the national air effort. A little over three weeks later, on July 7, another raiding force of 22 Gothas appeared over London during the morning and bombed at leisure without any significant interference from the defences. Lloyd George, the Prime Minister, appointed the South African Boer War veteran, Jan Christian Smuts, head of the inquiry committee, and less than two months later Smuts presented the government with his findings, condensed into two reports. The first of these detailed the sorry state of London's aerial defences, but the second report was to have much wider ramifications. It offered concise means of reorganising the whole British air services, with an overriding assumption that air power would one day cause the centuries-old concepts of army and naval power to be subordinated. It further recommended that the existing Air Board – a non-executive committee – be raised in status and powers to become a separate Air Ministry, administering all air matters, and thereby effectively creating a separate single air service.

The central motive for Smuts' recommendations was to unify air supply and planning towards a sustained bombing programme in 1918 against the German homeland. His views were based and shaped on one central false premise. Governmental statistics, wildly over-optimistic and unrealistic, had promised a production total of bombers for 1918 issue that would leave a 'surplus' of at least 3000 aircraft available for just such a bombing effort, over and above the anticipated needs of the existing squadrons. Trenchard, always realistic, knew that such production figures were figments of the politicians' imagination, and – foremost in his thoughts – was opposed to the suggestion of any form of change in overall administration at that particular point of the war. He was not opposed to having a separate air service – indeed this was his ultimate aim. But, being earthbound in reality, he feared the possible disruptive effects of any change in administration at a time when the British air services were facing admittedly superior German air power. His only quarrel therefore was with the timing of the proposed change. He was later to admit that Smuts' visionary proposal was correct in its timing: '. . . This made it possible to form the air service

on a sound basis when the Great War was finished, and I doubt now that we could have unified it then, with the opposition from the army and the navy we would have had, bearing in mind the terrific efforts made by the two older services to break us up *after* we had been amalgamated.' No less a force than Smuts in ensuring the proposed amalgamation was Sir David Henderson, the RFC's 1914 commander, of whom Trenchard admitted frankly in retrospect: 'Henderson had twice the insight and understanding that I had. He was prepared to run risks rather than lose a chance which he saw might never come again. He did so with no thought of self-interest, and it is doubtful whether the RAF and Britain realises its debt to him, which is at least as great as its debt to Smuts.'

As the autumn months of 1917 turned to winter, the Smuts Air Report was hotly debated in parliamentary circles, but eventually accepted and implemented, more for inter-party political expedience than any unselfish ideal of service to the future safety of the nation. Thus, based in the main on political self-seeking and an entirely mythical forecast

Below: Sopwith F.1 Camels of 8 Sqn, RNAS at Mont St Eloi, Christmas 1917. Nearest Camel is B6311. The Camel, which first entered operational service in Jun 1917, eventually claimed more combat victims (some 3000 claimed 'victories') than any other aircraft type, or any nation, during WWI.

Left: Maj J T B McCudden, seated in his 56 Sqn SE5A Scout, was credited with 57 victories before his death in a flying accident on Jul 9, 1918.
Above left: Harry Tate was the universal nickname for this RE8 two-seat reconnaissance machine, after a music hall comedian of the period.
Above right: Australian-born Maj Roderick Dallas, seen here in SE5A, D3511 of 40 Sqn on May 28, 1918. His accredited victory tally was at least 51.
Right: Capt Albert Ball, seen here seated in SE5, A4850 of 56 Sqn, RFC – the aircraft in which he died.
Below: Nieuport Scouts of 40 Sqn, RFC

'The Air Force to be established pursuant to the said Act shall be styled the "Royal Air Force"'.
King George V, March 7, 1918.

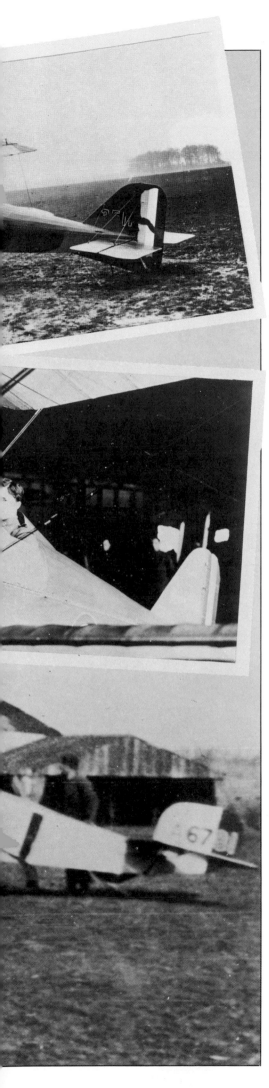

of aircraft production statistics, the seeds of a separate air service were sown. On October 16 Bonar Law informed the House of Commons that a bill to constitute an Air Ministry had been prepared for imminent introduction, titled the Air Force (Constitution) Act, and this bill passed through its various stages and received the royal assent on November 29, 1917, by which time it was known as the Air Force Act. This Act did not itself bring the Air Force into being, but empowered the King to do so. An Order in Council dated December 17 outlined the composition and duties of the Air Council, which was created on January 2, 1918. As first Chief of the Air Staff, Hugh Trenchard was appointed in December 1917, reluctant though he was to leave his operational command in France. He was succeeded by Major-General John Salmond on January 18, 1918. On March 7 King George V proclaimed his 'Will and Pleasure that the Air Force to be established pursuant to the said Act shall be styled the 'Royal Air Force'. Finally, on April 1, 1918, the Royal Flying Corps and the Royal Naval Air Service ceased to exist, and were both absorbed into the new, separately administered Royal Air Force.

Outside the corridors of power with their Babel of intrigue and political wrangling, the front-line squadrons of the RFC and RNAS simply accepted the fact that their equipment was by no means of the best, and continued to prosecute the war despite the ever-increasing odds against survival. A trickle of new units, freshly-equipped with the new designs of aircraft, began reaching France in the early months of 1917. 56 Squadron introduced the SE5 to the Western Front on April 7; 48 Squadron with its Bristol F2a two-seat fighters in March; and 70 Squadron, which exchanged its veteran Sopwith $1\frac{1}{2}$ Strutters for the vicious little Sopwith F1 Camel in July. The bomber and army co-operation units thankfully began to re-

Above: A Sopwith Pup, floated out to its parent ship on transit pontoons, about to be hoisted on board. By 1918 most ships of the British Fleet carried a quota of small fighting aircraft for reconnaissance, usually mounted on crude wooden platforms attached to forward gun housings.

place their out-dated BE two-seaters, but the new aircraft, RE8s designed by Farnborough, proved to be of little better performance or efficiency. Only the new De Havilland 4 two-seater promised well, though after its introduction to France – by 55 Squadron who flew to France on March 6, 1917 but did not see action until April – serious troubles requiring extensive modifications were encountered. Eventually the DH4 was to become recognised as possibly the finest two-seater bomber to see action with the British air services in 1917–18. Opposing the Allied airmen in 1917 were a host of well-equipped fighter units, whose pilots included some of Germany's greatest 'aces' – veterans of the air war who found a rich harvest of victims among the inadequately-equipped British units. Men like the Richthofen brothers, Werner Voss, Ernst Udet and a hundred others, piloting sleek Albatros and Fokker fighters, created havoc among the cumbersome Allied two-seaters and out-dated fighters of the RFC and RNAS, by attacking in formations and fighting teams, well-drilled in tactics of fighting partnerships. The day of the lone fighter was virtually over – safety lay in teamwork. As if epitomising the demise of the individual hunter, the RFC's contemporary leading 'ace', Albert Ball, died on May 7 after a sprawling series of clashes with units of *Jagdstaffel* 11. But on the same day a new pilot of 40 Squadron RFC claimed his first victim, and went on to become not only the British leading fighter pilot of the war, but also the acknowledged master of team tactics and fighting leadership. His name was Edward 'Mick' Mannock.

On August 1 1917 the RFC in France could muster a total of 51 squadrons, almost equally fighters and two-seat bombers or army co-operation types of aircraft, with an overall strength of 858 machines. Only five of these squadrons were RNAS, fighter units 'loaned' to the RFC to bolster its fighting strength. The bulk of RNAS squadrons were at this time based around the Dunkirk area, pursuing a day and night bombing offensive against German targets in occupied Belgium. They caused a large number of German defensive units to be employed in opposition which might otherwise have increased the fighting strength opposing the RFC in Flanders. In the wider context of the whole RNAS war effort, however, the units in France were virtually a side-show. In Britain a prodigious amount of naval air effort was at this time concentrating on the vital question of combating the German submarine threat to the country's very

Below: Short 320 seaplane, N4393, taxies away from the beach at Calshot on Feb 19, 1918, to undergo a series of torpedo-dropping trials.

existence. In the Mediterranean a large number of naval air units and personnel continued to harass the Turkish enemy. The year 1917 saw the static armies in France fight some of their bloodiest battles; Messines, Ypres, Arras, Passchendaele – and at the close of the year, Cambrai. In all of these the air crews kept faith with their trenchbound comrades-in-arms, and the majority of air operations were directly in tactical support of the PBI ('Poor Bloody Infantry'). On numerous occasions the single-seat fighters came down to zero feet to attack German troop concentrations and emplacements, on occasion flying so low that instances were recorded in German records of men being 'run over' and killed by aircraft wheels! The two-seater crews, ever-present in their RE8s and Armstrong Whitworth FK8s, maintained a constant 'umbrella' of artillery observation, infantry contact patrols, photographic reconnaissance and tactical bombing. In September 1917 alone these crews made 226 bombing raids by day and night, ranged heavy artillery guns onto 9539 targets, exposed 14,678 photographic

plates and issued to the Army 346,999 photoprints of German positions. The cost in casualties was high, with 214 men killed or missing. Casualties for the year amounted to 2094 men killed or unaccounted for. Depletion of the RFC's strength was further hastened in November 1917, when, due to the failure of the Italian Army to contain its Austro-Hungarian counterpart, a hastily-formed reinforcement force was withdrawn from France and sent to the crumbling Italian Front. The force included several front-line RFC squadrons, Nos. 28, 45 and 66 Squadrons all equipped with Sopwith Camels and 34 Squadron's RE8s.

Two events in 1917 were to have a profound effect on the war. In April America formally entered the fight against the Central Powers, though the immediate effect of her declaration as far as the British air effort was concerned was an abrupt reduction in the hitherto plentiful supply of essential materials for construction of new aircraft. The second event was the collapse of Imperial Russia, due to the 'March Revolution', which released enormous numbers of

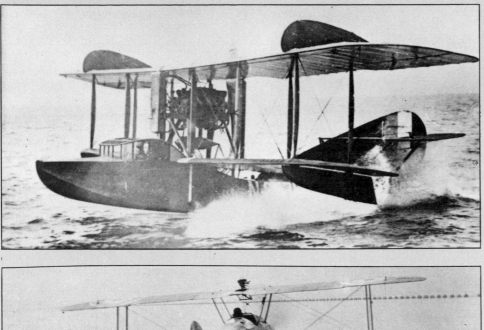

Left: Norman Thompson N2b trainer, N2571, 'unsticking' from the Solent, 1917 – one of RNAS Calshot's brood of training aircraft, nicknamed the 'Ruptured Duck'. . . .'
Below left: Sopwith 2F.1 Camel, N6603, piloted by Flt Lt Tomlinson, takes off from its wooden platform on HMS Pegasus (the former Great Eastern steamer, Stockholm). This particular 'Ships Camel' was also used aboard HMS Tiger and HMS Melbourne.

men and vast material in the German services for additional strength on the Western Front. Highly conscious of the potential of American reinforcement of the Allies in France, German authority redoubled its efforts to finish the war with a massive, decisive land and air offensive in early 1918. This was launched on March 21, and the initial impetus of the land forces was greatly enhanced by air services numerically superior to the RFC on that date.

In the ensuing weeks of the German assault, the British air crews flew unceasingly, bombing, strafing and bringing back immediate reports of the ever-

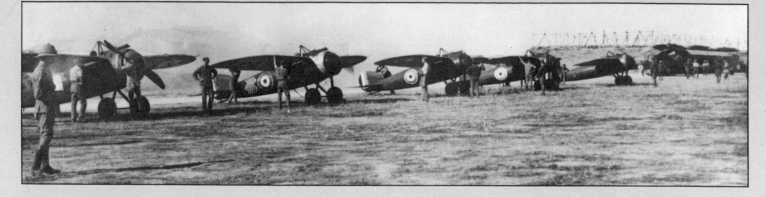

Above: Bristol M1c's of 72 Sqn in Mesopotamia, 1918. The Bristol M1 monoplane scouts were efficient and relatively fast.

changing pattern of the land struggle. The fluidity of this battle often meant that crews took off from a familiar airfield, only to have to return to a fresh field due to the rapid advance of German troops. Their sterling efforts were afterwards recognised as being the fine balance between a retreat and an utter rout of the gallant infantry facing vastly superior numbers in most sectors. If air power could not win the battle, it could at least prevent defeat. The exhausted crews, flying four and five sorties each day, pausing only for replenishment of fuel, ammunition and scant refreshment, had no interest in the machinations of the politicians in England, who chose this moment to create the new Royal Air Force by amalgamating its honourable forbears. Nor were they much impressed by the immediate clash of personalities amongst the new Service's chiefs in London. Trenchard, unable to continue working under Lord Rothermere, had tendered his resignation as CAS in March, though this was not officially announced until April. He was succeeded by Frederick Sykes, an unpopular figure, and this led to the resignation of Sir David Henderson. Finally, in April, Rothermere himself resigned. Such disharmony among the 'leaders' of the infant service was hardly the finest incentive for the rank and file crews in France, bleeding and dying in an all-out

attempt to retrieve a seemingly hopeless situation. The battle reached its peak on April 12, when the RAF flew more hours, dropped more bombs, fired more rounds of ammunition, and obtained more photographs than on any day since the commencement of the war. This direct intervention in the battle by aircraft undoubtedly tipped the balance, and German activity slowly slackened thereafter. The cost was high. More than 400 pilots and observers had died or were missing; over 1000 aeroplanes were written-off due to enemy action of some form. The birth of the new air service had been bloody but triumphant in purpose and effect.

The prospect of some form of strategic bombing of the German homeland and its war industry had been considered for several years. In 1916 No. 3 Wing RNAS had pioneered the practice, but was soon disbanded simply to reinforce the RFC and RNAS units elsewhere. In October 1917 Trenchard revived the idea by forming 41st Wing, composed initially of three bomber squadrons; this force became titled VIII Brigade in February 1918. In May 1918 it was absorbed into a virtually autonomous formation titled the Independent Force, with Trenchard as its commander. Eventually composed of nine bomber and one fighter squadrons, the Independent Force undertook 'long-distance' bombing with their DH4s, DH9s and the huge Handley Page heavy bombers, flying deep into the enemy's industrial zones, but also concentrating on German aerodromes. By virtue of the distances to

any worthwhile target, such raids were almost always unescorted by fighters. The only defence for the bomber crews against the ever-present horde of German fighters was a tight formation and thus concentration of the rear gunners' fire. An example of such odds was the proposed raid on Mainz on July 31, 1918 by twelve DH9s of 99 Squadron. Three DH9s left the formation early with engine troubles. The remaining nine then ran the gauntlet of at least 40 German fighters. The bomber leader decided to attack Saarbrücken instead of the primary target, but four DH9s were shot down before reaching this objective. The remaining five pressed on and bombed, then lost three to the fighters on the return leg of their perilous journey. The two survivors finally landed at base, and reported themselves willing to return 'to finish the job' – an example of the magnificent spirit which embued the bomber crews of the Independent Force. In its five months' existence, the IF's crews dropped a total of 543 tons of bombs – 160 by day and nearly 390 by night – 220 tons of which were released over German airfields. The price for these operations amounted to 328 men killed, wounded or missing, and 352 aeroplanes wrecked or missing.

The prelude to the final Allied victory came on August 8, 1918, when the British 4th Army spearheaded an advance near Amiens which was to continue gathering momentum until the final surrender of Germany in November. For this assault the RAF assembled its greatest strength possible, and on the eve of

Below: Line-up of 139 Sqn's Bristol F2b's in 1918, on the Italian front.

Top: Sopwith 2F.1 Camel at Mudros, late 1918, with its pilot, Maj Graham Donald. Note single Vickers gun.
Above: Pilot's dashboard of a Handley Page 0/400 heavy bomber, 1918; an array of leather-padded, plywood simplicity akin to the golden era of the automobile, and an illusion enhanced by the 'driving wheel' control column top.
Left: Pilot and Observer of a Bristol F2b of 11 Sqn, RAF, 1918.

Above: Pilots of 85 Sqn with their SE5A Scouts and multi-varied collection of unit pets, St Omer, France, on Jul 25, 1918.
Top Left: Maj Edward 'Mick' Mannock, VC, DSO, MC, acknowledged as the British leading fighter pilot with an accredited 73 victories in combat.
Top right: Maj Brian E Baker, DSO, MC in 1918 who commanded 141 Sqn at Biggin Hill. The Bristol F2b behind him displays the insignia of a fighting cock.

1

2

3

4

5

6

7

the advance this amounted to 93 squadrons, two independent Flights, and a total of 1782 aeroplanes available. Of these, nine fighter squadrons were allotted for direct co-operation with the initial assault, and these '... darted over the battlefield like dragon-flies over a pond ...' – attacking everything and anything in the path of the Allied infantry. German air opposition was fierce, and it quickly became necessary to have some fighters detailed to give top cover to the low-level strafing machines, but the pace of the latter's fighting did not diminish. By the end of August the Allied breakthrough was in full flood, and the RAF flew deeper into enemy-held territory, blasting a path forward and nullifying German air opposition wherever possible. Increasingly, the tactics evolved into massed formations of three, four or even five complete fighter squadrons making concentrated attacks on specific German aerodromes; while high above the infantry it was not uncommon for up to 100 fighters to be engaged in sprawling, wheeling dogfights, spread across miles of sky and cloud. The German infantry might have been in retreat, but the fighting fervour of its air services continued at full pitch until the very eve of Germany's capitulation. Despite rapidly deteriorating conditions of supply, fuel, maintenance and replacements, it can be truly stated that the German airman never gave up the fight until he was finally ordered to do so by the terms of the November armistice. Thus the RAF's final months of battle were against an opponent equally determined to win, and always ready to do battle.

The end to the fighting finally came at the eleventh hour, of the eleventh day, of the eleventh month of 1918. On that date, poised on the brink of peace, the Royal Air Force stood as the largest air service in the world. It comprised more than 290,000 men of all ranks, with 188 operational squadrons in existence, and an equal number of training squadrons with an overall strength of more than 3300 aeroplanes. It had reached this numerical peak in a little more than four years from the original 13 squadrons,

1: The rotary-engined Sopwith 7F.1 Snipe.
2: Sopwith F1 Camel of 46 Sqn, RAF, loaded with four 25lb Cooper bombs.
3: Members of the Women's RAF in 1918.
4: Lt A J Gaskin (r), and his new RAF uniform worn here by his sister! ...
5: Prince Albert of York (later, HM King George VI) (l) and his aide, Maj Sir Louis Grieg, MVO, in a Handley Page 0/400 bomber.
6: RAF mechanic, 1918, by an SE5A.
7: Sopwith 5F.1 Dolphins of the First Canadian Air Force sqn (No. 1), 1918.

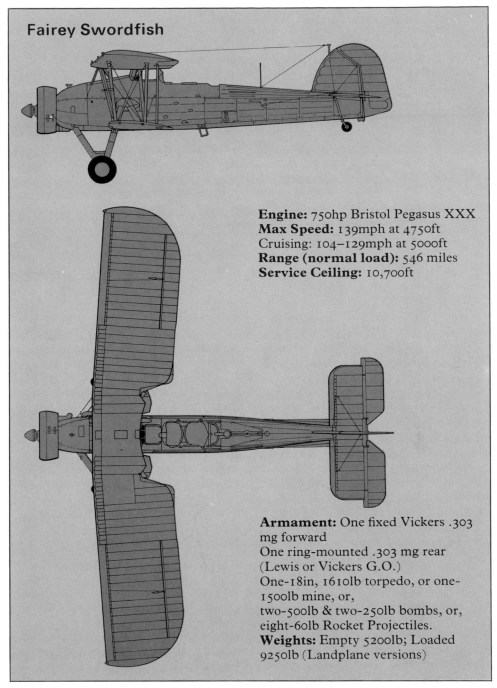

Fairey Swordfish

Engine: 750hp Bristol Pegasus XXX
Max Speed: 139mph at 4750ft
Cruising: 104–129mph at 5000ft
Range (normal load): 546 miles
Service Ceiling: 10,700ft

Armament: One fixed Vickers .303 mg forward
One ring-mounted .303 mg rear (Lewis or Vickers G.O.)
One-18in, 1610lb torpedo, or one-1500lb mine, or,
two-500lb & two-250lb bombs, or,
eight-60lb Rocket Projectiles.
Weights: Empty 5200lb; Loaded 9250lb (Landplane versions)

RFC and RNAS, and 2073 all ranks mustered for war in August 1914. In those four years of conflict in the skies, 9378 men died or were 'missing', while a further 7245 had been wounded. The crews had flown in open cockpits, lacking oxygen or heating equipment to protect them from the crippling effects of decreasing air pressure as they climbed towards the sun, and were denied even the life-saving comfort of a parachute in the event of damage to their all-too-vulnerable aeroplanes. Despite its physical strength, the RAF was nevertheless a mere eight-months' infant, standing unsteadily alongside its far older brother services; or as one wit put it, 'Cinderella, with two ugly great sisters ...' The parents of this healthy child had fought hard to prevent its birth at all, and were soon to continue trying to prevent the infant service ever reaching full maturity.

Such self-seeking squabbling amongst the Services' gold-braided 'brass-hats' and their political counterparts could not tarnish the record and sacrifices of the young air crews of the RFC, RNAS and RAF throughout the years of combat. These young men – many had enlisted immediately on leaving a school desk – had cheerfully accepted the fearful odds against survival in the new arena of the air; learned to survive only by the granite-hard lessons of personal experience in combat; and had formed the foundations of a service which could proudly stand alongside its 'elders'. The official air historian, Sir Walter Raleigh, in 1922, described their achievements in words that cannot be bettered, 'The air service still flourishes; its health depends on a secret elixir of immortality, which enables a body to repair its severest losses. The name of this elixir is tradition'.

Locust Years

The armistice of November 1918, though welcomed with heartfelt thankfulness by a nation numbed and weary of the years of slaughter and sacrifice, became merely the starting point for many years of difficulties for the recently-created Royal Air Force. The immediate effect of the tenuous peace was virtual decimation of its existing strength, as demobilisation of RAF personnel swiftly drained its manning. At the armistice date the RAF was composed of 27,333 officers – over half of these were trained pilots – and 263,837 non-commissioned men. By January 3, 1920, 26,087 officers, 21,259 cadets, and 227,229 non-commissioned ranks had left the service. Of the 99 squadrons along the Western Front in November 1918, only five still existed by October 1919, and these dwindled to just one

squadron, No. 12, by the end of that month. Everywhere the effect of the postwar rejection of war appurtenances was evident. It was not until August 1, 1919 that the first postwar permanent commissions list was published. It comprised a total of 1065 officers – a third of whom were of senior rank. In the same month new, distinctive rank titles for the RAF became official, replacing the Army ranks used since the RAF's inception in April 1918, a further stage in the consolidation of the RAF as a third, separate Service.

The continuing existence of the RAF as a separate force almost immediately became a bone of contention between the Admiralty and the War Office, each of whom pressed strongly for the retention of their 'private' air arms and the consequent dissolution of the RAF. In Jan-

uary 1919, Mr Winston Churchill had been appointed Secretary of State for both War Office and the RAF, a dual portfolio which suggested subordination of the air service to the Army, though Churchill's initial enthusiasm for the new Service prevented any serious intrusion upon its future. On January 11, 1919, Sir Hugh Trenchard once more became Chief of the Air Staff, and at Churchill's request, he compiled a memorandum outlining his personal proposals for the construction of the peacetime RAF. Restricted severely by the Cabinet decision to limit air estimates to £15 million per annum for the next five years, Trenchard based his proposals on constructing a permanent foundation for the RAF upon which future expansion could always be accomplished. Accordingly, he placed the bulk of his operational squadrons overseas to 'police' the many Imperial and mandated territories then within the aegis of the British government. These units of 'Air Control' soon provided the main *raison d'être* for the RAF's very existence in 'peacetime'. The greater, and more significant proposals of Trenchard's memorandum concerned the questions of training and technical development. Primarily determined to foster an 'Air Force spirit', Trenchard proposed the creation of an RAF College at Cranwell in Lincolnshire for training future permanently-commissioned junior officers. He inaugurated an Aircraft Apprenticeship scheme, whereby future skilled technical tradesmen for the RAF were to be enlisted as boys of 15–17 years of age

Below: Wings of peace. Felixstowe F5 flying boat, N4041, in Jan 1919.

Left: Vickers Virginia 'heavy' bomber of 7 Sqn RAF. The 'Ginnie' served the RAF faithfully for most of the 1920s.
Below left: Somaliland 'ambulance'. De Havilland 9 two-seat bomber, locally converted to carry casualties during the 'Mad Mullah' operations of RAF 'Z Force', 1920.
Below: Aircraft Apprentices at Halton, 1921, enjoying a tea break outside the 'Old Workshops' buildings still in use 55 years later . . . ! These boys, called Trenchard Brats, and their successors, were to form the technical 'spine' of the RAF in future years.

'The Royal Air Force depends on you far more than me.' Trenchard to the first cadets.

Below: DH9A's of 39 Sqn, based then at Spittlegate, near Grantham, Lincolnshire for the 1923 Hendon Air Display.

and given a three-years apprenticeship course prior to regular service in the RAF. For the latter he designated Halton Camp in Buckinghamshire as the future No. 1 School of Technical Training. Trenchard further recommended that an RAF Staff College be founded 'as soon as possible' and made several provisions for a limited variety of training establishments for flying, navigation, wireless, photography, naval and army 'co-operation' schools. Thus, within the stringent financial parameters imposed by the Treasury, Hugh Trenchard created what he personally termed, '. . . a very good cottage on the foundations of a castle. . .'

Of the $25\frac{1}{2}$ squadrons initially available to him, Trenchard based 19 abroad: eight in India, three in Mesopotamia, seven in Egypt, and one for general co-operation with the various naval bases. Only two squadrons of fighters were left for protection of the United Kingdom,

with a further two units for army co-operation, and $2\frac{1}{2}$ for Fleet liaison. His utter conviction that the future would bring a vast expansion of this meagre force enabled him to concentrate more assiduously on the matter of men to man the force. The proposed cadet college at the former RNAS airfield at Cranwell was officially opened on February 5, 1920, with Air Commodore C A H Longcroft as its first Commandant. Trenchard's dream of an RAF as a Service in its own unquestioned right, was exemplified by his earliest speeches to the first cadets to be trained there: 'The Royal Air Force depends on you far more than on me. The Service will be safe only when one of you takes over my chair as Chief of the Air Staff.' His words were prophetic; one of the cadets listening to him, Dermot Boyle, an Irish farmer's son, nearly 25 years later on January 1 1956, was appointed to that post – just six weeks before Trenchard

died. To complement the anticipated officer requirement of the early years Trenchard also inaugurated a Short Service Commission scheme in July 1919, whereby some 2500 temporary officers were required for a basic three years' term of service. Initially intended for ex-wartime pilots, the scheme was extended at the end of 1920 to include civilian candidates, and the terms of service to a four or five year period of active service, followed by four years in the RAF Reserve. Trenchard also emphasised the vital importance of provision for aeronautical research to keep the air service progressive and highly efficient.

On these limited but solid foundations the RAF began to consolidate during 1919–20. By March 1920 there were 33 squadrons established, though eight of these were still in the process of formation. The majority remained based outside Britain, and there was no immediate prospect of any enlargement of

Above: To replace the hitherto traditional three-man hand-swinging start-up procedure, the Hucks Starter was introduced in the 1920s – what might be termed early power-assisted starting . . .
Left: Another 31 Sqn Bristol F2b in India. The solar topees worn by the crew here were common headgear at this period.

the force due mainly to stringent financial provision. The defence policy adopted by the government assumed that there would be no major war involving Britain for ten years at the least. This idealistic hope caused many an ironic smile among the junior officers of RAF squadrons overseas. In fact the Royal Air Force had never ceased operational flying since the November 1918 armistice, and was to continue its constant operational commitments in various parts of the Empire until 1939 and the outbreak of World War II. Throughout

1919 the squadrons on India's North-West Province (now Pakistan) had been co-operating with the garrison army units in the apparently unending conflict with Afghanistan, while in Mesopotamia (later retitled Iraq) flying operations continued against rebel Arab chiefs of Kurdistan in the northern territory. Their aircraft were veteran wartime DH9As and Bristol F2bs using surplus explosive stores from the 1914–18 period. Maintenance facilities and accommodation were, at best, described as 'primitive'. It was the beginning of many lean years for the operational units of the RAF, during which they were expected to provide first-class air 'control' of the many turbulent areas under British administration with third-class equipment, paltry finance and constant inter-

Service bickering among the men in Whitehall. Inspired by Trenchard, and imbued with the unconquerable high spirits and ideals of youth, the young air crews accepted such conditions and never flagged in the pursuance of their assigned duties. This harsh experience of operating 'on a shoe-string' was to stand many of the more junior officers in good stead when, 20 years later, they had achieved high rank and were bearing heavy responsibilities in conducting the RAF's operations during the war against Nazi Germany.

Trenchard's task of building a separate service had myriad facets. Apart from the intrinsic needs of men, equipment and accommodation, he needed to convince not only political and Service opponents but also the nation itself of the

vital necessity for an independent air force. The British public, sickened by the years of carnage, was apathetic to anything resembling or connected with war. Rising unemployment, disillusionment, and general impoverishment provided more vital topics to consider. Accordingly, on July 3, 1920, the first RAF Tournament was held at Hendon. Later known as the RAF Pageant, and still later as the RAF Display, this annual showpiece for the air service was intended to serve three main purposes: to familiarise the public with the work and efficiency of its air force, to form a peak point for annual training of the RAF, and to provide a source of financial support for RAF charities. This first occasion attracted 60,000 spectators, and became an increasingly attractive and

attended function for nearly 20 years. The more immediate necessity for providing a genuine reason for the very existence of the RAF in 'peacetime' was partly solved by events abroad. In January-February 1919, a tiny force of DH9 bombers were able to provide conclusive support to the Army's Camel Corps and other ground forces in finally nullifying the rebel 'Mad Mullah' of Somaliland. The latter had defied a large garrison army's attempts to defeat him for nearly 20 years; the intervention of a handful of RAF aircraft played a major part in concluding this campaign in merely three weeks. This small example of the efficacy of air control exemplified the economy in time and finance in providing positive support to the governing bodies of the Empire's many territories.

In 1919 a proposal was made by the government that RAF units should be substituted for military forces in Mesopotamia, and that if the RAF supplied this main power, overall command should be entrusted to an RAF senior officer. With the existing RAF strength in the country at that time such a proposal was not practicable, but the principle was maintained until the following year, when the general equipment situation had improved, and was finalised at the Cairo Conference in March 1921, held to consider the whole question of the mandated territories of the Middle East. Trenchard, who attended this conference, proposed a force of eight squadrons to control Mesopotamia five of which (Nos 6, 8, 30, 55 and 84 Squadrons) were already stationed there. The

Below: The rigid airship R.33 at moorings.
Bottom left: The stalwart De Havilland 9A two-seat day bomber, in this case, E8650 of 84 Sqn, piloted by Flg Off (later, AVM) F F Inglis of A Flt, based at Shaibah, Persian Gulf. No. 84 Sqn's various Flts were distinguished by playing card insignia on the aircraft fins. Note spare wheel stowed, somewhat illogically, underneath the fuselage.
Bottom centre: With its stoic companion the DH9A, the Bristol F2b provided the bulk of operational RAF strength in overseas units throughout the 1920s. The 'Brisfit' left first-line service in 1932. Shown here is F2b, F4839 of 31 Sqn over Delhi, India, piloted by Flg Off Fresson, with Leading Aircraftman France.
Bottom right: Avro 504K trainer, 1924.

additional units – Nos 1, 45 and 70 Squadrons – were transferred to the area by early 1922, and actual control was not assumed until October 1, 1922 when Air Vice-Marshal John Salmond arrived to take up his appointment as GOC *all* forces in the theatre.

If the lessons of Iraq (Mesopotamia) strengthened Trenchard's hand in establishing the RAF as a new, potentially powerful factor in the context of controlling dissidents within a British-administered mandate or territory, they failed to make any impact on the hierarchy in the sub-continent of India. With more than a century of undisputed Army dominance in India, the meagre RAF force allotted to support the unceasing struggle with tribal rebellions against the White Raj was relegated to a completely subordinate level in all matters. Primarily, its finances were simply a very small part of the Army's annual budget, controlled by military accountants, despite the fact that in Britain and elsewhere the RAF had its own annual Air Estimate. Depending entirely on the largesse scantily provided by the Army were six squadrons – Nos 20, 31, 48, 97, 99 and 114 – by the close of 1919, known collectively as the India Group, and commanded by an Air Commodore (T I Webb-Bowen). Between them they were expected to be responsible for all necessary air operations in India, and particularly along the North-West Frontier Province – an area encompassing over 27,000 square miles of wild, unadministered territory alone, apart from the larger administered areas. Within the Province lived the largest tribal population in the world, conservatively estimated to number some 10 million, and including some of the world's finest and most merciless fighting men. Overwhelmingly Moslem in faith, and collec-

tively referred to as Pathans, these tribes were virtually a law unto themselves, tenuously allied by race and creed to the rulers in Kabul, and lived in the almost inaccessible hills and mountains on the northern border between India and Afghanistan. The squadrons' aircraft were of elderly concept and design – some Bristol F2bs of 20 Squadron still carried patched German bullet holes from 1918 combats – and were flown constantly with almost no back-up maintenance supplies due to the paucity of financial support. Life on the first-line units soon became a nightmare of continuous improvisation, whereby cannibalisation of two or three aircraft for spare parts was often necessary merely to put one 'serviceable' machine into the air. On February 1, 1920, No. 48 Squadron was retitled as 5 Squadron, and on April 1 99 and 97 Squadrons became 27 and

Below: Fairey IIID's of the first long-distance flight from Cairo to the Cape, 1926, seen here on their eventual return to Heliopolis, Cairo.

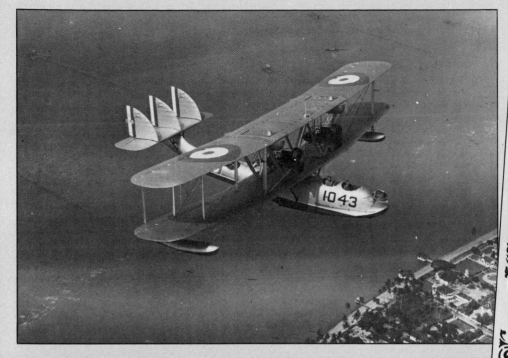

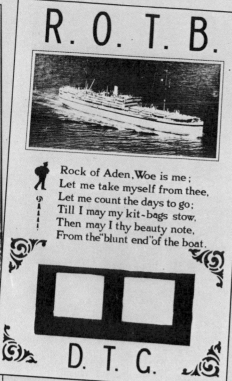

R. O. T. B.

Rock of Aden, Woe is me;
Let me take myself from thee,
Let me count the days to go;
Till I may my kit-bags stow,
Then may I thy beauty note,
From the "blunt end" of the boat.

D. T. G.

Above left: Hawker Hart of 11 Sqn skirting the high mountains of India's North West Frontier Province.
Above centre: The Supermarine Southampton is viewed here over the Mediterranean coastline near Alexandria, Egypt.
Above: 'Roll On That Boat' – the constant creed of the airmen posted overseas in the between-wars period. 'DTG' – 'Days to Go' – was carefully updated until the day of final departure to England.
Left: Vickers Valentia, K4634, named 'City of Lahore' of 31 Sqn in India. Primarily a troop-carrier, the sturdy Valentia also served as transport, supply vehicle, and even bomber throughout the 1930s and early war years of 1939–42.

Above: A 'signpost' erected at RAF Habbaniya, Iraq in the early 1920s.

60 Squadrons respectively. The change in 'labels' made no difference to the practical problems and the increasingly dangerous state of the aircraft finally climaxed in a storm of protest in Britain in 1922, when the Prime Minister was forced to send Air Vice-Marshal Sir John Salmond to India to investigate the scandal of RAF matters there.

Salmond's eventual report – a 40-page, highly detailed document – was submitted to the Viceroy of India in August 1922. The report particularly emphasised what its author described as, '. . . the existing low state of efficiency of the RAF in India with the causes which have led thereto . . .', and went on to suggest administrative measures '. . . without which the RAF cannot be main-

tained as an efficient fighting factor . . .'. Salmond also dealt with the possibilities of greater employment of the RAF in India, and the accruing benefits, both military and economic of such employment. He specified his evidence for stating that the RAF's efficiency was low by quoting the actual operational state as on August 23, 1922; 'The number of aircraft on the authorised establishment is 70 . . . the total number shown as serviceable (on this date) was seven; and of this number a percentage are so old and decrepit that they should have been already struck off charge.' The gist of the Salmond Report was to increase the number of resident squadrons from six to eight, to arrange a separate financial budget annually, to arrange an increase in rank and status for the RAF commander in India, and to discover a number of more efficient methods for the operational usage of the squadrons. His recommendations were accepted in principle, but it was to be several years before they were given full practical effect. Salmond's request for establishing a total of eight squadrons in India was simply a reiteration of Trenchard's original 1919 memorandum proposal, yet it was not until October 1928 that the two additional units – 11 and 39 Squadrons – arrived in India.

The plight of the individual airman serving in India in the 1920s was one of hardship, low pay with primitive living and working facilities. An overseas tour of duty was confirmed as a five years' stint after early 1924, which meant total separation from families for married men, while the bachelor had little off-duty recreation beyond that which he and his companions created for themselves. Life was almost wholly focused on the aircraft and work of the squadron,

yet with the traditional perverseness of the British 'regular' such conditions merely served to intensify his determination to enjoy himself despite his surroundings. Thus a spirit of comradeship was born which has never been surpassed in RAF history, though possibly equalled during periods of the 1939–45 war, and both officers and airmen worked in the closest harmony in achieving a relative peak of efficiency in both duties and play. The tone of the period is accurately reflected in the Service songs born in those years. With a traditional flavour of cynicism and fatalism, these became part of RAF folklore as the men created their own brand of humour and solace from stark surroundings and grim conditions. For the young officer fresh from England a tour of duty in India then was akin to stepping into the Kiplingesque atmosphere of the Victorian era. Steeped in centuries of long-held traditional social customs of the British Raj, the general off-duty rituals contrasted quaintly with the modern requirements of an air service, linked in a professional airman's mind directly with the obsolete equipment with which he was expected to carry out his duties.

As the financial strings were slowly loosened in Delhi, supplies of long-awaited maintenance spare parts began to reach the front-line squadrons in northern India, and the seldom-ceasing operations against dissident tribesmen continued apace. New aircraft to replace the aging DH9As and Bristol F2bs were not forthcoming, however, until late 1928, when 11 and 39 Squadrons introduced the Westland Wapiti IIa to the scene. Over the following four years Wapitis gradually re-equipped the other six squadrons, while several Vickers Valentia troop-carriers were brought into use as transport and occasional bombers. In early 1924 a brief air campaign against a specific tribal uprising, thereafter referred to as 'Pink's War' after Wing Commander (later Air Commodore) R C M Pink, was conducted solely by the RAF. The speedy and successful conclusion of this particular series of operations proved to be a turning point in the military attitude to the RAF in India, and slowly the squadrons began to be used to a greater extent in all operational campaigns in place of the cumbrous – and expensive – Army columns. Nevertheless, the air service in India continued to be last in the 'queue' for modern equipment until well after the outbreak of war in 1939. In December 1928 one compulsory innovation imposed on all air crews was the carriage of parachutes – a safety measure not as universally welcomed by the crews as

Left: FAA Fairey Flycatcher over the aircraft carrier Eagle.

Westland Wapiti IIa

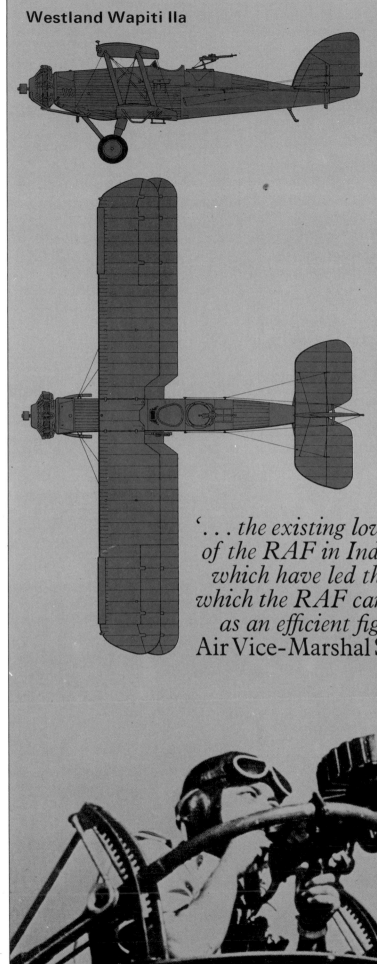

Engine: 550hp Bristol Jupiter VIII
Max Speed: 135mph at 5000ft
Cruising: 110mph
Range: 360 miles
Service Ceiling: 20,600ft
Armament: One fixed .303 Vickers mg forward
One Scarff Ring mounted .303 Lewis mg rear
Bomb load; 500lb under wings and fuselage
Weights: Empty 3180lb; Loaded 5400lb

Below: Westland Wapiti IIa, K1309 of 5 Sqn in India, piloted by Fg Off Emerton.

'*. . . the existing low state of efficiency of the RAF in India with the causes which have led thereto . . . without which the RAF cannot be maintained as an efficient fighting factor . . .*'
Air Vice-Marshal Sir John Salmond.

Left: The rear-seat Scarff Ring and Lewis gun of a Westland Wapiti IIa of 27 Sqn, India, 1938.

might have been expected. In the early 1930s the Wapiti dominated all eight main units, though by 1932, Nos 11 and 39 Squadrons had received the more modern Hawker Hart bombers. The first twin-engined, monoplane, all-metal bombers, Bristol Blenheim Is, reached India in May 1938 and began to re-equip 11 Squadron by July; but it was not until a year later that further Blenheims began to re-equip 39 and 60 Squadrons. In the autumn of 1936 many of the more prominent fighting tribes along India's North-West Frontier Province were brought to a fighting cohesion by the self-styled Faqir of Ipi, Mirza Ali Khan, who declared himself as 'Champion of Islam' and led an intensive holy war against the governmental authorities and forces. Operations against the Faqir and his followers continued for the next nine years, though on a dwindling scale after the commencement of World War II.

Throughout the 1920s the RAF in Iraq was faced with a task parallel to their comrades in India, that of quelling rebel tribesmen attempting to overthrow the constitutional authorities. A particular source of unrest in the northern territories was caused mainly by Turkey attempting to increase its own influence by undermining British authority. Tension reached its peak in the autumn of 1924 when the RAF was finally ordered to prevent a strong Turkish cavalry formation from crossing the existing border. It swept into action on September 14. Subsequent political settlements eased the Turkish threat to peace, only to be finally settled in June 1926. In the meantime the RAF in Iraq found itself in conflict with an equivalent to India's Faqir of Ipi. Sheik Mahmud, self-appointed 'King' of Kurdistan, began leading a series of uprisings to oust the government, with Turkish backing initially. From 1919 until his final surrender to the RAF, Sheik Mahmud instigated a spasmodic wave of insurrections and small wars against the British control and the newly-born Iraqi Government, to the extent that his RAF opponents jokingly referred to him as the RAF's 'Inspector of Training'. Mahmud eventually surrendered on May 13, 1931, but his example spurred several other independent sheiks to continue rebelling and fighting. In virtually all such operations the RAF's aircraft and armoured car units were called on to carry out bombing and fighting operations. The year 1928 saw a further instance of the recognition of air power as a decisive factor in control of the Empire, when the defence of Aden and its surrounding country was placed under the command of an RAF officer. For the next six years No. 8 Squadron fought a number of uprisings and projected invasions from the Yemen district. Elsewhere in the Mediterranean area the pattern was similar, with the RAF being on constant call for operations in Palestine, Egypt and the fringe countries.

In every operational area of RAF activity during its first decade of existence the common watchword was improvisation. Ever-conscious of the desperate lack of adequate finance, and the even greater menace of deliberate wrecking tactics by the Admiralty and War Office 'separatists', Hugh Trenchard's constant creed to his tiny air force was flexibility in all matters. Each member, from air rank to aircraftman, was expected to be able and willing to tackle any task needing attention, and not quibble over demarcation of individual trade parameters. With the lack of sufficient monies, and hence personnel, each man had to give priority to the task, not the laid-down 'rule book'. It was a 'shoestring' air force, but the esoteric spirit of pride in service and dedication evolved during those lean years – a characteristic of any small community when under common pressure of events – accorded precisely with the abstract ambition of Trenchard for the RAF and its future. Meanwhile he continued his crusade for an independent and expanding service. On April 4, 1922, the proposed RAF Staff College was established at Andover. In August of that year the Committee of Imperial Defence recommended the formation of 15 new squadrons for a projected Home Defence Force. This proposal was motivated more by the growing fears of France's aspirations in military strength than any specific sympathy with Trenchard's

Right: Fairey IIIF, S1373, of 202 Sqn based in Malta 1933.

dogmatic wishes. At this time France's air arm was numerically superior to any other European country, and at least three times stronger than the RAF in Britain. In June 1923, Stanley Baldwin, the new Prime Minister, announced his government's intention to create a Home Defence Force of 52 squadrons initially, an increase of 34 squadrons to the existing strength, which was to be implemented by 1930. On July 21 a sub-committee appointed to examine the relationship between the RAF and the Navy issued its report regarding the status and strength of a Fleet Air Arm. Based upon these recommendations the Fleet Air Arm was founded in April 1924, and Admiralty Fleet Order 1058/24 called for volunteers from navy officers for the new air arm. At the same time the RAF directed a small number of crews and technical tradesmen for FAA duties, and on June 16, 1924 the first 35 naval officers for flying instruction assembled at RAF Station, Netheravon; each was henceforth allotted a 'shadow' rank in the RAF for administrative and disciplinary purposes, though remaining naval officers in all other respects. These were not the first post-1918 naval officers to be given official flying instruction, however, as in April 1921 and January 1922 a total of 14 naval officers were given Air Observer training at Lee-on-Solent by the Navy.

If the fierce dogmatism of the Admirals, led vociferously by Lord Beatty, was to some extent mollified by this thin 'edge of the wedge' in obtaining naval control over Fleet aircraft, it was ironic that the FAA should then be virtually neglected by its own masters in terms of status and equipment for the next decade.

The projected Home Defence Force became a unified command in early 1925, with the title Air Defence of Great Britain (ADGB), under the initial command of Air Marshal Sir John Salmond. Of the 52 proposed squadrons (35 bomber and 17 fighter), it was intended that six should be units of the Auxiliary Air Force which was a part-time citizen formation similar to the Army's Territorial Force in concept. It came into being in

March 1925, with its first squadron (602) being inaugurated on September 12. The ADGB, with its headquarters at Uxbridge from 1926, was formed in two main sections: the Wessex Bombing Area (regular bomber units) and the Fighting Area (fighter squadrons). In 1927 the Auxiliary Air Force and its Special Reserve were designated No. 1 Air Defence Group and were added to the ADGB. Five years later the com-

Below: The final biplane flying boat to emerge from Short Brothers was the Singapore III. Here K3592 is seen on the Medway on July 26, 1934, its four 560hp Rolls-Royce Kestrel engines at full bore for take-off. Singapores finally equipped six RAF sqns at home and overseas.

mand reorganised, and those units within the Wessex Area and 1 AD Group were redistributed amongst the Western Area (with headquarters at Andover), Central Area (headquarters, Abingdon), and No. 1 AD Group (Auxiliaries). The Wessex Area soubriquet was discontinued, but the Fighting Area remained as before. In actual strength, as opposed to political pipedreams, the overall RAF in late 1924 comprised a total of 43 squadrons (18 of which were overseas), 18 Flights with the Fleet Air Arm, one Flight at Aden, an Inland Communication Flight, and a Night-flying Flight. The bland announcement by Baldwin of raising a further 34 squadrons within seven years, in 1923, hardly tallied with the finance provided by the annual Air Estimate, which in 1925 amounted to £21,319,300 – only a third of a million pounds more than the 1920 Estimate. This marked reluctance to spend the nation's money on ensuring an adequate air service was merely part of the contempporary apathy with all matters relating to the fighting services. The general mood was for disarmament in an idealistic attempt to promote a lasting peace in Europe. This fantasy was extended by the government of 1925, when its Chancellor of the Exchequer, Winston Churchill, amended the original 'Ten-year' estimate of non-aggression by allowing it to continue *ad hoc*, month by month, and used it as his basis for seeking financial cut-backs in defence expenditure. After Churchill's first, ill-fated Budget in April, in which he announced a return to the gold standard, he set about reducing public expenditure, with the services as a prime target for economies. Bolstered by the euphoric diplomatic agreements at Locarno that year, the unpredictable Chancellor reduced the Air Estimate to little more than £15 million. The 'Ten Year Rule' was altered on Churchill's initiative in 1928 to a continuing extension purely for his own political expediency, thereby providing him with an excuse to continue his meagre financial allotment to the RAF.

Trenchard, by now well-practised in thrift for his threadbare service, patiently continued to press for expansion and new equipment, if only on the lowest level permitted by the Treasury Shy-locks. Yet, despite the poor pay, dismal prospects for promotion, and bedrock levels of accommodation and technical facilities, the morale and enthusiasm of the men of the RAF remained astonishingly high. Trenchard's constant hope to create an independent 'Air Force Spirit' had found its fulfilment among the ordinary airmen and junior officers who, in the main, regarded their Service as a vocation rather than a prosaic 'career job'. It was as if each man understood the obstacles and disappointments constantly placed in the path of 'his' leader. This created a cohesive bond between all ranks in the patient battle for eventual survival of the infant service. This general feeling of stubborn pride and intense loyalty was summed succinctly by T E Lawrence in one of his many letters to Trenchard. Having enlisted as a ranker in the RAF through Trenchard's direct assistance, Aircraftman 2nd Class (AC2) Shaw (Lawrence's chosen pseudonym in the RAF) wrote; '. . . I've enlisted twice in the air force. I've seen from the inside the Turkish and Arab armies and something of the navy. The RAF is streets finer in morale and brains and eagerness

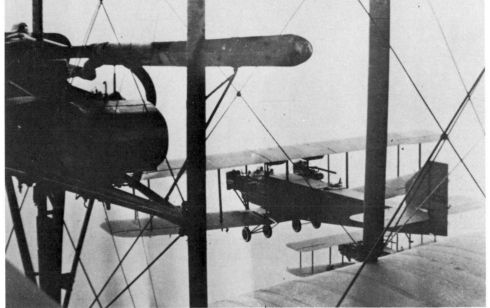

than the lot of them. Agreed, it's not perfect. It never will be. We grumble – over trifles, mainly customs of dress which you've inherited from the older services . . . . these silly details agitate our leisure accessory hours, but the actual *work* 99 per cent of the fellows enjoy. You have given us something worth doing. Of course you have enlisted some duds. There are dud Englishmen, but the average of the RAF is magnificent. The RAF is 30,000 strong, too huge for you to have personal contact with many of us; but there is not a single barrackroom in which your trumpet does not regularly sound; and these thousands of your champions find no opponents. We grouse and grumble at everything and everybody, except you.' This 'unsolicited testimonial', dated May 1928, expressed with moving sincerity, feelings shared by many thousands of anonymous airmen from Uxbridge to Hong Kong; the spirit of self-sacrifice in many things in order to preserve a Service in which each believed fervently.

The practical expression of this belief was exemplified from the earliest days of the RAF's post-1918 existence by a succession of pioneering flights and ventures. The immediate questions of communication between the many lands and territories within the British Empire provided ample opportunities to utilise the new element of air travel. Starting in early 1919, several individual long-distance flights were made or attempted between capital cities in the countries surrounding the Mediterranean; but the prime proposal by Hugh Trenchard was to establish a regular air trail from England to India, and eventually, Australia – the later-termed 'all-red route', referring to the pre-1939 world maps which usually marked all countries within the Empire in a red shading. The first stage of this proposed route was to establish a regular air trail between Cairo and Baghdad, partly to facilitate deliveries of fresh aircraft to Iraq for operational work, but also to inaugurate an air-mail routine schedule between the two cities. This was achieved initially by literally gouging a ground track, visible from the air, which could be easily followed by aeroplanes, across the desert wastes. Land convoys, accompanied by

aircraft from Nos 30, 47 and 70 Squadrons, carved out the first track in 1921, and the air route was officially opened on June 23 that same year. It ran from Heliopolis via Amman, Azrak, and Ramadi to Baghdad; a total distance of some 840 miles. The consequent air-mail schedule was maintained by 45 and 70 Squadrons – singly or in concert – until 1927, when the British civil Imperial Airways assumed responsibility.

By the end of 1925 a series of long distance Service flights began, primarily as experience in long haul formation flying but incidentally to illustrate the reliability of aircraft in sundry conditions of temperature and endurance. In September that year, four flying boats from RAF Calshot completed a 2500 mile cruise round southern England, Ireland and northern Scotland, while on October 27 a flight of three DH9As, led by Squadron Leader 'Maori' Coningham, completed the double trip from Cairo to Kano and back without mishap. In the following month a special flight of four Fairey IIIDs was formed at Northolt, commanded by Wing Commander C W H Pulford, for a Cairo–Cape attempt. Starting from Cairo on March 1, 1926, they returned to Cairo on May 27, were modified with floats in place of their land undercarriage, and then flew to Lee-on-Solent, England, arriving there on June 21 – a total of 14,000 miles by land and water without a serious hitch. Other long distance flights that year included a Cairo–Aden trip, and a round Mediterranean cruise by flying boats. Undoubtedly the outstanding achievement of this period was the 23,000 mile cruise undertaken by four Supermarine Southampton flying boats under the command of Group Captain H M Cave-Brown-Cave, from Plymouth to Singapore. Leaving Plymouth on October 17, 1927, the Southamptons reached their destination on February 28, 1928, on schedule. They then carried out further pioneering cruises round the Australian continent and to Japan, apart from survey flights to Calcutta, and additional trips to Australia.

A natural progression of all these flights was the attempt by the RAF to establish new world long distance flying records, and between 1927 and 1932 several such attempts were made by Service

Above: Boulton Paul Overstrand,
K4549, 'A' of 101 Sqn.

personnel in specially modified aircraft. Flying a much-modified Hawker Horsley, Flight Lieutenants C R Carr and L E M Gillman left Cranwell and finally alighted in the Persian Gulf after nearly 35 hours in the air, covering a distance of 3400 miles. This feat was eclipsed days later by Colonel Charles Lindbergh's epic solo trans-Atlantic flight. In April 1929, Squadron Leader A G Jones-Williams and Flight Lieutenant N H Jenkins, in a specially designed Fairey monoplane, flew non-stop from Cranwell to Karachi – a journey of 4130 miles. Tragically, these same officers were killed in December 1929 on their second attempt, crashing into a mountain near Tunis; but a second Fairey monoplane, crewed by Squadron Leader O R Gayford and Flight Lieutenant G E Nicholetts left Cranwell in February 1933 and reached Walvis Bay, South-West Africa, covering 5340 miles nonstop in 37 hours 25 minutes.

The quest by the RAF to expand its air frontiers was not confined to long range flying, but was extended in the pursuit of higher altitudes and greater speed. In 1927 the RAF competed for the first time in the bi-annual Schneider Trophy race for maritime aircraft. Held in Venice, the race that year was won by a Supermarine Napier S5 floatplane, piloted by Flying Officer S N Webster, whose average speed over the course of 217.35 miles was 281.49 mph – a new world speed record. In 1929 Flying Officer H R D Waghorn, flying a Supermarine S6, again won the trophy for Britain with an

average speed of 328.63 mph. In 1931 the trophy became Britain's permanent possession when Flight Lieutenant John Boothman, piloting an S6b, attained a winning average speed of 340.08 mph. Just weeks later Flight Lieutenant George Stainforth, of the same RAF High Speed Flight, in an S6b, became the first man to exceed 400 mph in the air; a record unbeaten in the world for the next 18 months. The many lessons learned from his experience in designing these ultra-high-speed monoplanes was to stand Reginald Mitchell of Supermarine's in good stead in the early 1930s. From this genesis was evolved Mitchell's Spitfire eight-gun monoplane fighter, which was destined to achieve near-immortality in the years 1939–45. Epitomising the RAF's motto, *Per Ardua Ad Astra*, almost literally, were the various experiments and trial flights attempting to reach the sub-stratosphere. At Farnborough, in September 1936, Squadron Leader F R D 'Ferdy' Swain, flying a specially-constructed Bristol 138 wooden monoplane, reached a new world record height of 49,967 feet. In June 1937, another Farnborough pilot, Flight Lieutenant M J Adam, climbed to 53,937 feet in the same monoplane. Both men had to be clothed in a particularly designed rubberised 'pressure suit' to withstand the effects of decreasing air pressure and increasing cold, which was oxygen-fed and curiously portentous in appearance of the garb used by the first American space pioneer-travellers three decades later.

Not all the RAF's major endeavours were crowned with unqualified success, however. The development of the rigid

airship which, during World War I, had been a major consideration by the naval air authorities, came within the aegis of the Air Ministry when future airship construction was transferred in October 1919. Unconvinced of any worthwhile service application for the monster 'silver queens', the Air Ministry undertook to complete construction of the R.38 as arrangements had already been made for its purchase by America. But, due to the financial stringency in air matters immediately after the Armistice, it was arranged to hand over all 'surplus' airships and projects to the civil aviation authorities. In January 1921, rather reluctantly the Air Ministry finally decided to allow its own plans for airships gradually to lapse. This decision was ostensibly justified when, on August 24 that year, the R.38 broke amidships while on trials over the Humber, near Hull, and killed 44 men aboard, including 16 officers and men of the US Navy, and Air Commodore E M Maitland, the foremost advocate of the British lighter-than-air vehicles. A revival of governmental interest came in 1922–23, and later still a new programme was instigated including the construction of two new rigid airships, R.100 and R.101. In August 1930, the R.100 made a successful flight to Canada and returned, but on October 4, only weeks later, the R.101 left her mooring mast at Cardington intending to fly to Egypt and, eventually, India. Just after 2 a.m. the following morning the giant airship hit a small hill near Beauvais, France and was completely destroyed in a holocaust of fire. Of its 54 passengers and crew, 47 perished in the flames, including Lord

Thomson, Secretary of State for Air, Air Vice-Marshal Sir Sefton Brancker, Director of Civil Aviation, and the noted airship captain, Major G H Scott. The R.101's spectacular demise marked the end of official interest in giant rigid airships.

In December 1929, Hugh Trenchard finally laid down his monumental task of nurturing and protecting 'his' service; preferring, in the interests of the RAF, to makè way for a younger man. His successor was Air Chief Marshal Sir John Salmond who, if not a visionary like Trenchard, possessed unequalled experience in practical air command, and was deeply committed to the cause of air power. Trenchard, dubbed 'Father of the RAF' by the press – despite Trenchard's detestation of the soubriquet – was raised to the peerage and continued fiercely to champion the need to recognise the supreme importance of air power throughout his remaining years. By the time of his death, on February 10, 1956, he was to witness undisputed proof of his constant creed. The nation buried him in Westminster Abbey, and during the 24 hours prior to his interment his catafalque was guarded alternately by ex-Halton Apprentice senior NCO's and Air Marshals – a fitting reminder of his breadth and depth of vision for the service to which he had given most of his life.

Salmond's immediate task parallelled that of his predecessor, attempting to satisfy all the operational needs required of the RAF from a government which refused to grant it adequate funds. The Air Estimate for 1930 was barely £21 million, and indeed was reduced in the fol-lowing year, when the international conference assembled at Geneva to consider general disarmament by the European nations. Britain's palpably weak military backing gave her little weight in arguing for any reduction in arms by her immensely stronger Continental confreres; and the withdrawal of Hitler's new Germany from the League of Nations in 1933 undermined any hope of a practical solution in this context. In March 1934 an air estimate of £20,165,600 was introduced, the Fleet Air Arm's appropriation from this topping £1 million for the first time. In debating this estimate, Stanley Baldwin continued to cling to the forlorn hope of at least a restriction in armaments within the European area, but promised that in the event of failure to achieve this objective the government would immediately proceed to strengthen the RAF to at least numerical parity with '. . . the strongest air force within striking distance of this country' – implying France. The myth of strength simply by numbers of aircraft had been consistently opposed by Trenchard, who had always urged the formation of well-trained squadrons manned by superbly-trained crews, and equipped with the best aeroplanes possible – quality before quantity.

Trenchard's fears for the quality of his equipment were well-founded at that time. Since 1918 the RAF had been forced to meet its commitments with obsolete aircraft originally designed for World War I operational needs. Throughout the 1920s its chief operational aircraft were the sturdy Bristol F2b and the ubiquitous De Havilland 9A – both two-seater biplanes. Heavy bom-bers were 1917-designed Vickers Vimys, or derivatives; fighter squadrons, least in Trenchard's priorities, were equipped with single-seat biplanes little better in design or performance than their 1917–18 predecessors. Partly due to the various governments' failure to provide sufficient finance, this situation was equally the result of governmental lack of practical support for Britain's private aircraft industries.

While the equipment position remained virtually stagnant, so too were the normal career prospects for the regular serving airman and junior officer. With pay at its lowest ever in RAF history, and promotion progress synonymous with that of a glue-footed sloth, it speaks volumes for the unforced sense of loyalty and vocation among the men of the RAF that they remained patiently devoted to their myriad tasks in a service which ostensibly offered them little material advantage. The lower echelons of the service were, by the early 1930s, beginning to swell with the graduates from Cranwell and Halton, young men deeply skilled in their trades and, in the main, imbued with the 'Air Force Spirit' so earnestly pursued by Hugh Trenchard. In particular, the ex-Halton Apprentices – dubbed sneeringly by the experienced adult-entry airmen as 'Trenchard's Brats', a 'label' soon proudly worn by all ex-apprentices – proved themselves a rock foundation for the technical backing of the RAF as it

'Ex-Brats' were to become outstanding
air crew leaders in the 1939–45 war, displaying unsurpassed courage and utter
devotion to their duties. Living conditions were sub-standard, uniforms and
equipment out-dated, discipline a bas-
tard mixture of Kipling's Soldiers Three
and Nelson's successors, officers of
middle-age, class-conscious and therefore seldom seen by their airmen beyond
compulsory parades, abysmal pay and
promotion outlook. Yet the younger airman and officer of the early 1930s were to
be the unshakeable spine of the RAF
during the early years of World War II –
and the bulk of its casualties during the
desperate years 1939–41.

On May 22, 1935, an announcement
was made simultaneously in both
Houses of Parliament giving the outline
to governmental proposals for greatly
expanding the RAF – twelve years after
the original 1923 proposals for a strong
air service. From the contemporary aircraft strength of 580 in the RAF (exclud-
ing the Fleet Air Arm), it was intended
to triple this total within two years –
thereby achieving theoretical parity with
France and the recently announced
Luftwaffe in Germany. In general effect
this proposal meant forming 71 new
squadrons for defence of Britain in
1935–36. In July 1935, supplementing
this decision, the Secretary of State for
Air, Cunliffe-Lister, stated that 2500
pilots and 20,000 other additional personnel were required to be recruited to
the RAF. To pay for this tripling of RAF
strength, an extra £5½ million was approved by the reluctant Treasury. Only

now was the wisdom of Trenchard's original concept of creating 'a good cottage on the foundations of a castle' to become appreciated. Having consolidated its hallmark of quality of men and prepared its 'bases', the adolescent RAF could now expand to the true strength and size which Trenchard had always advocated. As part of the new enlarging service establishment, the Air Defence of Great Britain Command (ADGB) ceased to exist in July 1936. In its place, the RAF in Britain was re-organised into four new Commands: Bomber, Fighter (which included Army co-operation and the Observer Corps), Coastal, which was responsible for all land-based and flying boat stations, including shore training of Fleet Air Arm units, and Training Command which, with a few exceptions, took control of all training units (flying and technical) within the United Kingdom.

On the matter of actual equipment, the state of the RAF's operational potential was vividly demonstrated on July 6, 1935, when King George V reviewed his air service at Mildenhall and Duxford. A total of 37 squadrons (356 aircraft) assembled for ground inspection by the King at Mildenhall in the morning, and then 20 of the squadrons executed a near-immaculate fly-past in salute at Duxford in the afternoon. Every aeroplane on view this day was a biplane; indeed, the latest design, placed on a stand at Duxford for close inspection, was the Gloster F7/30 – the forerunner of yet another biplane, the Gloster Glad-

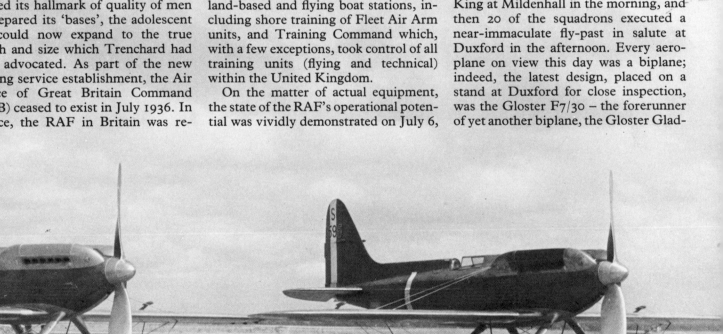

iator fighter. In squadron service the fastest fighter was the Gloster Gauntlet, capable of well over 200 mph but armed, like its 1917–18 predecessors, merely with twin machine guns. Three squadrons flew the aesthetically beautiful Hawker Fury I, but the remaining fighter units were mainly equipped with the obsolescent Bristol Bulldog. The bomber units were led by two squadrons of Handley Page Heyford biplanes, backed by the stalwart Hawker Harts, Audaxes, and Demons of the remaining units. None could reach a speed of 200 mph. The Heyfords could only just top 100 mph with a normal bomb load of approximately 3000 lb over a potential range of about 900 miles. In the 17 years since the 1918 Armistice, the only real progress in design and concept of the RAF's first-line aeroplanes had been in aero engines and a variety of minor items relating to safety and reliability. Armament had virtually stagnated, overlooking the basic requirement of any operational aircraft as a vehicle for offensive weapons. Fighting and bombing tactics were regarded as simply an extension of the drill square.

If officialdom was complacent with such a state of affairs within the nation's first-line defence, many private aircraft manufacturers were already attempting to rectify the situation by private venture designs for modern, all-metal monoplane fighters and bombers. Most significant among the many designs in embryo were the Hawker Hurricane and the Supermarine Spitfire. The Hurricane's origins could be traced to October 1933 when a 'Fury Monoplane' design, incorporating a Rolls-Royce Goshawk engine was first projected. In January 1934 it was decided to replace the Goshawk powerplant with a new Rolls-Royce engine, the PV.12, later to be named 'Merlin'. After further modifications and reappraisals of armament, the prototype Hurricane IK5083, made its initial flight on November 6, 1935, and within seven months the Air Ministry had placed a contract for 600 production machines. The Hurricane marked several 'firsts' in RAF history. It was the first operational fighter capable of speeds in excess of 300 mph, and the service's – indeed, the world's – first eight machine-gun first-line fighter. It entered service with 111 Squadron in late 1937. The Supermarine Spitfire – arguably the most beautiful fighter ever designed – was the creation of R J Mitchell, designer of the Schneider Trophy winning floatplanes, and the prototype, K5054, made its initial flight on March 5, 1936. Like the Hurricane, it was powered by a Rolls-Royce Merlin, and carried a battery of eight .303 machine guns in its slender wings. In its production form, the Spitfire entered RAF service with 19 Squadron at Duxford in August 1938.

For the bomber units too, modern designs were soon to be projected and progressed. In the autumn of 1936, Air Ministry specifications were issued calling for several heavy, all-metal, monoplane bombers. Of these, the Short Stirling was designed from its outset as a four-engined monoplane bomber – the first such to enter RAF service – while two other projects, the Handley Page HP 56 and Avro Manchester, were originally intended as twin-engined bombers, but were later re-designed for four engines resulting eventually in the Handley Page Halifax and Avro Lancaster. The first Stirling prototype, L7600, made its first and only flight in May 1939 when it crashed on landing. The second prototype, L7605, did not fly until shortly after the outbreak of war, but production Stirlings first entered service with 7 Squadron at Leeming in August 1940. The second four-engined 'heavy' to join the RAF Bomber Command was the Halifax, which first flew in its prototype form (L7244) on October 25, 1939, and entered service with 35 Squadron at Leeming in November 1940. Like the original Handley Page project, the Avro Manchester was designed to have twin Rolls-Royce Vulture engines. The Avro design team had serious doubts about these powerplants from the outset, and, while proceeding with the Manchester as originally conceived, also drew up plans for a four-engined version, titled Manchester III, powered by Rolls-Royce Merlins, in 1939. The team's doubts were amply justified after the Vulture-engined Manchesters entered service in November 1940. And their conception of the 'Manchester III' quickly became the Avro Lancaster – the finest bomber produced by Britain for operations in World War II.

The vital necessity of protecting Britain's ocean life-lines of merchant shipping, though primarily the task of the Royal Navy, was catered for in RAF Coastal Command by the introduction of the four-engined Short Sunderland flying boats in the summer of 1938. They soon began to replace the out-moded biplane flying boats already equipping the squadrons. In the same year the relatively small Army Co-operation element of the RAF began to receive its first monoplanes – the peculiarly-shaped Westland Lysanders. That time and money was expended on a concept of aerial warfare relating directly with World War I tactical appreciations merely exemplified the contemporary

Right: Probably the most adaptable design of the inter-war years was the classic Hawker Hart bomber, which entered RAF service in Jan 1930. From its basic design flowed a host of variations such as the Demon, Audax, Hector etc. Eventually replaced by its stable-mate, the Hind, in 1936, Hart continued in service in India and Egypt into the 1940s. No. 18 Sqn, depicted here, was reformed in Oct 1931 with Harts.

thinking of much of the Army's hierarchy. As interim measures, RAF Bomber Command began receiving several twin-engined and single-engined metal monoplane designs including the Armstrong Whitworth Whitley, Handley Page Hampden, Vickers Wellington, and Bristol Blenheim – all of which were destined to bear the brunt of war operations between 1939 and 1942 while awaiting replacement by the newer generation of four-engined heavy bombers. Of these, the Blenheim was the most numerous in use pre-1939, but almost equally numerous was the Fairey Battle,

Below: Last of the peacetime biplane bombers for the RAF was the Handley Page Heyford. In this view of K3503, a modified enclosed cockpit has been added, while the standard under-gunner's 'dustbin' turret is fully extended. Capable of carrying a bomb load of over 3000lb, the Heyford could only reach a speed of 140mph and a range of less than 1000 miles.

of which the RAF possessed nearly 1500 by September 1939. Totally unsuited for its allotted task, being too slow, poorly armed, and relatively lightly war-loaded, the Battle was to become a coffin for its gallant crews in the clashes with the Luftwaffe in May 1940.

Prime emphasis for the 1935–36 expansion plans was placed on greatly bolstering the Home Defence air units, and on generally improving conditions of service for airmen and officers in the junior ranks, the latter as an incentive to recruiting. In 1935 the RAF comprised 45,000 officers and airmen, and it was proposed to increase this total during 1936 to 50,000, the bulk of the increase being non-commissioned airmen. The 1936 Air Estimate for the RAF was set at £39 million (with an additional £3 million from Navy Estimates for the Fleet Air Arm), and a slight increase in pay was envisaged for all ranks. The Chief of Air Staff was given an annual 'rise' in salary of £25! Weekly pay for a Leading Aircraftman, with three years

seniority in a Grade 1 trade – a skilled fitter – was 42 shillings (£2.10), while a Flight Lieutenant on completion of four years service from promotion to Flying Officer was granted £1.3.6d per day (£1.17). The official demise of the 'dog-collar' tunic and breeches and puttees for everyday wear by airmen came in 1936, when an Air Ministry Order, dated April 2, introduced a new Service Dress for every non-commissioned airman below the rank of Sergeant, comprising an open-neck tunic with blue shirt and black tie, and trousers. Also 'introduced' was the Field Service side-cap for working hours – a revival of the original Royal Flying Corps side-cap, which the RAF re-introduced yet again in the early 1970s. The official description included the quaint, yet serious information that the new FS Cap '. . . can be adapted for use as a flying helmet. . .' In the event, the dog-collar tunic – so heartily condemned by T E Lawrence in the 1920s – continued to be used as a working jacket by many regular-serving air-

Right: Crews of 201 Sqn's Saro London flying boats on the shingle beach of RAF Calshot, early 1938. Fourth from left is Pilot Off Denis Spotswood, eventually to become ACM Sir Denis, CAS.

Above: Yet another derivant of the Hart was the FAA's Hawker Osprey. The example, K3626, pictured here is accompanied by an echelon of naval Hawker Nimrod fighters.

men until well after the outbreak of war in 1939.

No sooner had the expansion of the RAF begun in 1935, however, than it was called upon to strengthen Britain's defences in the Middle Eastern theatre, due to Italy's declaration of war against Abyssinia. Five light bomber and four fighter squadrons – their aircraft dismantled and crated – sailed from Liverpool on October 4, and eventually were dispersed around various key stations from Aden to Alexandria, ready for protection of British interests in the area. In addition three flying boat squadrons

arrived in the zone, and units of the Fleet Air Arm were brought to a readiness state. The 'emergency' lasted – for the RAF – until the summer of 1936, when the fighter squadrons began returning to England. Remarkably, the general public, though well-informed of the steps undertaken by its Army and Navy to counteract any escalation of the Italian invasion of Abyssinia, were told little of the RAF's part in the matter. Possibly the government's wide publicity for the proposed increase of taxpayers' money on air defence of the UK – £88½ million in 1937 and £111½ million in 1938 –

clashed with such an immediate depletion of the existing RAF defences at a moment's notice.

By April 1937 the expansion scheme was gathering momentum, and RAF strength stood at 100 squadrons in the United Kingdom (on paper), 26 squadrons based overseas, and 20 with the Fleet Air Arm. The Navy's long and bitter struggle to attain sovereignty over the latter reached part-fruition when on July 30, Prime Minister Neville Chamberlain, announced that complete control of the FAA was to be given to the Admiralty, which would supply all per-

Above: The Hart's successor, Hawker Hind. K6783 is pictured in Jun 1937, when serving with 62 Sqn, based at Cranfield. Under the lower wing can be seen a Light Series Bomb Carrier.

sonnel henceforth for air units of the Fleet, and accordingly would take over control of the air bases at Ford, Lee-on-Solent, Worthydown, and Donibristle for training of naval personnel. Nevertheless, RAF Coastal Command, on which the Admiralty had cast covetous eyes, remained firmly under the aegis of the Air Ministry, albeit with co-operation links with naval operational commands. Still highly conscious – some might say, obsessed – with the policy of attaining sheer numerical strength, an agreement for buying aircraft from the USA was inaugurated in April

1938, and in June it was announced that 400 aeroplanes (half of these Lockheed Hudsons, and the remainder trainers) had already been purchased. It was the start of an increasing dependence on American-built aeroplanes to maintain the RAF's strength during the next few years. This had the reciprocal benefit to America of virtually revitalising her small aircraft industry when British-financed aircraft factories were quickly built to cope with the large demand from British governments. Further impetus to the hasty re-arming of the RAF came with the September 1938 Munich Crisis,

when Britain came to the very brink of war with Hitler's Germany over the Führer's territorial ambitions in Europe. Neville Chamberlain's apparently 'weak' ploy of appeasement – and, incidentally, the sacrifice of Czechoslovakia – may have found little favour among the armchair hawks of London's military and naval clubs, but it gave an unprepared RAF at least a year's 'breathing space' in which to continue expanding and arming for the perhaps inevitable war to come. The Admiralty, now aware of its responsibilities to the minute naval air arm it had fought to

Left: The first all-metal cantilever monoplane heavy bomber for the RAF was the Fairey Hendon, which entered service with 38 Sqn at Mildenhall, Suffolk in Nov 1936. Its performance was little better than the biplane Heyford, and carried only half the Heyford's bomb load at little better speed, though over slightly increased range.

Above: Contemporary with the beautiful Hawker Fury II was the Gloster Gauntlet, last open-cockpit fighter for the RAF. In 1937, at least 19 squadrons flew Gauntlets; the example here is from 46 Sqn, based at Kenley.

possess but failed to nurture, announced in December 1938 that the Fleet Air Arm was to be enlarged from 3000 to 10,000 officers and men; and that the six aircraft carriers already in service were to be supported by a further seven carriers.

With the 1939 Air Estimate in excess of £200 million for the RAF, new organisations and extension to the service's establishment mushroomed swiftly.

Below: Pilots of 87 Sqn run to their Gloster Gladiators at Debden, Essex for a 'scramble, interception take-off. The unit's green 'snake' marking was derived from its 1918 original 'S' insignia. Last RAF biplane fighter, the Gladiator gave gallant service in the 1939–41 period in France, Norway, Egypt, Greece, Crete and Malta.

New flying training schools were opened, and three separate Commands were added – Balloon, Maintenance, and Reserve Commands. On June 28 King George VI gave Royal Assent to the formation of the Women's Auxiliary Air Force, and by September the first trained WAAFs were being posted to RAF stations to supplement war establishments of personnel. This initial 'invasion' of a hitherto all-male community was received with mixed feelings generally, and it should be noted that the WAAF was not *legally* admitted to the Armed Forces of the Crown until June 1941. If many more senior officers and NCOs had distinct reservations about women in uniform in 1939, within a year they were to change such opinions after witnessing the calm courage of 'mere adolescent girls' during the Luftwaffe's devastating bombing of Fighter Command's bases during the Battle of Britain. The second week of August 1939 saw the RAF in Britain undertake its biggest annual air exercises, when 1300 aircraft, 53,000 men, 110 guns, 700 searchlights and 100 barrage balloons

participated in the final peacetime 'war' lasting just four days. Within two weeks, on August 31, following the order for general mobilization, all RAF reservists were called to the colours, and the RAF worldwide was placed on a war footing. On that date the RAF could claim a total of 157 squadrons – nearly 2000 first-line aircraft, with almost 8000 more aeroplanes in reserve. Of these, 34 squadrons were at bases scattered throughout the Empire, while only 40 squadrons were equipped with fighters overall. And 28 of the total squadrons were still equipped with out-dated biplane fighters, bombers or flying boats. For home defence, 400 Hurricanes and 270 Spitfires were officially on strength. The remaining fighters were either out-moded biplanes or temporarily converted twin-engined bombers, such as the 396 Gloster Gladiators and 111 Blenheim 1Fs shown on official strength records. For offensive operations, RAF Bomber Command possessed nearly 600 Hampdens, Whitleys and Wellingtons, but the predominant designs available in greater numbers were Blenheims and Fairey Battles.

On September 1, 1939 Hitler's armies attacked Poland, and the RAF put into effect its pre-laid plans to detach an air formation of short-range bombers to France. Accordingly, the same day, orders were sent to No. 1 Group, Bomber Command for Operation 'Panther' – the code name for the move of ten Battle squadrons to France. On the following day, all ten units – 160 Fairey Battles – headed across the English Channel and landed in the Reims area, where they immediately prepared for their role as direct tactical support of the British Expeditionary Force (BEF) due to follow shortly. If the many years of procrastination by successive governments had not prepared the RAF for a European war in terms of actual equipment, at least the men of the RAF were of superb quality. Commanded and controlled by veterans of the first war in the air, and manned largely by products of the visionary Trenchard's various training schemes of the 1920s and early 1930s, the RAF in the autumn of that fateful year could hardly have been bettered in terms of skill, practical experience, and indomitable faith in itself. The cruel test of its abilities was yet to come.

Right: The last biplane Hawker fighter to see RAF service was the Fury II interceptor, first equipping 25 Sqn (illustrated) in late 1936. A maximum speed of 220mph-plus, and a service ceiling of almost 30,000ft, made the Fury II an ideal defender for its day. Already, however, the prototype Hawker Hurricane and Supermarine Spitfire were in embryo.

Debacle

As the Prime Minister's clipped, nasal speech announced to the world Britain's declaration of war against Germany on Sunday morning, September 3, 1939, the RAF, fully mobilised since August 31, swung hastily into action. Under the Bomber Command 'Scatter' plan, most bomber squadrons were dispersed to strange airfields, and crews stood by in 'Readiness' state awaiting operational orders. Just after noon a solitary Blenheim of 139 Squadron left Wyton to reconnoitre elements of the German Fleet based at Wilhelmshaven. Reaching its objective, the Blenheim crew spotted several warships, but were unable to pass this intelligence immediately. Their

wireless equipment had frozen. Elsewhere, Hampdens from 49, 83 and 144 Squadrons were seeking vainly to bomb German naval vessels, but they either brought their loads back or jettisoned them into the North Sea on the return journey. On September 4, Blenheims from 107, 110 and 139 Squadrons attacked several enemy capital ships near Wilhelmshaven while 14 Wellingtons, from 9 and 149 Squadrons, simultaneously tried to bomb two warships near Brunsbüttel. Of the 29 bombers engaged in these attacks, seven failed to return, and the out-dated General Purpose (GP) bombs used simply failed to achieve any worthwhile damage. Navi-

'. . . *an incredible combination of luck and judgment'.*
Blenheim leader's report on navigation to the target.

Below: Fairey Battle, K9438 of 88 Sqn at Boscombe Down during the Aug 1939 annual air exercises. All too soon the Battle units were to face grim reality in France . . .

Bottom: Hurricanes of 85 Sqn at Lille, late 1939 which were still to be tested in full combat with the Luftwaffe . . .

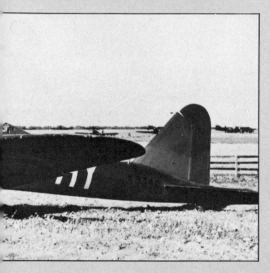

gation to the target by the Blenheim force had been '. . . an incredible combination of luck and judgment', in the words of the leader's report. These initial raids, made in atrocious weather conditions, exemplified the next few months of the bomber offensive: totally ineffective bombs, poor navigation, over-optimistic expectations of results. Only the superb courage and determination of the individual crews provided shining relief in an otherwise gloomy vista. Further reconnaissance sorties – by bombers, unescorted, and in broad daylight – finally brought disaster in December, when the Luftwaffe's fighters cut a crippling swathe through the rigidly-held, tight formations of Wellington bombers. Bomber Command's implicit faith in the unescorted daylight bomber being able to defend itself providing a 'tight formation' was kept – a legacy of the 1918 tactics evolved by Trenchard's Independent Force bomber crews – was shattered although further sorties of this type continued to be despatched thereafter. The command's overall dilemma lay in the fact that it was simply understrength in terms of aircraft available to pursue any far-reaching bombing offensive. Of the 33 first-line squadrons available on the outbreak of war, ten had gone to France with the BEF. The remaining squadrons were wholly equipped with twin-engined, relatively short-ranged Blenheims, Whitleys and Wellingtons. None of these could do more than prick the outer fringes of German territory from UK bases. Equally restrictive was the governmental policy imposed on the bomber chiefs to restrain bombing permitting only German naval targets to be bombed. In the interests of conservation of the relatively small bomber force, at least until the promised four-engined 'heavies' such as the Short Stirling were in frontline use, Bomber Command had little choice but to waste energy – and precious crews – in face-saving flights over western Germany, dropping propaganda leaflets. The 'phoney war' on the Western Front in 1939–40 applied to the skies above it as well.

The building of a strong, effective Bomber Command was necessarily slowed by the even greater necessity of establishing an immediately effective home defence system within Fighter Command. The looming threat of an estimated force of 2000 long-range Luftwaffe bombers outweighed all other operational considerations in the mind of the commander, Hugh Dowding, who had pressed strongly before the war for a force of at least 53 fighter squadrons, equipped with the latest Hurricanes and Spitfires, for effective defence of the United Kingdom. In September 1939 he had only 35 squadrons, of which 27 were equipped with Spitfires and Hurricanes.

Top left: Fairey Battle of 12 Sqn, France.
Top right: Hawker Hurricane L1628 of 87 Sqn, in which Sqn Ldr W E Coope force-landed in Belgium on Nov 4, 1939. It was the first of several Hurricanes interned by (then) neutral Belgium.
Far left: Bristol Blenheim IV of 139 Sqn over France, early 1940. The Blenheim units suffered high casualties during the imminent blitzkrieg . . .
Below: Hurricane I, P2617, with fixed pitch two-blade Watts propeller, in France Feb 1940. Morale among the crews was still high.

Of these, four Hurricane squadrons accompanied the BEF to France that month, further reducing the strength of the UK fighter shield. Dowding, utterly convinced of the storm to come, proceeded to fight tooth and nail, not only to increase his understrength command, but to ward off the many demands from other commands and the government to detach fighter squadrons to other duties. By December 1939 Dowding, with backing from the Chief of Air Staff, Newall, obtained an additional 18 squadrons. Most of them were half-formed and equipped with crudely converted Blenheim I and Fairey Battle bombers. By May 1940, however, four Blenheim units had been transferred to Coastal Command, and two others sent to France. But nine squadrons had converted to Spitfires or Hurricanes, leaving Dowding with only 47 frontline squadrons.

Part of Dowding's overall task interlinked with the role of Coastal Command – protection of shipping in coastal waters, and naval ports and bases. Coastal Command's air strength at the beginning of the war comprised 20 squadrons – eleven equipped with Avro Ansons, one with Lockheed Hudsons, two with Short Sunderlands, and the rest with obsolete biplane flying boats and torpedo 'strike' aircraft. Thus, during the early months Dowding was forced to assign a handful of frontline fighter squadrons to the defence of key naval bases, such as Scapa Flow. The Admiralty, having fought for decades to possess its own, independent air service, had made no provision for air cover of its own vital bases. Chief area for Coastal Command's role was the North Sea, through which German naval warships and submarines had to travel to reach the open ocean, and the first months of the war saw Coastal's mainly obsolescent aircraft engaged in virtually unending reconnaissance over the North Sea waters, apart from myriad divergent tasks in co-operation with mercantile and naval shipping. The growing menace of the German U-boat was difficult to counter with the existing anti-submarine bombs then in use, which were completely ineffective, and attention was given to developing an airborne depth charge. It was a period in which Coastal Command, though unable to contribute very much to the many Royal Navy successes against the enemy's shipping, was building the foundations of its own later success in the air-sea war. Germany's invasion and annexation of Norway and Denmark in April-May 1940 – an object-lesson in the dominating effect of air superiority on the success of any land or sea battle – intensified Coastal Command's operational commitments, but extra stress was placed on Hugh Dowding's Fighter Command. The Luftwaffe now had bases from which its long-range bombers could reach any part of the UK's eastern coastal areas.

In France the Battle squadrons of the Advance Air Striking Force (AASF) and their two Hurricane squadrons, 1 and 73, found little action during the winter of 1939–40, beyond occasional reconnaissance sorties and some spasmodic clashes with the Luftwaffe. The other squadrons of the BEF's Air Component, composed of Blenheims, Lysanders, and Hurricanes, flew a steady routine of tactical support to the Army, but were equally free of any major involvement with German fighters and bombers. The 'Phoney War' abruptly altered in the dawn of May 10, when German troops and their Luftwaffe 'umbrella' began a devastating blitzkrieg ('lightning war') against the Low Countries. With a preliminary concerted attack on 70 airfields in France, Belgium and Holland – nine of which housed RAF aircraft – the Luftwaffe created havoc, but the RAF luckily suffered little damage. Every fighter squadron flew from dawn to dusk that day, some pilots putting in six or seven sorties before nightfall. The Battle crews were also out, seeking the German advance columns and attempting to bomb these from low level. Of the 32 Battles despatched that day, thirteen were hacked out of the sky by mobile 88mm flak guns and roving Messerschmitt fighters, and the survivors were all damaged. It was an ominous portent of the imminent fate of all Battle crews in France. That night Wellingtons of Bomber Command were sent to attack the German-held airfield at Waalhaven, near Rotterdam, and this form of additional offensive by bombers based in England continued for several nights. The following day saw 114 Squadron (Blenheims) virtually destroyed on its own airfield. Other Blenheims and Battles continued to suffer high casualties in their attempts to harass the ever-advancing Germans. At dawn on May 12, nine Blenheims of 139 Squadron strafed a column of troops on the road from Maastricht to Tongres – and were swamped by a horde of Messerschmitt Bf 109s, losing seven to the agile fighters. Throughout the day the Battles, Blenheims and Hurricanes tried again and again to destroy the already captured bridges across the Albert Canal. Five Battles from 12 Squadron set out on a suicidal mission to bomb two bridges at Vroenhoven and Veldwezelt, only to be met by a veritable wall of 88mm flak. Four Battles were shot down. The fifth managed to stagger part-way home before force-landing. In the leading Battle of one sub-Flight, Flying Officer Donald Garland and his Observer, Sergeant Tom Gray, perished but were honoured with a posthumous V.C.

Elsewhere that day Bomber Command Blenheims were valiantly attempting to break the bridges over the Meuse, but no damage was achieved, and ten of the 24 Blenheims failed to return. Fifteen AASF Battles raiding targets near Bouillon lost six of their number to marauding Messerschmitts and deadly accurate groundfire. The loss rate for May 10–11–12 was frightening – 40 per cent, 100 per cent, and 62 per cent respectively. Of nearly 140 bombers serviceable on the morning of the 10th, the AASF was reduced to 72 by dusk on the 12th. Pausing briefly to recuperate on May 13, every available aircraft was flung into the battle for the Sedan bridgehead on the 14th. The French air service tried first, and was so severely mauled that it flew no more sorties that day. In the late afternoon the entire AASF's bombers made their attack – 71 Blenheims and Battles from 12, 105, 139, 150 and 218 Squadrons – and 40 never came back, the highest loss rate ever experienced by the RAF to date. With no alternative, the remnants of the AASF squadrons were forced to retreat, moving westwards on May 16 to rough grass airfields in the Troyes area. From there only isolated sorties, mainly by night, were flown, but the relentless advance by German troops forced their further

withdrawal on June 3 to fresh airfields in the Le Mans district. The swan-song of the bombers came on June 13, when ten patched Battles strafed troops along the banks of the Seine. Two formations, totalling 38, bombed German positions by the Marne, and lost six aircraft to the 88mm flak crews. Forty-eight hours later the hopeless position of the survivors was so evident that an order was given for all remaining serviceable bombers to return to England. The pitiful procession of scarred Battles and their exhausted crews crossed the Channel and landed at the first airfield they could find. Between May 10 and June 15 alone the AASF had lost 115 aircraft and almost as many crews – virtually the entire strength available on the opening day of the German blitzkrieg. The evidence of the bomber crews' valour lay in a hundred wrecked and burned bombers strewn in the valleys and forests of France. Added to these smouldering memorials to raw courage were the pyres of the British-based bomber crews sent to bolster a bombing offensive doomed from the outset.

If the tragic bomber casualties caused concern in London, the plight of the fighter units became a nightmare for Hugh Dowding, who had emphasised constantly that the real battle for survival would be over England, not France. His visionary forecast – largely ignored by Whitehall – was now only too obvious. From the first day of the German onslaught France became an ever-increasing drain on Dowding's already slender command, and he fought a daily, almost hourly battle with the government and his superiors at Air Ministry, trying desperately to prevent more precious fighters being thrown into the hopeless French campaign. Despite personal assurances by Winston Churchill, who had been appointed Prime Minister of a new government on May 10, Dowding continued to be ordered to despatch more fighters to France. When Oper-

Left: Once the fury of the German onslaught in the Low Countries erupted in May 1940, the few Hurricane squadrons in France were in constant action. Here, Sgt 'Sammy' Allard of 85 Sqn is greeted on his return from a sortie during which he destroyed two enemy aircraft.
Below: Flt Lt John Ignatius 'Iggy' Kilmartin of 1 Sqn, a unit which claimed 100 victims before its eventual return to England in Jun 1940.

ation Dynamo – the evacuation of the BEF from Dunkirk – commenced fully on the evening of May 26, the Army and Navy insisted upon constant air cover over the evacuation area. This task was impossible to achieve from airfields 50–60 miles away with the available aircraft strength of Fighter Command. The onus of providing air protection for the Dunkirk evacuation fell on Keith Park, the brilliant New Zealander commanding Fighter Command's No. 11 Group, who could only muster some 200 fighters. Using one or two squadrons, Park succeeded in providing at least a form of continuous cover. His pilots, mostly unblooded in combat, cheerfully accepted fighting odds as high as 50 and even 100-to-one, as they tackled the huge arrays of Luftwaffe bombers and fighters attempting to annihilate the BEF on Dunkirk's beaches. Inevitably, many German bombers hit their target – sheer weight of numbers prevailed – but it is little realised how much greater the assault from the air might have been had it not been for the RAF's unceasing defence. Backing the fighters were a motley collection of aircraft from other commands – Skuas, Lysanders and Ansons, crewed by anyone available. They faced terrifying odds.

The combination of fighting over every facet of the BEF's initial battles and eventual retreat to and evacuation from Dunkirk, was costly for Dowding's pilots. From May 10 until the end of Operation Dynamo, 432 Hurricanes and Spitfires were expended. The whole campaign of the blitzkrieg cost the RAF as a whole, 959 aircraft, of which 477 were fighters of all types. The 66 additional fighters lost in the disastrously brief Norwegian venture – 32 of which were fighters – meant that in a mere 40 days the RAF had expended the equivalent of more than 40 complete squadrons of aircraft and crews. The original Hurricane squadrons of the AASF and Air Component had created a legend for courage in France as well as a fighting record which was unsurpassed. By May 24 No. 1 Squadron alone had lost a total of 38 Hurricanes, but the original pilots, who were withdrawn to England on that date and replaced by fresh men, had claimed nearly 100 victims in air combat. With its sister unit, 73 Squadron, it continued the rearguard fight until June 18, when the last surviving aircraft and personnel finally left French soil for England. In England the exhausted crews were quickly rested and re-formed. Decimated squadrons were either re-equipped or dispersed to form new units. Aircraft factories were urged to step up production to the highest possible figures. With a triumphant German military juggernaut less than 20 miles from Dover, and a massive Luftwaffe regrouping and re-equipping well within bombing range of any point of southern England, it could only be a matter of time before the real battle for Britain's survival – indeed, her very existence – would begin.

The projected invasion of Britain – Operation Sea Lion – though already outlined, was not seriously undertaken until after Hitler's offer of peace terms to England on July 19, 1940. In the meantime the Luftwaffe, now based in northern France, rested and eager for further operations, used only a fraction of its strength to harass southern England. This totally unexpected lull in air operations gave Dowding a slim opportunity to rebuild and consolidate the thin ranks of Fighter Command. Extending his area of defences along the whole of the southern counties, Dowding worked incessantly to strengthen the fighter squadrons. His main deficiencies were trained pilots rather than aeroplanes.

Nearly 300 combat-tested fighter pilots had been irretrievably lost in the French debacle, and the ever-expanding RAF training schemes could not replace such men overnight. Replacements were culled from every possible source. Bomber and reconnaissance pilots were hastily converted to Spitfires and Hurricanes. The Fleet Air Arm 'loaned' trained men. The flying training schools gave up experienced instructors wherever they could possibly be spared without disrupting the steady flow of embryo pilots. Not all the frontline squadrons were inexperienced. Many had fought in France and over Dunkirk, while 'salting' many of the other squadrons were the veterans of the French campaign who had given the vaunted Luftwaffe its first, bloody taste of the RAF's mettle. On the eve of what Winston Churchill termed the Battle of Britain, the fighter pilots were supremely confident and ready for the fray.

Below: The poignant remains of a Hurricane in France reflects the bitter but hopeless task which faced the few squadrons fighting Germany's military might in France in May–Jun 1940. Bottom: L–r: Sgt Pilkington; Flt Lt 'Ginger' Paul; Fg Off 'Fanny' Orton; and Fg Off Edgar 'Cobber' Kain – all of 73 Sqn. Kain, a New Zealander, became the first five-victory RAF 'ace' of WWII, and claimed 17 victories in all before his death in a flying accident in Jun 1940.

So Few

The aerial struggle in the skies of southern England during the high summer of 1940 – now immortalised in the nation's history as the Battle of Britain – was primarily a triumph for the RAF Fighter Command. In its four months duration a total of 3080 pilots – for the most part young, eager men – fought a daily contest of wits, skill and matchless courage with an equally skilled, determined opponent, the Luftwaffe. For the Germans it was simply another stage in their fanatical leader's grandiose plan of world domination. For the RAF the conflict was a desperate defence of its homeland and heritage. Yet if the self-sacrifice and astounding prowess of the fighter pilots – the 'Few' as Churchill was to title them – earned undying fame so deservedly, it was not wholly and simply their individual and corporate deeds which were responsible for the defeat of the projected German invasion of Britain. Magnificent as it was, their succinct role was one of defence. With the Army only slowly recovering from the shambles of the French disaster, and the traditional first-line defence of the

Royal Navy powerless to turn back any air armada, the only offensive weapon available to Britain was its relatively small, comparatively inexperienced RAF Bomber Command. While 'Dowding's Chicks' flung themselves daily against seemingly impossible odds in the ever-blue skies, the bomber crews hit back each night: battering potential invasion embarkation ports in France and Holland, disrupting lines of communication, and giving the German population a foretaste of the meaning of total war. Elsewhere, the thinly-spread Coastal Command crews continued their vital task of protecting the merchant shipping supplying Britain's vital war materials and food. On the ground the men and women of the balloon barrage, radar stations (known then as RDF – Radio Direction Finding) and sector control rooms played their vital parts. Meanwhile the 'ordinary' airmen and airwomen of the servicing crews worked without pause, providing a truly magnificent backing for the exhausted fighter pilots. Indeed, without this unceasing back-up ground maintenance,

the fighters' eventual triumph would not have been possible.

By June 19, 1940 the remnants of the RAF in France had found their way back to England. At Fighter Command's headquarters at Bentley Priory, Stanmore, Hugh Dowding was already preparing for the inevitable aerial onslaught against Britain by the Luftwaffe. His task appeared hopeless. The German military machine now occupied countries in a semi-circle around Britain's east and south coasts, stretching from Norway to western France. All were potential springboards for an intensive bombing assault on the United Kingdom. The best intelligence reports available to Dowding gave the Luftwaffe's estimated strength as well over 2000 operationally fit aircraft, some 60 per cent of which were bombers. Against this array, Dowding could only produce about 1200 trained pilots and just over 800 aircraft – of which less than 600 aeroplanes were considered first-line machines. Fighter aircraft production was already receiving top priority, but trained pilots were in desperately short supply. Dowding's

Left: AM Sir Keith Park, commander of No. 11 Group in 1940, and Dowding's chief lieutenant.
Below left: Over Dunkirk and the English Channel the few Boulton Paul Defiant crews secured initial successes. Seen here, Sqn Ldr Philip Hunter, (3rd from left standing) and his 264 Sqn crews.
Below: An underground fighter control room – nodal point of Fighter Command's defence system.
Right: Pilots of 151 Sqn (Hurricanes) at North Weald in Jul 1940. Fourth from left is Sqn Ldr E M Donaldson, OC Sqn; while fifth from left is Wg Cdr Victor Beamish, cdr of North Weald Station.
Below right: ACM Sir Hugh Caswall Tremenheere Dowding.

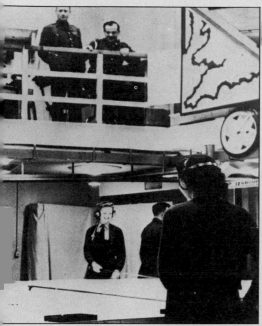

command was composed of four main Groups, Nos. 10, 11, 12 and 13. Of these, 11 Group, commanded by Keith Park, was responsible for the prime battle area of south-eastern England, including London and the bulk of Fighter Command's fighter stations. Covering the western counties was 10 Group; and 12 Group, commanded by T L Leigh-Mallory, was responsible for the Midlands and the northern areas of East Anglia. North of 12 Group's territory was 13 Group, a safeguard against any possible intrusion from the Luftwaffe based in Norway. Two other Groups, 9 and 14, for the defence of north-west England and Scotland, were still in the process of completion. At the very heart of the command's overall defence system was the network of radar detection stations spread thinly along the southern and eastern coasts of Britain. Each was linked to the command Group and Sector controllers, who were in direct contact with the fighter squadrons both on the ground and airborne. This 'early warning' system, instigated in May 1937 when the first station at Bawdsey was inaugurated,

gave barely adequate but vital warning of any aircraft approaching Britain's shores, thereby enabling the fighter controllers to despatch available fighters to intercept accordingly. Forewarned, Dowding's command robbed the Luftwaffe pilots of any hoped-for surprise tactics in attack. Their height, strength and direction were already known and transmitted to the fighter pilots in the air.

Operations against England were started by the Luftwaffe on the night of June 5–6, a modest bombing raid against airfields near the east coast. They became more intensive in late June with a series of daylight attacks against Allied merchant shipping in the English Channel. Fighter Command was forced to retaliate in some strength, and the consequent clashes gave the confident Luftwaffe its first inkling of the fierce defence they were to encounter during the coming months. Flying some 600 sorties each day, the RAF fighter pilots became accustomed (if such a description can ever be used) to the sight of layer upon layer of black-crossed opponents in awesome array – odds never before met in the history of air warfare. On June 30, a week after the end of the French campaign, Hermann Goering, head of the Luftwaffe, issued general directions for air operations against England, with the RAF's destruction as the prime consideration. On July 11 he gave specific orders for attacks on the Channel convoys in order to draw out the RAF fighter force. After Hitler's appeal for 'peace' with England on July 19, and Britain's categorical refusal three days later, the Führer ordered his military and naval commanders to proceed with Directive No. 16 – 'a landing operation against England' (Operation Sea Lion) – which he had originally ordered on July 16, three days *before* his offer of peace terms to Britain. The prerequisite to any such invasion – air superiority over southern England – was boastfully promised by Goering, who issued final orders on August 2 for *Adlertag* (Eagle Day) – in which RAF Fighter Command was to be destroyed. This was eventually set to begin on August 13.

To the fighter pilots of the RAF these machinations within Germany's military high command, even had they been known, were of less immediate importance than the already heavy air offensive increasing daily from across the Channel. Flying four and five sorties daily, they desperately flung themselves against formations of 100 or more Luftwaffe bombers, heavily escorted by wheeling *jagdstaffeln* (fighter units) of Messerschmitt Bf 109s and Bf 110s. Tactics

*Far left: Two pilots from 43 Sqn: Flt Lt
Peter Townsend (l) and the South
African, Flt Lt Caesar Hull.
Above left: Flt Lt A W A Bayne, DFC
of 17 Sqn in the cockpit of his Hurricane.
Above: Adolph Gysbert Malan, DSO,
DFC who fought with 74 'Tiger' Sqn
throughout 1940.
Above right: Spitfires of 610 Sqn, 1940.
Below: Flt Lt Ian 'Widge' Gleed, DFC
in Hurricane P2798 of 87 Sqn. Gleed,
who fought in France, the Battle of
Britain, and throughout 1941–42,
became Wg Cdr with the Desert Air
Force and was eventually killed in combat
on Apr 16, 1943.*

were empirical at first. The prewar
'pretty' tight Vic-formations, so restrictive of initiative, had been abandoned
after the fall of France, and individual
squadron commanders adopted individual techniques according to the situation
confronting them. In the main these
comprised headlong plunges into the
heart of the Heinkel and Dornier mass
formations, followed by an individual
free-for-all hunt for targets by each
pilot. It soon became policy by the command to 'ignore' the German fighter escorts and concentrate on the bombers,
whenever this was practicably possible.
The strain on the Spitfire and Hurricane
pilots mounted swiftly, with physical
and nervous parameters being reached
within weeks of such continuous combat. Constant flying and fighting at high
altitude and battle damage resulting in
potentially dangerous landings, and not

uncommon parachute descents in the
midst of fighting sapped the pilots' energy. In the RAF's favour was the knowledge that pilots were fighting above
their homeland. They could be retrieved
if they were forced to abandon their aircraft. The psychological reaction to this
knowledge was some comfort to the
hard-pressed fighter pilots. Dowding,
for his part, had wisely refused to commit the 20 squadrons then responsible
for defence of areas north of 11 Group's
zone of responsibility to the developing
main battle in the south. Instead he used
these 'backwater' units as turn-round
replacements for combat-weary and depleted squadrons, which were sent to the
relative safety of the north to rest, recuperate and replenish aircraft and personnel. This system prevailed throughout the battle.

The preliminary month of fighting –

*Right: H M Stephen, DSO (l) and
J C Mungo-Park, DFC, both high-
scoring pilots of 74 'Tiger' Sqn in 1940.
Mungo-Park was killed in action on Jun
27, 1941 over France.
Far right: Sqn Ldr (later, A Cdre) Alan
Deere, DSO, DFC who flew with 54 Sqn
in 1940. His numerous escapes from death
– including many bale-outs by parachute
– were legendary. A New Zealander, 'Al'
Deere first joined the RAF in 1937.*

from July 10 to August 10 – resulted in the loss of 227 Luftwaffe aircraft against RAF losses of 96. These figures did not account for the many other German bombers which returned to their French airfields bullet-riven, seriously dam-aged, and often bearing dead or woun-ded crews. Nor do they differentiate be-tween RAF fighters totally destroyed and aircraft, however seriously damaged, which were salvaged and rebuilt. What such figures do reveal is the deter-mination, skill and valour of the fighter pilots in tackling frightening odds and winning the battle of attrition in the air. Principal targets for the Luftwaffe were the RAF fighter bases and, initially, the mast towers of the radar early-warning stations in south-east England. Even with the advan-tage of hindsight, it remains a matter of some astonishment that in 1940 the Luftwaffe's intelligence service was lacking in precise information as to which were the key RAF fighter bases. Though most airfields received raids of high intensity during August and Sep-tember, a great deal of German effort was dispelled on minor, even relatively unimportant targets, leaving Fighter Command to continue the fight if only with slender ground organisations in-tact. Even more astonishing was the fact that the Luftwaffe's high command nourished a dangerous illusion that such

misdirected attacks on non-essential airfields were successful in crippling RAF defence capabilities, prior to the projected *Adlertag* assault. Bolstered in this belief by over-optimistic claims of enemy aircraft shot down by the German fighters, Goering complacently pushed ahead plans for the 'decisive air struggle' in mid-August. On August 12 large-scale raids were made against the airfields at Hawkinge, Lympne, Man-ston, and naval installations at Ports-mouth, and other attacks were made on the various radar stations in Kent and Hampshire. The fighting that day was the fiercest to date, resulting in 22 RAF fighters being lost, but over 30 Luftwaffe aircraft were shot down. The damage caused on the ground, by no means small, was cleared and repaired by the indefatigable ground crews, and – with the exception of the radar station at

Ventnor, Isle of Wight – they were in working order by the following morning.

Adlertag – August 13 – dawned mistily with a fine drizzle of rain, leading to a postponement by Goering of the original start-time of 0730 hrs until 1400 hrs. He had assembled impressive strength for the assault, comprising nearly 1300 bombers and 1000 fighters, the bulk of which were based in northern France. To combat this armada Dowding could only muster 23 squadrons in 11 Group, with some 36 more squadrons scattered throughout the other three Groups. The total was some 1100 fighters, little more than 700 of which were immediately available for operations. The planned massive assault by the Luftwaffe started in error, when 55 Dorniers of KG2, led by Oberst Johannes Fink, set out at 0730 hrs to bomb Eastchurch airfield, not having received the postponement sig-nal. The Dorniers reached their objec-tive, plastered Eastchurch fairly thor-oughly, and were jumped by Spitfires on their return journey, losing four bomb-ers. At the amended zero hour of 1400 hrs, 23 Messerschmitt Bf 110 twin-engined fighters set out for Portland. Their task was to draw the RAF fighters into combat, after which the main bomb-er formations would strike during the period in which the Spitfires and Hurri-canes were refuelling. The Bf 110s suc-ceeded in their prime task, but they were attacked by three Spitfire and Hurricane squadrons from Exeter, Warmwell and Tangmere which outnumbered the Ger-mans by two to one. The Messerschmitts

*Left: Some of 601 Sqn, AAF's Hurricane
pilots during the Battle. Dubbed 'Week-
end Fliers' before the outbreak of war,
the AAF crews achieved fighting records
second to none throughout 1939–45.*

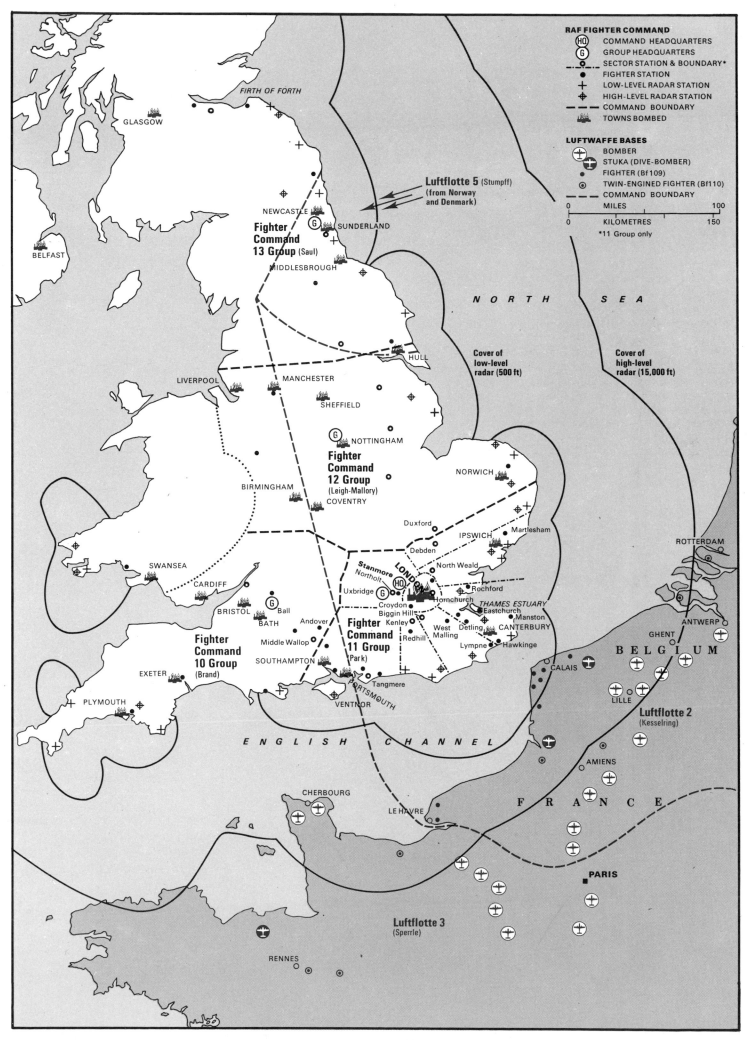

RAF FIGHTER COMMAND
- (HO) COMMAND HEADQUARTERS
- (G) GROUP HEADQUARTERS
- SECTOR STATION & BOUNDARY*
- FIGHTER STATION
- LOW-LEVEL RADAR STATION
- HIGH-LEVEL RADAR STATION
- COMMAND BOUNDARY
- TOWNS BOMBED

LUFTWAFFE BASES
- BOMBER
- STUKA (DIVE-BOMBER)
- FIGHTER (Bf 109)
- TWIN-ENGINED FIGHTER (Bf110)
- COMMAND BOUNDARY

MILES 0 — 100
KILOMETRES 0 — 150
*11 Group only

FIRTH OF FORTH

GLASGOW

BELFAST

NEWCASTLE

Luftflotte 5 (Stumpff)
(from Norway
and Denmark)

Fighter
Command
13 Group (Saul)

SUNDERLAND

MIDDLESBROUGH

NORTH SEA

HULL

Cover of
low-level
radar (500 ft)

Cover of
high-level
radar (15,000 ft)

LIVERPOOL

MANCHESTER

SHEFFIELD

NOTTINGHAM

NORWICH

Fighter
Command
12 Group
(Leigh-Mallory)

BIRMINGHAM

COVENTRY

Duxford

IPSWICH   Martlesham

ROTTERDAM

Debden

Stanmore
Northolt

LONDON

North Weald

SWANSEA

CARDIFF

Uxbridge

Rochford

ANTWERP

BRISTOL   Ball

BATH

Andover

Croydon
Biggin Hill
Kenley

Hornchurch

THAMES ESTUARY
Eastchurch

Manston

CANTERBURY

GHENT

BELGIUM

Middle Wallop

West
Malling

Detling

Fighter
Command
10 Group
(Brand)

Redhill

SOUTHAMPTON

Fighter
Command
11 Group
(Park)

Lympne

Hawkinge

CALAIS

LILLE

Luftflotte 2
(Kesselring)

EXETER

PORTSMOUTH

Tangmere

VENTNOR

PLYMOUTH

ENGLISH   CHANNEL

AMIENS

CHERBOURG

LE HAVRE

FRANCE

Luftflotte 3
(Sperrle)

PARIS

RENNES

finally limped back to their Caen base. Five German aircraft were lost and the remainder were riddled with machine-gun fire. Their effort was in vain. The 'follow-up' bombers did not attack until three hours later, by which time the RAF fighters were again ready for them. As wave after wave of Junkers 87s, Heinkels, and their Messerschmitt Bf 109 escorts crossed the Channel and attacked various airfields, the RAF fighters cut them up. In all, 484 bombers and about 1000 fighters crossed the English coast that day. The RAF shot down 34 and lost 13 Spitfires and Hurricanes. Dozens of other German bombers, slashed and semi-crippled by the fury of RAF's defenders, staggered back to France, witnesses of the continuing potency of RAF Fighter Command.

Bad weather the following day precluded any attacks in strength, and save for a brief 'nuisance' raid on Manston, the day passed relatively quietly. August 15 started with equally bad weather conditions, but quickly changed to a bright summer's day. Accordingly, the Luftwaffe set out again to destroy the

Above: Pilots of 41 Sqn at Hornchurch, Sept 1940. The unit commander, Sqn Ldr D O Finlay, DFC (standing centre) was a prewar Olympic Hurdles champion. Second from left, standing is Norman Ryder; second from right is E P 'Hawkeye' Wells – both stalwart members of 41 Sqn throughout the Battle. Above right: Hurricanes of 615 Sqn get away from Northolt in Oct 1940. Right: Spitfire I flown by Colin Gray of 54 Sqn, Hornchurch, Apr 1940.

RAF fighter airfields. By dusk, after a day of unceasing combat and interceptions, the RAF optimistically rejoiced in announcing claims for an unprecedented 182 German aircraft shot down. The true figures were 55 Luftwaffe machines brought down, against an RAF loss figure of 34. Again, the German crews' identification of targets was poor. Instead of the designated objectives of Biggin Hill, Kenley and similar key fighter bases, the bomber crews had attacked Croydon, West Malling and other less vital airfields. That same day Goering, in conference with his air commanders, directed that all future raids were to concentrate solely on destruction of RAF Fighter Command's aircraft, bases and production factories. He also made the major error of ordering a cessation of attacks against the chain of radar stations, as he was apparently ignorant of the true importance of this warning and tactical guidance system to the RAF fighters. For the remainder of August, therefore, the RAF's fighter stations suffered heavily. Particularly badly hit –

though typical of many other bases – were Hornchurch and Biggin Hill, which suffered devastatingly accurate bombing raids on August 31. Hornchurch, a sector station with four squadrons, was caught napping in the afternoon by KG2's Dorniers, whose bombs were falling across the airfield before the ground alarm had sounded. Frantically attempting to take off among the bomb bursts were three Spitfires from 54 Squadron, when a stick of bombs landed squarely between them. One Spitfire, piloted by Sergeant Davies, was literally blown into an adjoining field; a second, piloted by Pilot Officer Edsell, had both wings shorn off and crashed; the third fighter, with Flight Lieutenant Al Deere in the cockpit, was thrown upside down as it became airborne, and skidded across the field on its back for hundreds of yards. Amazingly, all three pilots es-

Below: The brief pause between sorties, as the faithful erks refuel, re-arm Hurricanes of 601 Sqn, AAF at Tangmere in the summer of 1940. Pilot at left is Max Aitken, son of Lord Beaverbrook.

caped with minimal injuries, and, indeed, were airborne again next day, continuing the fight. Biggin Hill, still groggily recovering from three consecutive damaging bomb attacks the day before, was again hit on this day with appalling results. With the air station already bereft of gas, water, electricity and telephone communications, and with over 60 personnel dead from the previous raids, the few buildings still standing were razed to the ground by more bombs on the 31st, and the operations building, the nerve centre for the station's three fighter squadrons, were wrecked. A courier, despatched from Kenley to reestablish communication, was horrified at what he found, '. . . the airfield was like a slaughterhouse . . .' Dazed and shocked, the airmen and airwomen of Biggin Hill retrieved what they could from the wreckage, and set up a temporary 'operations room' in a nearby village shop, thereby enabling one squadron to be controlled for further operations.

In the 14 days from August 24 to September 6, the main period of assault against Fighter Command airfields, the RAF lost 103 pilots killed and 128 seriously injured, with an overall loss of 466 Spitfires and Hurricanes either written-off charge or in need of major repairs. The grim pace of the endless fighting was taking a stark toll of Fighter Command machines and, particularly, pilots. Utterly exhausted and depleted squadrons were being continually rotated with ostensibly 'fresh' squadrons from the quieter sectors in the north, but the limits of human endurance were fast approaching. Then, fortuitously for

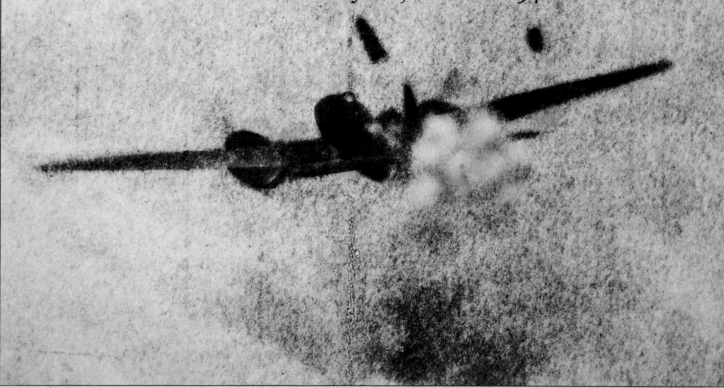

'I gave him a two-second burst and his starboard engine erupted . . .'
A Heinkel III 'buys it', Summer 1940.

'...the airfield was like a slaughterhouse...'

Left: 'And left the vivid air signed with their honour...' Vapour trails of combat over Kent in the high summer of 1940 recall Stephen Spender's lines...
Below: Pilots of 32 Sqn relaxing between sorties at Hawkinge on Jul 31, 1940. In background is Hurricane P3522, GZ-V; its trolley accumulator is plugged in for immediate start, and pilot's parachute pack on the tailplane ready for fast donning.
Above: Hurricane of 32 Sqn lets down at Biggin Hill on Aug 15, 1940.

Dowding and Park, Goering ordered a complete switch in tactical objectives. From September 7 all efforts were to be channelled into devastating London by day and night. In fact, London had already suffered several isolated raids, but this new directive provided a great measure of relief to the hard hit Fighter Command operational structure, though only a modicum of ease for the pilots who were now called upon to defend the heart of the British Empire.

One major reason for this new de-cision was the depredation being caused by the squadrons of RAF Bomber Command, who almost nightly were raiding French ports and even Berlin itself. Hitler's avowed intention to invade Britain still held, and during late August and early September many French and Dutch ports were filling with a host of invasion barges intended to convey the eventual landing forces. 'Operation Sea Lion' – the code name for the actual invasion, had been set for September 15, on the assumption that Goering's boast

Below left: As the pilot climbed out of his cockpit, the ground erks moved in.
Below: Plt Off Albert G Lewis climbing out of his 85 Sqn Hurricane after combat.
Below right: Spitfire pilots of 19 Sqn. The sqn CO, Sqn Ldr B J 'Sandy' Lane, DFC is seated on wing root, top left.
Far right: Men of 92 ('East India') Sqn, with Cdr John Kent. At Kent's right elbow is Brian 'Kingpin' Kingcombe.

Below: Spitfire I of 19 Sqn, Duxford being refurbished between combats. Note 'blown' canvas covers of wing gun ports and ammunition replenishment boxes in foreground.

that his Luftwaffe would crush the RAF would be implemented. Photo reconnaissance by RAF aircraft revealed the gradual build-up of the invasion barge fleet, and Bomber Command set out to nullify this threat. Night after night Hampdens, Whitleys, and Wellingtons unloaded their bombs over the tightly packed barge concentrations, creating havoc. The determination of the bomber crews to match the efforts of their fighter comrades were exemplified by two crew members who were awarded a Victoria Cross each for these operations. On the night of August 12–13, Flight Lieutenant Roderick Learoyd of 49 Squadron was the last of a formation of Hampden bomber pilots to attack the vital Dortmund-Ems Canal. He ran the gauntlet of terrifying flak and groundfire to place his bombs in the right place, and then piloted a shattered aircraft back to Scampton to eventually land safely. On the night of September 15 Sergeant John Hannah, a wireless-operator/air-gunner in an 83 Squadron Hampden bombing barges in Antwerp harbour, fought a horrifying fire in his aircraft and succeeded in quenching the blaze single-handed. Only 18 years old, the young Scot was the youngest man ever to receive an air VC.

Sunday, September 15 – the date originally planned for Germany's invasion of England, now postponed – saw the air struggle reach its peak. Throughout the day the Luftwaffe despatched hundreds of bombers in wave after wave, protected above by Messerschmitt Bf 109 fighters,

DURING SEPTEMBER LUFTWAFFE BOMBERS DROPPED JUS'
BOMBS ON THE CAPITAL. THIS GRUESOME FIGURE

all heading for London. Their crews were under the illusion prompted by faulty German intelligence that RAF Fighter Command was virtually a non-effective force by now. This illusion was cruelly shattered when the Luftwaffe neared London. Throughout the afternoon more than 300 Hurricanes and Spitfires hacked the unwieldy bomber formations to shreds and took a bloody toll. By evening 56 German bombers had been destroyed, while several dozen others had wearily reached their bases, nursing dead engines, dangling undercarriages, bullet-riven fuselages, and dead or dying crew members. From London to the Channel, the afternoon was a constant battle scene, with RAF fighters and their opponents weaving fantastic contrail patterns of grim beauty in the brilliant blue skies. No German formation remained unmolested; few German machines were left totally unscathed. The cost to the RAF was 26 pilots killed. At the end of the day the jubilant RAF pilots totted up their claims, and a figure of 185 German aircraft brought down was eventually announced, a tally understandably overestimated in the heat, cut and lightning thrust of fierce combat. Whatever the figure, it was undeniably Fighter Command's greatest single day of success, despite the five-to-one odds encountered. This date remains today as Battle of Britain Remembrance Day, on which annual commemorations are made in tribute to the fighter pilots of 1940.

During the rest of September the assault on London continued by day and night, but with gradually reducing impact. The pace of air fighting remained as fierce as before, but the transition from day to night bombing – necessitated mainly by weather conditions as autumn gave way to winter – brought little relief to the citizens of London and its suburbs. During September Luftwaffe bombers dropped just over 7000 tons of high explosive and incendiary bombs on the capital. This gruesome figure increased to more than 9000 tons in the month of October. By November, however, the threat of an invasion had finally receded. Indeed, Hitler himself cancelled Operation Sea Lion on October 12. The 'thin blue line' of Dowding's fighter pilots had convinc-

ingly quashed any hope of a German occupation of Britain forever. In achieving this they had suffered grievous losses. Of the 3080 pilots who flew at some period of the battle, 481 had been killed, captured or were in unknown graves, while a further 422 had been wounded or seriously injured. Of the survivors, more than 800 were to die in action during the remaining war years. Beyond these tragic statistics were the many pilots whose potential future greatness, skill and experience was to be denied to Fighter Command during the subsequent years of combat. Among them were Eric Lock, Caesar Hull, Archie McKellar, 'Willy' Rhodes-Moorhouse, and a hundred others, whose instinctive qualities of leadership and personal prowess were sacrificed in the supreme effort of that summer. From the battle rose many of the RAF's most prominent leaders of the war – 'Sailor' Malan, a legend in his own lifetime; Roland Tuck, the ever-aggressive hunter; Douglas Bader; 'Widge' Gleed; Max Aitken – the list is long. And it should never be forgotten that nearly 500 of Dowding's pilots were not British-born, but had come eagerly from every corner of the world to join the fight against Nazism – from Poland, France, Belgium, Canada, New Zealand, Czechoslovakia, South Africa, Rhodesia, Australia, Jamaica, Palestine, and the neutrals, Ireland and the USA. With very few exceptions, all were young, at the height of their physical peak, and wholly committed to the task of defeating Hitler's vaunted Luftwaffe and the shadowy threat of Nazi domination of their freedom. Winston Churchill, in one of his carefully dramatic phrases, immortalised Dowding's pilots on August 20, 1940, when he said: 'Never in the field of human conflict was so much owed by so many to so few'. It must remain a simple statement of fact that the Battle of Britain was not won solely in the air. Many thousands of men and women on the ground, each in their own manner, contributed to the final victory. Yet their collective endeavours and sacrifices were towards one purpose – support and implicit faith in the handful of young men who daily placed their lives in jeopardy to preserve their homeland and inheritance. It is to those men that the accolade of posterity must be given.

Above: Eric 'Sawn-Off' Lock.
Above centre: Hurricane pilots of No. 1 Sqn, RCAF.
Above right: Pilots of 46 Sqn.
Below: Sqn Ldr Roland Tuck, OC of 257 Sqn and Flt Lt P 'Prosser' Hanks.
Below right: Plt Off E Q 'Red' Tobin, an American serving with 609 Sqn.

VER 7000 TONS OF HIGH EXPLOSIVE AND INCENDIARY
NCREASED TO MORE THAN 9000 TONS IN OCTOBER.

'Never in the field of human conflict was so much owed by so many to so few'. Winston Churchill.

Road Back

In November 1940, as the severely mauled Luftwaffe turned to night bombing in preference to the daylight struggle, Hugh Dowding, chief architect of the Fighter Command victory, was quietly replaced as C-in-C by Air Marshal Sir William Sholto Douglas. The brilliant 11 Group commander, Keith Park, whose tactics had virtually ensured that victory, was also hurriedly succeeded by his chief critic, Leigh-Mallory, the former 12 Group chief. Though both Dowding and Park were victims of internal jealousies and ill-founded criticism in their handling of the Battle, it was nevertheless a period of shift in aim for Fighter Command. The German night blitz on British cities was under way, creating fresh problems of defence for the fighters as they attempted to conquer the problems of seeking and destroying an enemy operating in the inky

95

Left: Battle of Britain 1940, by Paul Nash.
Below: 609 Sqn pilots in 1941. Standing, l-r: Bob Boyd; Baudouin de Hemptinne (Belgian); Peter MacKenzie; Paul Richey; John 'Bish' Bisdee; Jean 'Pyker' Offenberg (Belgian); Jimmy Baraldi. Sitting, l-r: Vicki Ortmans (Belgian); Tommy Rigler; Keith 'Skip' Ogilvie (Canadian); Bob Wilmet (Belgium). The pets were 'Flying officer de Goat', 'Spit', and 'Peter' (Sailor Malan's dog).
Bottom: A section of 122 Sqn's Spitfires taking off from Fairlop satellite airfield to Hornchurch, Jun 1942.

THE GERMAN NIGHT BLITZ ON BRITISH CITIES WAS
UNDER WAY , CREATING FRESH PROBLEMS OF DEFENCE
FOR THE FIGHTERS AS THEY ATTEMPTED TO CONQUER
THE PROBLEMS OF SEEKING AND DESTROYING AN
ENEMY OPERATING IN THE INKY CLOAK OF DARKNESS.

*Above: The superb Eric Kennington
portrait of Sqn Ldr Richard Playne
Stevens, DSO, DFC.
Above right: Night fighter pilots of 85
Sqn relaxing prior to a night flight.
Second from right is Sqn Ldr Peter
Townsend, DSO, DFC, with his
Alsation dog, 'Kim'.
Below: Hurricane night stalker about
to roll down the runway for a patrol
over London, 1941.*

cloak of darkness. Possessing no aircraft specifically designed or equipped for such a task, Fighter Command had to improvise, employing day fighters in a role for which they were never envisaged. Sholto Douglas, however, was an exponent of the offensive, whose principal aim was to begin the long road back by using his fighters to 'lean forward' into Europe, rather than vegetate in defensive attitudes. Such an offensive policy had two main objectives; to cause the Luftwaffe to maintain a large defensive force chained down in France, and to give the RAF fighter pilots an offensive initiative both in practice and morale. The beginning of this fresh policy came on December 20, 1940, when two Spitfires of 66 Squadron crossed the Channel and strafed the German-occupied airfield at Le Touquet. Although they merely damaged two grounded aircraft and some buildings, it was the start of an ever-increasing offensive by Fighter Command.

On January 10, 1941, a new tactic was inaugurated – 'Circus 1'. Using a single Blenheim bomber unit (114 Squadron), escorted by no less than nine fighter squadrons, the 'Circus' had a simple aim – to force German fighters into the air in circumstances ostensibly favourable to the RAF fighters. In a modest way, this first foray succeeded in its purpose, due mainly to the unreadiness of the Luftwaffe fighter arm for any defensive role. The Circus operations, which were to continue on an increasingly large scale throughout the first half of 1941, were simply massed fighter offensive sweeps using bombers as a bait to bring up the Luftwaffe in retaliation. This forced German fighters into battle on RAF terms. If the theory was impeccable, the practice fell short of perfection. Nevertheless, these operations gave invaluable experience to fresh pilots commencing their operational careers and gave birth to new variations in fighting tactics and means of leadership within Fighter Command. Whereas previously RAF fighters had mainly continued using the pre-1939 methods of tight, inflexible formations in 'Vics' of multiple-threes, harsh experience had shown the dangerous ineffectiveness of such formation flying. Henceforth, RAF fighters 'borrowed' the tactical methods of their Luftwaffe opponents, whereby the Spitfires and Hurricanes fought in pairs, a 'leader' being closely protected and backed by a No. 2, or wing man. Two such pairs flew in 'Finger Four' loose formation, thus providing a new tactical fighting unit. Thus the No. 1 fighter became the fighting, killing partner. His No. 2 wholly concentrated on the protection of his leader's tail and fending off opposition. The other significant innovation was an adaption of 12 Group's

Above: Douglas DB-7 'Havoc' night fighter of 23 Sqn, based at Ford.

theories during the Battle of Britain, where three or four fighter squadrons were grouped, usually on the same airfields, as a Wing led operationally by a Wing Leader – a wing commander with fighting experience. The initial wing leaders – Douglas Bader and 'Sailor' Malan – set a standard of fighting prowess and leadership which was to be richly embellished by their successors throughout the subsequent years.

Further adaptations of the basic offensive policy were soon instigated. Pure fighter sweeps over Nazi-occupied France – known as 'Rhubarbs' – were occasionally complemented by specific anti-shipping strikes along the French, Belgian and Dutch coastlines, operations known as 'Roadstead'. The already weak and poorly-organised Luftwaffe fighter defences in France were further depleted in June 1941. On June 22 Hitler's main strength was pushed forward across the borders of Russia – Germany's 'second front' had become a reality. Though any weakening of German fighter opposition might logically have been welcomed by Fighter Command, in fact it now became doubly necessary to attempt to pin down strong Luftwaffe forces in the occupied countries in order to relieve some of the pressure on Britain's latest partner in the war against Nazism. Immediate fighter aid for Russia was implemented by the allocation of large numbers of Hawker Hurricanes to the Soviet Union. Indeed, nearly 20 per cent of all Hurricane production was sent to Russia. To teach the Russians how to operate Hurricanes, No. 151 Wing, comprised of 81 and 134 Squadrons, sailed from Liverpool on August 12, bound for Vaenga airfield near Murmansk. The Wing remained in Russia until late November, during which time its pilots accounted for 15 German aircraft destroyed, four more probably destroyed, and a further five

seriously damaged – all for the loss of one Hurricane pilot killed. Between sorties, instruction in handling Hurricanes was given to Russian pilots, and the first Russian Hurricane squadron was officially formed on October 18.

By the summer of 1941, with the main German concentration of force aimed at defeating Russia swiftly, the nightly blitz on Britain eased considerably. In just over a year's operations the Luftwaffe's bombers had achieved considerable success in terms of destruction of property and civilian casualties. In opposition the RAF had waged a long, frustrating campaign in the night skies, with little initial success. In mid-1940 RAF night fighters *per se* simply did not exist. Instead a number of hasty improvisations – converted Blenheim bombers, Boulton Paul Defiants transferred from their day role, Hawker Hurricanes and a few Spitfires, and a motley variety of second-line machines – were pressed into service. Just prior to the war, a handful of Blenheim IV bombers had been fitted with the promising A.I. (Airborne Interception) radar sets. Ground controllers were intended to guide an aircraft to within striking range of any hostile aircraft by night. For the following year continuous experiments and trials gradually ironed out the myriad 'bugs' in the new 'black boxes', but still achieved no positive successes. On July 22, 1940 the first tangible result came when an A.I.-equipped Blenheim of the Fighter Interception Unit, Tangmere, intercepted a Dornier bomber and claimed it as probably destroyed. When the real night blitz on London and other major cities commenced in September, however, the RAF night fighters continued to grope helplessly in the night air – seeing little and gaining no victories.

With the improved A.I. Mk IV, however, success came on November 20 when Squadron Leader John Cunningham and his radar operator, Sergeant Phillipson, flying one of the newly-issued Bristol Beaufighters, intercepted a Junkers 88 and shot it down. Night victories began to come spasmodically as the Beaufighter crews gained experience in handling their new machines and the improved radar sets. In January 1941 the night fighters claimed three; in February, four; in March, 22; in April, 48; and in May, a total of 96 Luftwaffe bombers were destroyed. Such results were a culmination of many months of patient trial and error, demanding the utmost skill and resolution from the fighter crews. Yet it should be mentioned that not all such successes were achieved by radar-guided aircraft. One of the most successful individuals in the midnight combat arena was a Hawker Hurricane pilot, Richard Playne Stevens of 151 Squadron, who, without benefit of radar, claimed 14 victims alone.

By mid-1941 Fighter Command was steadily expanding in strength. The night fighter element was equipped mainly with Bristol Beaufighters – pugnacious-looking 'destroyers' carrying four 20mm cannons and six .303 Browning machine guns, the heaviest

Left: Sgt Thorsteinn Jonsson, the only RAF pilot from Iceland joined in Jul 1939. Flying successively with 17, 111, and 65 Sqns, he scored five victories, was awarded a DFM, then commissioned.
Above: Messerschmitt Bf 109F receives its death blows from a Flt Sgt Spitfire pilot.
Below: Pilots of 133 Sqn – the second of three all-American 'neutrals' formed within the RAF 1940–41. Despite their country's legal neutrality then, 'Old Glory' is proudly fluttering on its staff at dispersal.

'punch' fitted to an RAF fighter throughout the war. The day fighters were still predominantly Spitfires and Hurricanes. But they were improved versions from the machines that had won the 1940 battles. Machine guns gave way to 20mm cannons in the Spitfire Vb and Hurricane IIc, with slight up-rating of their Merlin engines. The Hurricanes were now relegated in the main to low-level attacks, often fitted externally with bombs. A new design, from the same stable as the Hurricane emerged, the mighty Hawker Typhoon, a brutish-looking four-cannon fighter powered by the revolutionary Napier Sabre engine. The 'Tiffie' entered front-line service with 56 and 609 Squadrons at Duxford in July 1941, but it was to be many months before the flying and maintenance snags were finally eradicated. The load-carrying capability, high speed, and ability to absorb terrifying punishment in damage marked the Typhoon as a tough 'war-horse' which was to play a vital part in the 1944 land campaign in France. Another fresh design, of which much was expected, was the twin-engined Westland Whirlwind, the first examples of which had reached the RAF in June 1940. However, the sleek Whirlwind was only used by two squadrons, 137 and 263, where it was confined to long-range escort and ground-attack roles. Thus, the onus of pure fighting remained on the superb Spitfire, which was continuously modified and embellished throughout the war. By Christmas 1941 Fighter Command could count 100 front-line squadrons available for operations, but the cross-Channel offensive had already encountered a new menace when, in September, pilots first reported meeting a new Luftwaffe

fighter, the Focke-Wulf 190 radial-engined design. Though only introduced slowly into Luftwaffe service, the Fw 190 was clearly superior to any RAF fighter in use, proven by its increasing casualty figures. The RAF's answer to the deadly Focke-Wulf was basically an improved Spitfire, the Mk IX, capable of speeds topping 400 mph at 25,000 feet, examples of which entered service with 64 Squadron in early 1942. At low levels the Typhoon proved equal to the Fw 190, though not superior in performance range.

While the day fighters mounted mini-armadas in offensive sweeps across France, battling the Luftwaffe's *jagdgeschwadern* in sprawling, sudden-death combat, the night fighters of Fighter Command continued to expand their efficiency and methods. To the Beaufighters and Douglas Havocs already in operation were added De Havilland Mosquito IIs in 1942. This classic, all-wooden construction machine, with its astonishing speed, manoeuvrability, and heavy fighter armament, proved ideal for the latest extension of the night role, intruding over enemy airfields by night. Though originally pioneered in a combat role by the Sopwith Camels of 151 Squadron in late 1918, the task was only reintroduced in serious form in early 1942. Equipped with a crew of two, the Mosquito quickly established a record of high achievement, roaming the Continental airfields individually and creating havoc wherever it struck. In the following years the intruder Mosquitos became the scourge of the Luftwaffe, ever-present, ever-deadly. Their arrival in Fighter Command coincided with a resurgence of bombing attacks on many cathedral cities in southern and eastern

England, reprisals for the mounting Bomber Command's offensive over Germany. Of the relatively small numbers engaged in these so-called 'Baedeker' raids, 40 were clawed out of the sky by the much-improved night fighter defenders by midsummer.

Probably the high peak of day fighter activity in 1942 was reached on August 19, when a mainly Canadian land force was despatched on a probing attempt to land on French soil at Dieppe. This 're-hearsal' for the invasion of occupied Europe provided Fighter Command with a practical opportunity to test Luftwaffe opposition over any Allied beach-head, and a total of 56 squadrons of Spitfires, Hurricanes, and Typhoons were detailed to provide a fighting umbrella over the barge-filled invasion fleet. They were complemented by a further nine squadrons of Mustangs, Bostons and Blenheims which would provide reconnaissance, smoke screens and tactical support bombing to the troops. Just after dawn the troops were put ashore in the face of murderous resistance. Hurricane fighter-bombers attempted to blast a path through the concrete fire positions of the German coastal defences. High above in the bright sky the wheeling Spitfires were soon engaged by hordes of Luftwaffe fighters, and a continuous battle waged for the next few hours. As the fighters exhausted their fuel and ammunition and swung out of the fight to return to base, reinforcements took their places and continued to thwart the several hundred German bombers attempting to interfere with the land struggle. Air combat was fierce, and the combat area became a 'box of sky', several miles wide, and layered from ground zero to 30,000 feet – a flashing, wheeling, tracer-crossed, three-dimensional cube of intense life or death endeavour. At any given moment nearly 600 RAF fighters were in bitter conflict with almost equal numbers of Focke-Wulf 190s and Messerschmitt Bf 109Gs and Fs – numbers not seen together since the high summer of 1940. By 1400 hrs the withdrawal of the heavily-mauled ground troops was completed, but the Luftwaffe continued to harass the returning landing craft until late afternoon. As the bright sun finally set that evening, Fighter Command had lost 106 aircraft, but claimed 91 German aircraft destroyed, and a further 190 possibly destroyed or badly damaged.

Left: The Russian Ambassador, Maisky, presenting Wg Cdr Ramsbottom-Isherwood, DFC with the Order of Lenin. Similar awards had just been made to (l-r) Plt Off C Haw; Sqn Ldr A G Miller; Sqn Ldr M Rook – all four pilots having served in Russia with No. 151 (Hurricane) Wg in 1941.

Supermarine Spitfire IXE

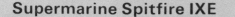

Engine: One-1710hp Rolls-Royce Merlin 63 or 63a
Max Speed: 408mph at 25,000ft
Range: 980 miles (max)
Service Ceiling: 44,000ft
Armament: Two-20mm Hispano cannon
Two .50 Browning mg
Weight: 7500lb (loaded)

Left: Spitfire II, P7895 of 72 Sqn, 1941, carrying the Fighter Command distinguishing band around its rear fuselage.
Far left: The night shift of ground crew overhauling Spitfire V's in a hangar.
Below: No. 452 Sqn, a Spitfire unit comprised almost entirely of Australian pilots. Its commander, Sqn Ldr R W Bungey, RAAF is 9th from left. Fourth from left is Flt Lt (later Wg Cdr) Brendan 'Paddy' Finucane, DFC who scored 32 victories before his death on Jul 15, 1942. Second from right is Keith 'Bluey' Truscott, DFC, a well-known Australian football player.

In fact, the true German figures were 48 destroyed and 24 seriously damaged. The mathematics of the air battle were not as important as the lessons learned in covering a land invasion. Nor could they mar the fact that the aerial umbrella had been almost entirely successful in stopping the Luftwaffe. If this heartened the Allied war chiefs in their forward planning for the actual invasion of Europe, an event just 48 hours before Dieppe was an even greater portent of the eventual destructive use of Allied air power. On that

Below: Just some of the hundreds of fighter pilots who supported the ill-fated Dieppe 'invasion' operation in Aug 1942. All had to fly through a curtain of groundfire, and fought heavy formations of Luftwaffe fighters – casualties were high. . . .

day the Spitfires of Fighter Command had been escorts to a new weapon of war – the brightly polished B-17 Flying Fortresses of the American Air Force, setting out on their first tentative sorties, the trail blazers for the mighty formations which were to devastate Germany for the balance of the war.

In November 1942 as command of the fighters passed to Trafford Leigh-Mallory, Fighter Command was rapidly attaining its zenith in strength of numbers. With over 100 first-line squadrons continuing to hack at the Luftwaffe across the Channel, the basic command structure had greatly expanded with new airfields and, particularly, specialist training units. Notable among them were the Air Fighting Development Unit at Wittering and the Fighter Leaders' School at Aston Down, which pro-

vided a fine honing of the command's fighting edge. Increasingly through the summer and autumn of 1943 Fighter Command's Spitfires overlapped with the USAAF's P-51 and P-47 long-range fighters in providing fighting cover to the thickening stream of American heavy bombers pounding targets far into Germany. The daylight combats with the Luftwaffe kept constant pressure on the German fighter arm. Equally depleting of Luftwaffe strength were the many low-level strafing sweeps undertaken by both British and American fighters, zero-height surprise assaults which left a trail of burning and broken machines, men and buildings in their wake. Yet the German air arm was far from defeated. Factory production of a high order produced huge numbers of replacements. Meanwhile the early American day-bombing sorties, unescorted during the final stages, had to run a murderous gauntlet of German fighters defending the Reich, and sustained crippling casualties.

Behind the scenes, while the daily fighting continued in the blue arena over France, plans were already afoot for the long-awaited return to Europe by the Allied armies. With a target date set for the early summer of 1944, the proposed invasion forces were slowly assembled and organised into preparatory battle formations. The prime need to establish complete air supremacy over the Luftwaffe in France – a lesson exemplified by the Luftwaffe's failure in 1940 – led to a complete reorganisation of Fighter Command, beginning in June 1943 when No. 2 Group, Bomber Command, composed of all the existing light

and medium day bombers, was put under the aegis of the fighter commander. By November Fighter Command as such was dissolved, and its place was taken by two new formations: the 2nd Tactical Air Force, and a revived Air Defence of Great Britain. All but Air Defence came under the command of the recently-created Allied Expeditionary Air Force, commanded by Leigh-Mallory, which included the US 9th Air Force. Thereafter the former 12 Group commander, Air Marshal Roderic Hill,

Right: Spitfire Vb, R6923, QJ-S of 92 Sqn, 1941. Arguably the most aesthetically pleasing fighter design of all time, the Spitfire was described by the artist, Sir William Rothenstein as, '. . . pretty and precious-looking as a cavalier's jewelled rapier.'

104

De Havilland Mosquito FB VI

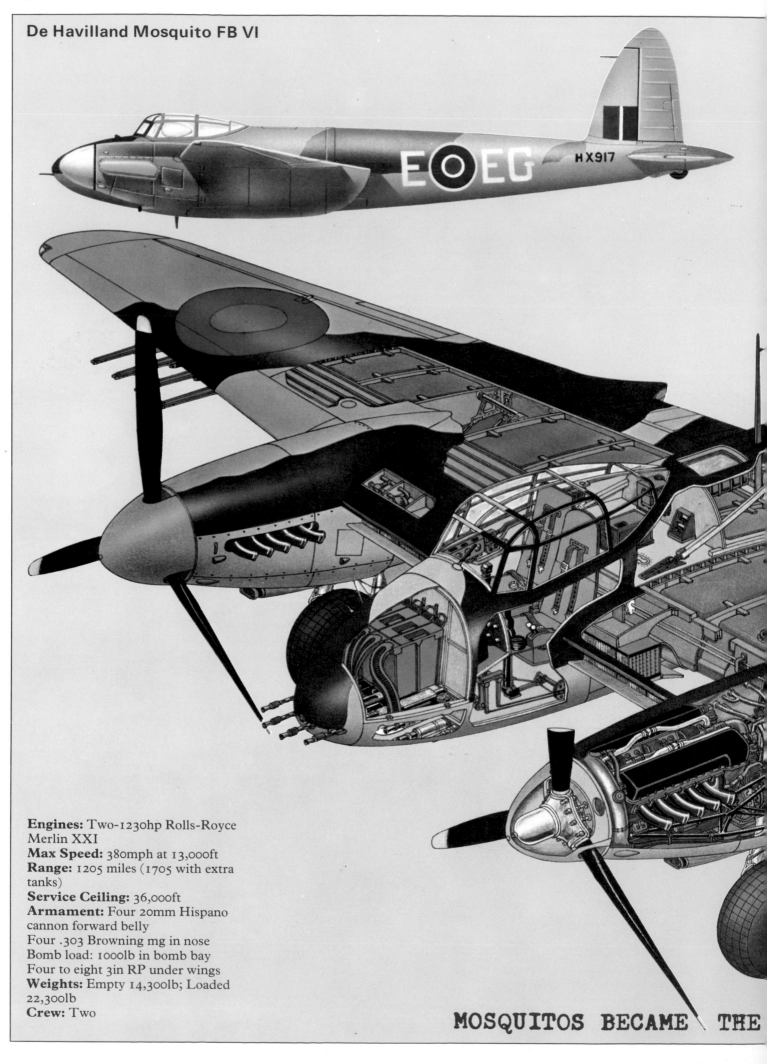

Engines: Two-1230hp Rolls-Royce
Merlin XXI
Max Speed: 380mph at 13,000ft
Range: 1205 miles (1705 with extra
tanks)
Service Ceiling: 36,000ft
Armament: Four 20mm Hispano
cannon forward belly
Four .303 Browning mg in nose
Bomb load: 1000lb in bomb bay
Four to eight 3in RP under wings
Weights: Empty 14,300lb; Loaded
22,300lb
Crew: Two

MOSQUITOS BECAME THE

SCOURGE OF THE LUFTWAFFE, EVER-PRESENT, EVER-DEADLY.

was appointed C-in-C, ADGB, with an operational strength of only 10 day and 11 night fighter squadrons with which to defend the United Kingdom – a fifth of the former Fighter Command numerical strength. He continued to provide offensive sorties across the Channel and was responsible for operational training of the fighter forces building up in reserve for the coming year's battles. It was a prodigious responsibility, despite the decline of Luftwaffe activity over Britain. It became a greater problem at the turn of the year, when German bombers re-opened their nightly assaults on the UK with the 'Little Blitz' which lasted from January 21 until late April 1944. By 'borrowing' other night fighting units, Hill was able to have 18 squadrons on his Battle Order to combat this fresh assault: eleven A.I.-equipped Mosquito squadrons, five A.I. Beaufighter units, and two Mosquito intruder squadrons. The first heavy assault – 447 German bombers attacking London on January 21 – was wildly inaccurate due to the many countermeasures set up, and 25 were lost. This pattern of confusion in target location by the German bomber captains, and a concentrated, smoothly efficient night defence organisation, resulted in the loss of almost 200 Luftwaffe machines by early April, a loss the Germans could ill-afford. Their bomber crews had been harried from take-off to final landing, first by Mosquito intruders over their own flare-paths, and then by night fighters waiting to pounce once they were across the coast of England. In addition, anti-aircraft guns, searchlights, and a panoply of ingenious countermeasures added sorely to their problems. It proved to be the final bomber offensive by the Luftwaffe against Britain.

Above: HM King George VI greeting Spitfire pilots on Apr 29, 1942. The fighter pilots' flying clothing, included the yellow-doped life-preserver inflation waistcoat – known as a 'Mae West'.
Right: Spitfires of 332 (AH), 411 (DB) and 56 (US) Sqns, of 2nd Tactical Air Force (TAF) in Jun 1944, employed as air support for the Normandy invasion. 'Servicing Commandos' belt up 20mm cannon shells for the aircraft guns.
Below right: North American Mustang fighters of 19 Sqn, 1943.
Below far right: Hurricane IIb, BE417, AE-K of 402 Sqn, RCAF at Warmwell, 1942 receiving its additional load of two 250lb GP/HE bombs.

As D-Day, June 6, 1944 approached, Roderic Hill's responsibilities grew heavier still. Air defence to obviate any German air reconnaissance over the huge array of land and sea forces assembling in southern England was crucial. By the end of April Hill instituted a tight system of standing patrols, with high and low level fighter sweeps continuously covering the North Foreland to 50 miles south of the Isle of Wight; this permanent vigil was kept right up until the actual invasion date. His ploy was completely successful, in that of the 125 Luftwaffe reconnaissance sorties attempted during the final six weeks, virtually none were permitted to cross the English coast. In the first days of June the fighters kept up a continuous rain of bombs and rockets on the whole stretch of radar posts along the French shorelines, until by dusk on June 5 all was ready for the following morning's Operation Overlord – the invasion of Normandy. The air power assembled for this operation was the greatest ever seen. At the finger tips of Air Chief Marshal Sir

Above: Wg Cdr A G Page, DFC in his Spitfire IXe, fully weighted down with one 500lb (centre) and two 250lb bombs (under wings) in addition to the aircraft's normal armament in 1944 in France. Note black and white 'invasion' stripes, applied to all 'invasion' aircraft during the initial stages of the Allied invasion operations.

soon relieved of their tensions. No opposition was forthcoming on the day. The Luftwaffe in France, battered and depleted by the previous year's constant struggle with the RAF, was overwhelmed. Air supremacy belonged wholly to the Allied air formations. Maintaining constant strong patrols above the tide of invasion, shipping churning its inexorable path across the Channel to Normandy, the outriding fighter squadrons were sent in to blast a free way forward for the beach-bound infantry. Hawk-eyed Spitfire and Typhoon pilots pounced on any German movement, blasting it with a storm of rocket and cannon fire, and strafing every path or road showing German troop reinforcements. As evening came on that first day, and the day fighters returned to base, the night fighters took up the task of constant protection. By June 10 a Canadian fighter wing was operating from the beach-head, the first of a flood of other tactical fighter units to take over French landing strips hacked out of the countryside to operate in direct support of the ground armies.

Arthur Tedder, the Deputy Supreme Commander of all the forces involved, were 2000 British and 1300 American fighters, a third of the 9210 aircraft directly involved in 'Overlord', apart from the heavy strategic bombers which were to play a massive supporting role of their own. Expecting massive Luftwaffe opposition, the fighter commanders were

As direct control of the invasion air cover was transferred to the Continent, Roderic Hill's defence force in England received an abrupt challenge. In the early hours of June 13, four isolated robot flying bombs 'put-putted' their

Above: The brutish Hawker Typhoon four-cannon fighter which entered service in Jul 1941 but only commenced full operations in the following summer. During the Allied advance across France, 1944–45, Typhoons were used extensively as 'long-range artillery'.

implacable track over Kent and Sussex and then dived to explode in suburban areas. This tiny quartet of V.1 flying bombs were the only arrivals from an originally planned wave of 500 to open the terror assault envisaged by Hitler. Over the previous months Allied bombers had blasted dozens of suspected V.1 launching sites, thereby seriously impeding progress of the terror programme. But on June 15 a further 244 V.1s left their ramps, 144 of which crossed the English coast, and 72 of these exploded in the greater London area. Hill immediately put Operation Overlord/Diver into action – a prearranged programme of co-operation in defence between the ADGB, Anti-Aircraft Command and Balloon Command. Allotting eight day fighter squadrons – Spitfire IXs and XIVs, Typhoons and Tempests – plus four Mosquito night squadrons, Hill concentrated on the nullification of this latest form of air bombardment. The V.1 was basically a bomb containing 1870lb of high ex-

Below: Typhoon pilots of 198 Sqn, commanded by Wg Cdr Johnny Baldwin, DSO, DFC (9th from left).

plosive, with crude jet propulsion power, simple cruciform wings and control surfaces. Its wing span, merely $17\frac{1}{2}$ feet, and maximum speed in the region of 400 mph, made the V.1 a difficult target for the fighters. Even if a fighter caught up with the robot, once within practicable firing range (some 200 yards was the ideal position), a fighter was likely to suffer from the effects of its target exploding. For the next two months V.1s continued to rain down on England. London alone received the equivalent of 100 tons of high explosive on average for each 24-hour period. The ADGB's fighters patrolled around the clock, seeking, chasing and destroying, but the assault did not slacken noticeably. One new weapon in the ADGB's armoury became effective in early August, when Flying Officer 'Dixie' Dean of 616 Squadron, based at Manston, scored the first success for a revolutionary new design of fighter, the Gloster Meteor I jet. In clearly defined areas, the fighters were free of anti-aircraft fire and balloons, and stepped up their efforts until, by the beginning of September, with the Allied armies in France breaking through towards the launching sites and causing their withdrawal inland, the V.1 battle was virtually won, though spasmodic attacks continued unevenly until late March 1945. By then, of the 10,492 V.1s actually launched – 3000 of which never reached England – the fighters had accounted for 1846, while guns and balloons had brought down a further 2109.

Even as the V.1 onslaught began to fade, an even greater menace was added to the terror blitz – the V.2 rocket. In the early evening of September 8 the first

V.2 fell in Chiswick. It was the harbinger of a mighty generation of vehicles which would eventually lead to man's first faltering steps into space. This latest opponent was impossible to intercept by existing defences. Only by destruction of its launching sites could the V.2 be nullified, and accordingly Bomber Command was brought in to obliterate the rocket bases. Fighters assisted by becoming dive-bombers, blasting every site known within their range, and any suspected storage and transportation depots and sites. On March 27, 1945 the last V.2 fell in England. Some 1115 rockets, each bearing a ton of high explosive, had been delivered. Meanwhile, in October 1944, the Allied Expeditionary Air Force headquarters was disbanded, its invasion task completed. At the same moment, Fighter Command was reconstituted, and the ADGB label dissolved.

While Roderic Hill's relatively small fighter force in England fought its battles with the mechanical menace of Hitler's terror weapons, the RAF's fighters of 2nd TAF on the Continent made their vital, massive contribution to the gigantic land struggle for the liberation of Europe and the invasion of Hitler's Reich. In the main, Luftwaffe opposition during the remaining months of 1944 was relatively weak and uneven. Most remaining German fighter forces were by then engaged almost wholly in attempting to halt the awesome armadas of Allied bombers which daily pounded the Reich. Thus the many hundreds of Spitfires, Typhoons, Tempests and Mustangs were left largely free to wreak a terrible havoc among the German infantry resisting the Allied break-out

from the Normandy beach-heads. In early August, rocket-laden Typhoons blasted a massing German tank movement, and by sheer fury in attack and explosive power drove the Panzer division into retreat. This tactic was repeated all along the shallow fighting zone until the eventual breakthrough by the Allied armies. Once the battle moved out into more open country, Allied fighters ranged far and wide ahead of the infantry, attacking all modes of transport and means of communications behind the crumbling German Front. Flying at times as many as 1200 sorties a day, the 2nd TAF fighters meted out a perpetual reign of destruction and death to everything which moved or retaliated. Targets were smothered in a holocaust of rocket and cannon hail. Little escaped the eyes of the roving fighter pilots, whose free-wheeling aircraft pounced on the slightest hint of German occupancy of any house, wood, copse or ditch, creating a harvest of slaughter and demoralisation. The vital aid to the armies of photo-reconnaissance was accomplished by complete wings of Mustangs and Spitfires allotted to individual military formations. This enabled the army commanders to have immediate in-

Above right: Sqn Ldr Joseph Berry, DFC of 3 Sqn, who destroyed 61 German V.1 ('Diver') pilotless bombs in four months in 1944. In Oct 1944 Berry became OC 501 Sqn in Europe.
Right: A night-fighting De Havilland Mosquito tests its four 20mm cannons and four .303 Browning machine guns.
Below: Gp Capt (later, AVM) J E Johnson, DSO, DFC, in France, 1944, when leader of a Spitfire Wing.

telligence concerning the ground in front of them and the likely opposition to be met.

The chief danger to the marauding fighter pilots was the highly accurate anti-aircraft flak defences – mobile 88mm and 103mm gun teams able to encircle any important objective at a few hours' notice and put up a deadly curtain of shells through which any attacking fighter had to penetrate. Nevertheless, the Luftwaffe occasionally made last-ditch forays in relative strength, but was overwhelmed. On April 30, 1945 a mass air battle resulted in the fighters of 83 Group claiming 37 German fighters destroyed without any loss to itself. Even the rare appearance of the jet Messerschmitt 262 made no impact. Raw courage and determination by the dwindling German fighter pilots could not compensate for utter inferiority in

numbers, complete breakdown in reinforcement supplies, and virtual lack of overall direction. By May 1945 the vaunted Luftwaffe was broken, decimated on the ground and in the air; retaining only the fierce pride and royalty of a tiny band of dedicated fighter pilots who fought on until the bitter end.

On May 8, 1945, Germany signed its unconditional surrender and the work of the fighter pilots of the RAF in Europe was done. Their contribution to the final victory had been no mean effort. A protracted, remorseless fight had been maintained at great cost. Nearly 4000 pilots of Fighter Command had been killed. A further 2000 were injured or taken prisoner. If the price of such sacrifice was freedom, then the fighter pilots epitomised the type of youth who provided the shield preserving that elusive ideal for future generations.

Bomber Assault

For the first three years of World War II, RAF Bomber Command might have been likened to a sleeping giant, fitfully dozing through the opening rounds of the conflict, gathering muscle power and energy, waiting impatiently for the right tools and opportunities to implement its potential, awesome might. At the start of hostilities the command was in a state of transition, hastily expanding to meet its commitments, with obsolescent aircraft in its squadrons awaiting replacement by the long-range, heavy bombers still being developed. Its crews, superbly trained to peacetime standards, had little if any practical experience of night bombing with its associated problems of accurate navigation and target-finding. The contemporary policy which advocated daylight bombing, unescorted by fighters, was sustained by a complacent

belief that such bombers would 'always get through', despite the glaring lessons of the 1918 Independent Force. In September 1939 Bomber Command had only 53 squadrons. Of these, only 33 were considered fully operational, and ten of these were immediately despatched to France to accompany the BEF. The squadrons' aircraft were Blenheims, Hampdens, Wellingtons,

Whitleys and Fairey Battles – all at least six years old in concept, all twin-engined (except for the single-engined Battles), and none capable of carrying a worthwhile warload of bombs over a significant range. For defence of these daylight bombers, the Hampdens and Battles relied on hand-operated single machine guns – a concept directly linked with the 1916–18 bombers – while the remainder had power-operated gun turrets fitted with .303 Browning machine guns.

With little more than 300 first-line bombers based in Britain, Bomber Command was clearly incapable of pursuing any true bombing offensive against Germany at the outbreak of war, while the potential bomber force of the Luftwaffe – nearly 1500 machines which might be launched against Britain's civil population in 'retaliation' – obviated any desire by the British government to aggravate the 'opposition'. Hence, on September 1, a policy was adopted restricting British bombers to attacks on units and installations of the German Fleet. If the Luftwaffe commenced unrestricted bombing of Britain, such targets were

OPERATIONS RECORD BOOK.

Appendix _Appendix H_   R.A.F. Form 541.

DETAIL OF WORK CARRIED OUT.

From _2304_ hrs _3 / 9 / 39_ to _2759_ hrs. _3 / 9 / 39_   By _139 Sqdn._   No. of pages used for day _1_

Aircraft Type and No.	Crew.	Duty.	Time Up.	Time Down.	Remarks.	References.
Blenheim Mk. IV. N6215.	F/O McPherson. Cdr. Thompson. c/2. Arrowsmith.	Photo. Reco.	1200.	1650.	Duty successful. 75 photos taken of GERMAN fleet. The first Royal Air Force aircraft to cross the GERMAN frontier.	

then to include German industrial plants and objectives. Conservation of the meagre bomber force available was a necessity born of the locust years of peace, during which parsimonious and idealistic politicians had studiously ignored Hugh Trenchard's constant plea for an effectively strong bomber force, capable of attacking any would-be European aggressor. Thus, throughout the winter months of 1939–40, RAF bombers were despatched in tiny formations, and even singly, on what were termed 'armed reconnaissance' sorties – daylight operations, with bomb bays loaded, seeking the German naval forces. Blissfully maintaining the 'tight formations' advocated by the bomber hierarchy, the young crews were quickly disillusioned about their defensive capabilities. On September 29 eleven Hampdens of 144 Squadron attempted a raid near Heligoland, only to be swamped by Messerschmitt fighters; five bombers were lost. On December 14 twelve Wellingtons of 99 Squadron penetrated the Schillig Roads trying to bomb German surface vessels, but again the Messerschmitts cut a swathe through their formation, destroying five and forcing a

Top: The official Operations Record Book entry for the first Bomber Command operation of WWII; Blenheim IV, N6215 of 139 Sqn, Wyton, set out at mid-day on Sept 3, 1939 to reconnoitre the German Fleet dispositions.
Left: Avro Lancasters of 50 Sqn en route to Germany.

sixth Wellington to crash in England on its return. Undeterred, four days later 24 Wellingtons from 9, 37 and 149 Squadrons set out on an armed reconnaissance of the Schillig Roads and Wilhelmshaven, though two of these soon returned with mechanical troubles. The remaining 22, in a close-formation in a blue sky bereft of cloud, were a perfect target for the Messerschmitt Bf 109s and Bf 110s under the operational control of *Jagdgeschwader 1*'s commander Carl Schumacher. After weathering a storm of anti-aircraft fire, the neat array of Wellingtons finally turned for home – only to run straight into the guns of Schumacher's men. In wave after wave

the Luftwaffe's fighters ripped the bomber formation to shreds as it fled across the open sea. Within 30 minutes the battle was over. Ten Wellingtons had been shot down, two had ditched with ruptured fuel tanks, and a further three eventually crash-landed on the English coast. On balance, the Wellington's air gunners had sent two Bf 109s into the sea.

The disastrous results of these (and other) daylight raids revealed the inadequacy of the 'unescorted bomber' theory, and forced the RAF to restrict its bombing to night raids in future. In particular the December 18 sortie highlighted the vital need for self-sealing fuel

tanks for bombers, and the limitations of existing gun turrets in manoeuvrability and firing range when confronted with fighters using long-range cannons. The change from daylight to the relative safety of night operations saw the bombers used, initially, simply to scatter tons of propaganda leaflets – code-named 'Nickels' – across western Germany. Regarded by the Air Ministry as valuable 'exercises' in training the crews for night work, these paper bombing raids mainly revealed further inadequacies in the equipment of the aircraft. In bitterly icy weather conditions during those first months, crews froze, instruments ceased to operate, hydraulic pipelines operating

Far left: Some of the damage caused to Whitley V, N1377, DY-P of 102 Sqn by atrocious weather conditions over Germany on the night of Nov 27, 1939.
Left: 'Two-six!' – the traditional yell in the RAF for 'All hands to help', exemplified here by the combined effort to wheel in a 1000lb HE bomb to the bomb bay of an Armstrong Whitworth Whitley bomber.
Right: The air crew about to climb in to their Wellington bomber for night ops.
Below: Vickers Wellington II, virtually the backbone of Bomber Command's early years of night operations. Nicknamed 'Wimpy' – after the contemporary Popeye cartoon strip character, J Wellington Wimpy – this particular example, W5379, served with 12 Sqn and flew 15 operational sorties before being lost on the night of Oct 10, 1941.

turrets, controls and operating systems became blocked with ice. Navigation remained crude by later standards, based almost wholly on 'dead reckoning' calculations. Accurate radio aids were not yet available. Little opposition was met from German night defences, but a far more implacable foe was the deadly grip of Europe's worst winter for decades. Chief exponent of the leaflet sorties was the Whitley bomber, which could seldom achieve an operational ceiling higher than 17,000 feet due to the crippling weather conditions. Engines quickly became fractious, control surfaces were enveloped in thick ice coatings, oxygen and wireless communication lines refused to operate. Temperatures inside the unheated fuselages sank to a level where human flesh instantly froze to any metal object if a glove were inadvertently removed. Electrical storms in the upper atmosphere merely added hazard to hazard as the bomber crews diligently pursued their allotted tasks. The leaflet 'campaign' finally ended on April 6, 1940, as emphasis for bomber operations changed to the more vital task of laying sea mines around the enemy's ports and naval installations. The cost of the paper raids was not light – some six per cent of all aircraft despatched on such operations since the outbreak of war – but a number of lessons were learned, resulting in improvements in crew comfort and aircraft equipment.

In the spring of 1940, Bomber Command, in anticipation of its expected expansion in strength, inaugurated its own

Left: Bristol Blenheim IV of 88 Sqn being armed at Swanton Morley, Norfolk. Right: The Boston, one of the war's outstanding twin-engined bombers. The Boston was originally ordered by France. The contract was taken over by Britain and the RAF in 1940.

Operational Training Units, in which bomber crew members could complete their training prior to joining operational squadrons; the first OTU's, Nos 10 to 17 inclusive, opened in April. Within days Bomber Command shouldered a new responsibility. On April 9, German forces invaded Norway, thus posing a fresh threat to Allied shipping in the North Sea, and providing the Luftwaffe with new springboards for possible bombing operations against Britain. Wellington and Whitley units were quickly despatched to northern Scotland for operations against German shipping off the Norwegian coast, but the few sorties flown were soon nullified by the swiftness of the German campaign in Norway. Hardly had the German occupation of Norway and Denmark been completed than the main assault against France began; on May 10, 1940, massive

German forces swung in to attack the Low Countries. Facing the RAF's detachments in France – the AASF and Air Component of the BEF – were *Luftflotten* 2 and 3 of the Luftwaffe, composed of 1486 bombers and assault aircraft, backed by 1264 fighters. This blitzkreig had been expected for months by the RAF, and a three-fold plan for Bomber Command had been prepared. The AASF Battles were to tackle opposition in the southern sector; Blenheim squadrons based in Norfolk, Suffolk and Essex would attack in the northern area of the battle; and 16 squadrons of 'heavy bombers' in England would undertake raids against the industrial targets in the Ruhr area. Two Blenheim squadrons already in France were decimated within 24 hours of the start of the German onslaught. Seven aircraft of 139 Squadron were lost in a vain attempt to bomb

bridges near Maastricht on May 11. That same morning the Dornier 17s of KG2 delivered a surprise bombing attack on 114 Squadron based at Conde Vraux and destroyed virtually the entire unit on the ground.

Bomber Command's planned 'strategic' offensive against Germany's oil and steel plants commenced on the night of May 15–16, when nearly a hundred Wellingtons, Whitleys and Hampdens set out from English airfields to attack the Ruhr. Only 24 of the crews claimed to have located their designated targets due to the dense haze over the objective. Subsequent night raids during May and June fared no better. Difficulties in accurate navigation and precise target location greatly diminished the intended effect of such sorties. On May 27 Operation Dynamo – the evacuation of Allied troops via Dunkirk – accelerated, and during the succeeding nine days the bomber crews of the RAF contributed their share of raids against German troops outside the town and their reinforcement and supply lines. The results were poor. Committed as it was to helping to stem the German tidal wave, Bomber Command was given an additional task at midnight on June 10; Italy declared war on France. Two Wellington squadrons, 99 and 149, were immediately sent to Salon in France with the intention of bombing northern Italy, but due to direct opposition from French authorities they were not able to despatch any aircraft until June 15. Meanwhile the Whitleys in a force of 36 aircraft, detached to the Channel Islands en

Below: Another Bomber Command stalwart in the early years of the war was the distinctively shaped Handley Page Hampden. Here, AE196 of 408 ('Goose') Sqn, RCAF is being prepared for operations at Syerston on Aug 12, 1941.

FACING THE RAFs DETACHMENTS IN FRANCE - THE AASF
AND AIR COMPONENT OF THE BEF - WERE LUFTFLOTTEN 2
AND 3...1486 BOMBERS AND ASSAULT AIRCRAFT
BACKED BY 1264 FIGHTERS.

118

Above: A touch of private humour by a Wellington bomber skipper. Personal 'art' insignia were widely applied by bomber crews as the war progressed.

route, crossed the Alps on the night of June 11–12 and bombed Turin and Genoa. By June 18 all RAF units had been evacuated from France, and on the 22nd France capitulated to the Germans. Apart from the horrific casualty rates sustained by the AASF, Bomber Command had lost 162 aircraft since May 10 – the equivalent of nearly ten complete squadrons and their crews. Yet, despite the outstanding courage of the crews, the command had achieved nothing of consequence.

Throughout the subsequent Battle of Britain, Bomber Command, flying almost nightly, concentrated mainly on destroying the assembling invasion fleet

in French and Dutch ports. Bombers continued to raid Germany, including the first night attack on Berlin on the night of August 25–26. These latter raids soon encountered their first taste of enemy night fighter opposition. The first bomber to be lost, a Whitley, fell to a Messerschmitt Bf 109 piloted by Werner Streib on July 20. The small nucleus of a night fighter defensive force was being built up in Germany, including early trials of ground radar control for the fighters by the autumn of 1940. Over the coming four years of the aerial struggle the unceasing race for supremacy in the night skies above Germany was to become the major facet of the bomber's war. Equally significant, however, was the introduction of the new bomber aircraft 'generation' to Bomber Command when, on August 2, 1940, the first Short Stirling – indeed the RAF's first four-engined monoplane heavy bomber – was issued to 7 Squadron at Leeming. Shortly after, in November, two further new designs joined the ranks of the command, when the first Avro Manchester and Handley Page Halifax joined 207 and 35 Squadrons respectively. All three were harbingers of the heavy bombers intended to implement the command's long-term objective of destroying Germany's industrial capacity for war. The actual process of converting from a mainly twin-engined, medium range force to the four-engined, long-range bomber formation was to be a protracted business, not fully accomplished for another two years. In the interim Bomber Command was forced to soldier on with its Hampdens, Wellingtons and Whitleys, and to a lesser extent, Blenheims.

If the issue of fresh, more potent air-

craft was slow, the progress in pure armament for the bombers had accelerated by the close of 1940. At the outbreak of war the command's chief warloads comprised a variety of the outdated General Purpose (GP) high explosive bombs varying from 250lb to 1000lb, although the majority of aircraft in use could not accommodate the largest of these. Ineffective against any armoured objective – such as a capital naval ship – the GP series of bombs were unable to produce any significant damage to important targets due to the low content (less than 40 per cent of total bomb weight) of actual explosive material. The early introduction of a larger, more efficient bomb – the 2000lb Medium Capacity (MC) bomb – showed an increase by half of actual explosive content of a more destructive nature. By early 1941 the High Capacity (HC) bomb had made its debut when, on March 31, two 4000lb HC bombs were dropped on Emden by specially-modified Wellingtons. The 4000lb bomb – colloquially known as the 'Cookie' or 'Dangerous Dustbin' was simply a thin-cased can of high explosive. With over 80 per cent of its weight actual explosive filling, it was primarily intended as a blast bomb for release among high density building complexes such as factories and industrial estates. With no pretensions to ballistic beauty, the Cookie proved so effective in this role that, in an enlarged version, it continued in operational use until the end of the war.

These new weapons were complemented by an increasing variety of incendiary bombs. Standard and most effective was the hexagonally-shaped 4lb Incendiary – a simple stick of highly

imflammable magnesium derivative which burned fiercely on contact and was difficult to extinguish. Others included 30lb incendiaries, often with explosive charges which could scatter the burning content over a wide area.

The increasing responsibilities of various members of a bomber crew, particularly after the introduction of the larger aircraft, led to a recognition of distinct aircrew 'trades'. Prior to September 1939 the only categories of air crew recognised by outward insignia were pilot and observer, and from 1923, the volunteer air gunner who was non-commissioned in rank was allowed to wear a brass 'winged bullet' badge on the tunic sleeve. This category of crew, always of non-commissioned rank, became the first of the new generation of distinct crew categories when, in November 1939, an Air Ministry Order

(AMO) authorised qualified air gunners to wear the cloth badge of an 'AG' above the tunic breast pocket, in the same manner as the pilot's 'wings' or the Observer's 'Flying O'. At about the same time, air gunners were granted minimum rank of sergeant, with restricted prospects of further promotion to Flight Sergeant and Warrant Officer. In anticipation of the introduction of four-engined heavy bombers, a new aircrew category, Flight Engineer, was inaugurated in March 1941, with an appropriate flying badge and temporary rank of SNCO. In September 1942 the former role of the Observer was officially replaced by that of Navigator, though observers who had qualified for their 'Flying Hole' badge prior to September 3, 1939 were permitted to continue wearing the former insignia – a jealously guarded privilege which most such men

Above: Avro Manchester over Germany, 1941.
Right: Air crew transport was hardly luxurious in 1940–41! No. 83 Sqn (Hampdens) crews climb aboard the 'bus' outside their Scampton hangar for transportation to the aircraft dispersals. Flying clothing here is a mixture of Irvin 'Para-Suits' worn over Irvin flying jackets and/or overalls.
Below: Blenheim IV's of 235 Sqn on course for France 1941.

Avro Lancaster B1

Left: Avro Lancaster B'1, NG358 of 15 Sqn, based at Mildenhall, Suffolk with fin bars painted in yellow to denote a G-H formation leader.

Above: Threading in the .303 machine gun ammunition belts to the nose turret of Lancaster ED763, KC-Z of 617 Sqn at Woodhall Spa, 1944. Total 'ammo' capacity was 14,000 rounds.

LANCASTERS SERVED FROM JAN 1942, IN A TOTAL C
COMMAND'S BOMB TONNAGE THROUGHOUT THE ENTIRE
NINE OF THE TOTAL OF 32 VCs AWARDED TO AIR CR

Left: The pilot's dashboard in a Lancaster bomber.

Engines: Four-1460hp Rolls-Royce Merlin 20 or 22

Max Speed: 275mph at 15,000ft (fully loaded)

Cruising, 200mph at 15,000ft 245mph at sea level

Range: 2530 miles (7000lb load) 1730 miles (12,000lb load) 1550 miles (22,000lb load)

Service Ceiling: 19,000ft

Armament: FN5 nose turret with two .303 mg

FN50 mid-upper turret with two .303 mg

FN20 tail turret with four .303 mg

FN64 ventral turret with one .303 mg (early models only)

(Above was standard on introduction; later, nose turrets were often deleted and faired over, ventral turrets removed, newer-type mid-upper turrets installed – some having twin .50 mg)

Bomb load: 8000lb (initially), up to 22,000lb (special modified versions only)

Weights: All-up 65,000lb; Tare 37,000lb.

Crew: Seven.

SQUADRONS, AND DROPPED JUST OVER 60% OF BOMBER
NEARLY 4000 WERE LOST, MAINLY IN ACTION, WHILE
EMBERS DURING 1939-45 WERE AWARDED TO LANCASTER CREWS.

retained. Other distinct aircrew members were later created – such as Radar Operator and Bomb Aimer – as Bomber Command, and the RAF generally, made increasing use of more sophisticated equipment and methods.

A particular feature of the many hundreds of young volunteers for air crew duties with the RAF, especially Bomber Command, in the early years of the war was the high proportion of Empire citizens who travelled halfway across the globe to fight the Nazi threat to Britain. Canada, Australia, New Zealand, South Africa, Rhodesia and a host of smaller countries provided a wealth of eager men, while even neutral Americans, thinly disguised as 'Canadians', willingly offered their services. The eventual contribution in men alone was prodigious, and a hard core of courageous men provided for every facet of RAF activities throughout the war. In addition, refugees from the many countries already under Nazi occupation willingly

swelled the ranks of the flying crews and maintenance staffs. Eventually, several units composed of 'non-British' nationals were formed as separate entities within the overall aegis of the RAF. The Canadians formed a complete bomber Group within Bomber Command, manned and financed almost wholly by Canada. In general mixed national crews soon became the norm on most bomber squadrons, and indeed were considered by many senior bomber veterans to be the best type of crew to captain.

Throughout 1941 Bomber Command continued patiently to attempt its expansion plans in the face of increasing demands for diversion of its bombers to other duties. The Admiralty, absorbed almost entirely in its campaign against the German submarines threatening Britain's lifelines of merchant shipping, pleaded strongly for bomber squadrons to be employed against the U-boat bases, and especially the German capital ships, *Scharnhorst* and *Gneisenau* and *Prinz*

Eugen, based at Brest. Equally concerned with the battle of the Atlantic was Coastal Command, whose lack of long range aircraft was only partly solved by the few Short Sunderlands available. Resisting the various moves to deplete Bomber Command's first-line strength, its commander, Richard Peirse, agreed to allot a proportion of bomber operational sorties to pounding the U-boat bases and, particularly, the capital ships in Brest harbour. Bombers flew a proportion of roughly ten sorties against Brest to every attack on the more important U-boat pens then being constructed around Biscay and western France – a priority of targets virtually dictated by the Navy.

Operations by the new Short Stirling, Handley Page Halifax, and Avro Manchester aircraft also began in 1941. The results soon gave cause for concern: the Manchester with its twin Rolls-Royce Vulture engines, though basically a fine design, was simply unreliable on oper-

ations; the Stirling, a strong and manoeuvrable giant, lacked a safe service ceiling, leaving it prey to anti-aircraft fire and roving German fighters. Another disappointment lay in the design of the Stirling's lengthy bomb bay. Capable of lifting some 14,000lb in bomb load, in fact the long narrow bomb cells could not accept the 4000lb HC blast bomb for internal stowage. This restricted it to the less-effective 2000lb store as its largest single bomb. Even the Halifax, in its initial form, proved troublesome in general handling, and was soon modified in many respects to improve its all-round performance. By the end of the year Bomber Command had a paper strength of 58 squadrons. Of these, seven were non-operational, and 23 were still operating the doughty Wellington. Three squadrons each of Stirlings, Halifaxes and Manchesters represented the 'new' generation of bombers – the balance comprising Blenheims, Douglas Bostons, Hampdens and a single squadron of American B–17 'Flying Fortresses'. Clearly, the plan for a massive aerial onslaught on Germany was still incapable of fulfilment. Yet a portent of the future lay with one of the temporarily non-operational units, 44 Squadron, which began replacing its war-weary Hampdens in December 1941 with a new four-engined design, the Avro Lancaster. Originally designed as an 'Avro Manchester III' employing four Rolls-Royce Merlin engines in late 1939, the design was renamed 'Lancaster' and put into production quickly to replace the ill-fated Manchester with its recalcitrant Vulture twin-engines. By early 1942, 44 Squadron was sufficiently familiar with its new aircraft to undertake initial operations; the first sortie was a 'soft run', laying mines in the Heligoland Bight on March 3–4. The Lancaster gradually replaced most designs in Bomber Command, to become the outstanding bomber of the war.

If the new bombers held hope for an imminent bombing offensive of worthy proportions, capable of influencing the war, the actual bombing results during 1941 told a different tale. Navigation, target location and actual bombing were all dismally unproductive. A detailed analysis of 100 raids in September was made from photo reconnaissance reports and photographs, and it was plain that only a third of the crews who had claimed to attack any target had come within five miles of the objective. Over the Ruhr this proportion was one-tenth. The vast damage claimed, and eloquently broadcast by the news media, simply did not exist in reality. No blame for this state of affairs could be fairly placed upon the bomber crews, who con-

tinued to operate as best they could with the equipment they had. Radio and radar aids to navigation, so sorely needed, had yet to be introduced. The dilution of the main bomber effort caused by consistent diversions to naval targets at the insistence of authorities outside the command prevented a steady gain in succinct experience for its main role. In the year 1941 Bomber Command dropped a total of 31,704 tons of bombs, but had suffered totals of 333 aircraft crashed and 701 'missing' – almost 21 aircraft and crews for every full week of the period. And, despite the tragic lessons of 1940, a third of those listed as 'missing' occurred on daylight sorties. In all, close to 4000 individual crew members had died or become prisoners of war in the space of a single year of mainly non-effective bombing results – a sacrifice made infinitely more poignant by the cheerful eagerness with which the youthful crews had set out, attempting to accomplish their given missions against the odds. Despite this catalogue of frustration and individual tragedy, the year was not entirely a sombre one in the overall picture for Bomber Command. During the latter half of the year operational trials had been made with a new radio aid to navigation – code-named *GEE* – which held promise of, at least, improvement in target location. In November 105 Squadron received its first example of the revolutionary De Havil-

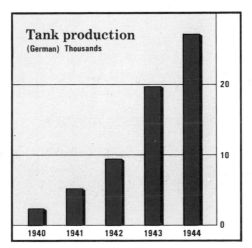

Bombs dropped on German targets
Thousand tons

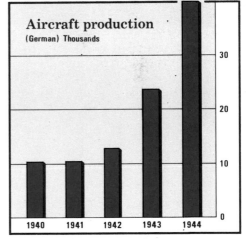

Aircraft production
(German) Thousands

Tank production
(German) Thousands

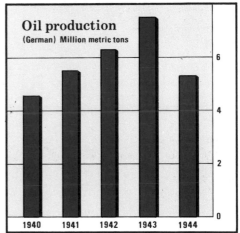

Oil production
(German) Million metric tons

Top left: Short Stirling of 7 Sqn at Oakington.
Top centre: Result of a direct hit by Halifaxes and Lancasters on an ammunition and explosives depot north of Falaise, 1944.
Top: Handley Page Halifax B.111, MZ759, NP-Q of 158 Sqn, its wings aflame, seconds before its final plunge.
Left: Stirling crew after a mission.

Left: 500lb MC/HE bombs descending from the bay of a 98 Sqn N. A. Mitchell aircraft, FV914.
Right: AVM Don Bennett with Gp Capt Johnnie Fauquier, DSO, DFC, RCAF (centre) in front of Avro Lancaster KB700, 'Ruhr Express'.
Below: Douglas Bostons of 88 Sqn.

land Mosquito all-wood bomber – the harbinger of a host of Mosquito bomber versions which were to become a major factor in the strategic bombing offensive against Germany.

A turning point for Bomber Command came on February 20, 1942, when a new commander took up his appointment – Air Marshal Arthur Harris. Only six days previously a directive emanating from the Air Staff and sanctioned by the War Cabinet, ordered Bomber Command to commence a prolonged, specific offensive against Germany, with '. . . the morale of the enemy civil population and in particular of the industrial workers . . .' to be its chief focal point. In more popular terminology, it was a policy for 'area bombing', whereby large targets, such as industrial towns and cities, were to become primary targets for night bombing. Selection of targets was restricted to the range of *GEE* – at most, 400 miles – thereby covering the cities in west and northwest Germany, and most of the existing industrial complexes. This policy remained in force for nearly two years, an open acknowledgment that precision bombing of specific targets was simply not within the command's capability. Of the 38 fully operational squadrons able to carry this intention into effect, fourteen were equipped with four-engined heavy bombers. The bulk were still using ageing Whitleys and Wellingtons. Adding to Harris's problems were the continuing demands upon his strength in crews and aircraft for tasks outside the command, not only from Coastal Command and the Admiralty. A steady stream of men and machines were also being diverted to the Middle

Above: The multi-role DH Mosquito, LR356, YH-Y of 21 Sqn is captured on film during a 'Noball' (anti-rocket base) operation in 1944.

East campaign. With little more than 300 bombers actually available on any given night, Harris implemented the new bombing policy by making devastating fire raids on the cities of Lübeck and Rostock. A particular sortie designed mainly to test the new Lancasters was undertaken on April 17, 1942, when Squadron Leader John Nettleton of 44 Squadron led twelve Lancasters – six each from 44 and 97 Squadrons – on a low-level daylight raid deep into enemy territory to bomb the M.A.N. Diesel Works at Augsburg. Four aircraft of Nettleton's leading formation were shot down by fighters of the Richthofen *Geschwader* before reaching the target, while a fifth was brought down over the target. Two of the 97 Squadron formation were also shot down during the approach to Augsburg. The five surviving Lancasters, each bearing battle scars, finally returned to England where Nettleton was quickly awarded a Victoria Cross for his leadership and courage. It is no criticism of the crews' sublime courage and determination to say that this raid caused only negligible damage to the target, and merely re-emphasised the pointless sacrifices inherent with daylight, unescorted bomber raids against pinpointed targets. Had the Lancasters

achieved maximum destruction of the objective, their loss rate was one which the overall command could never have supported for any length of time without completely dissipating its entire strength.

Harris's personal conception of his task could well be summed up in the phrase 'the big fist'. With a profound faith in the power of destruction of huge high explosive bombs, such as the 4000lb and 8000lb HC types now available, he fervently adhered to a policy of saturation bombing of large targets. Though having no part in formulating the area bombing principle directed by Whitehall, he was nevertheless its greatest exponent. With this foremost in his mind, though equally determined to prove the capability of his command and thus challenge those who wished to assign the bomber units to other duties, Harris conceived the famous 'Thousand Plan', or 'Operation Millenium', as it was code-named. The choice of target was to be either Cologne or Hamburg with weather conditions on the night providing the final decision. Harris's intention was to despatch 1000 bombers on a controlled, high density raid in the hope of causing maximum damage. Until this time no RAF raiding force had ever exceeded 230 aircraft on a single operation of this nature. By a feat of organisation involving every available unit, both operational and training within Bomber Command, Harris finally 'found' his

GREAT BRITAIN

HIGH WYCOMBE
(HQ RAF Bomber Command/
HQ US 8 Air Force)
SUNNINGHILL PARK
(HQ US 9 Air Force)
BUSHY PARK
(HQ US Strategic Air Force)

F R A

Seine

1 INDUSTRIAL TARGET
1 RAILWAY TARGET
1 OIL TARGET

MILES
0

KILOMETRES
0   30

28 Oscherleben (aircraft)
29 Dessau (aircraft)
30 Essen
31 Dortmund
32 Duisburg
33 Düsseldorf
34 Cologne
35 Bonn
36 Möhne Dam
37 Wuppertal
38 Eder Dam
39 Sorpe Dam
40 Kassel (aircraft)
41 Leipzig
42 Dresden
43 Liegnitz
44 Berlin
45 Rostock

46 Peenemünde (V-bombs)
47 Stettin
48 Erfurt
49 Gotha (aircraft)
50 Schweinfurt (ball-bearings)
51 Fürth
52 Nuremberg
53 Regensburg (aircraft)
54 Augsburg (aircraft)
55 Munich
56 Ulm
57 Stuttgart
58 Ludwigshafen
59 Saarbrücken
60 Bochum
61 Karlsruhe
62 Friedrichshafen

63 Chemnitz
64 Prague
65 Wiener Neustadt (aircraft)

Railways
1 Frankfurt
2 Hanau
3 Aschaffenburg
4 Koblenz
5 Oberlahnstein
6 Giessen
7 Siegen
8 Schwerte
9 Soest
10 Hamm
11 Löhne
12 Osnabrück
13 Rheine
14 Bielefeld

15 Altenbecken Neuenbecken
16 Seelze
17 Lehrte
18 Hameln
19 Paderborn
20 Bebra
21 Stendal
22 Halle
23 Gera
24 Breslau
25 Minden
26 Mulhouse
27 Freiburg
28 Offenburg
29 Rastatt
30 Karlsruhe
31 Heilbronn
32 Treuchtlingen
33 Pasing
34 Munich

35 Rosenheim
36 Salzburg
37 Strasshof
38 Würzburg
39 Mannerheim
40 Darmstadt
41 Mainz
42 Bingen
43 Vienna
44 Munster

Oil
1 Wesseling
2 Reisholz
3 Dülmen
4 Gelsenkirchen
5 Salzbergen
6 Nienburg
7 Farge
8 Heide
9 Hitzacker

10 Dollbergen
11 Derben
12 Pölitz
13 Salzgitter
14 Lützkendorf
15 Leuna
16 Ruhland
17 Böhlen
18 Rositz
19 Mölbis
20 Zeitz
21 Brüx
22 Neuburg
23 Freiham
24 Linz.
25 Moosbierbaum
26 Korneuburg
27 Floridsdorf
28 Schwechat
29 Lobau
30 Ploesti

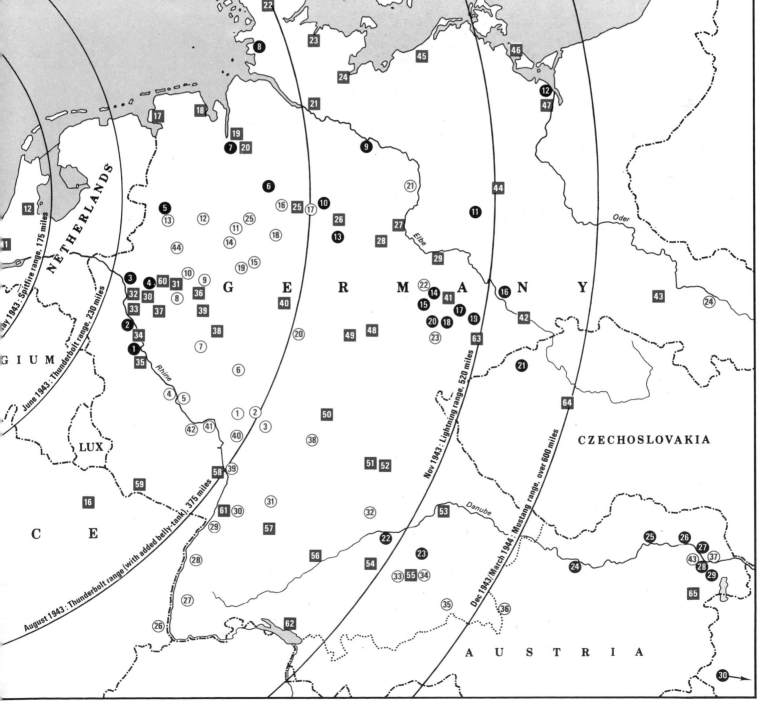

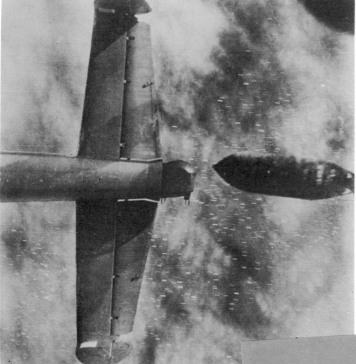

Above: A Lancaster rear gunner ('Arse-End Charlie') about to get grey hairs as a 1000lb MC/HE bomb from an overhead Lancaster plunges down.
Above centre: Douglas Bostons of 88 Sqn taxiing at Hartford Bridge, Jun 1944 fitted with chemical containers and four under-fuselage nozzles for laying smoke screens across the invasion beach-heads in Normandy.
Above right: A Mosquito of 464 Sqn at Hunsdon gets a thorough engine check.
Right: l-r: Fg Off T N Scholefield; Fg Off I Hamilton; F. Sgt R T Hillas; F. Sgt F E Hughes; Sgt R H Burges; F. Sgt K E Stewart and Sgt J D Wells; all of 467 Sqn RAAF. Photo taken after this crew's operation on the night of May 11–12, 1944 in the Lancaster behind them, R5868, PO-S – ostensibly this Lancaster's 100th operational sortie. This aircraft is now preserved at the RAF Museum at Hendon.

thousand bombers. On the night of May 30–31, 1942 a total of 1046 bombers, manned by both experienced and student crews (from the command's OTU's) set out for Cologne, preceded by 88 aircraft on intruder and diversionary sorties to confuse the German defences. In a time lapse of just 103 minutes, at least 910 of the bombers dropped their bomb loads of incendiaries and HEs into the heart of the cathedral city and devastated 600 acres of public buildings, factories and houses. German casualties amounted to nearly 5000, of whom 469 had been killed – ten times the *total* casualties inflicted in 107 previous raids on Cologne. RAF losses amounted to 41 bombers 'missing'' three intruder aircraft lost, and a further seven bombers

which crashed in the UK on their return: a loss rate to the bombers of 3.9 per cent, well within the '100 bombers' which Churchill had been 'prepared to lose'. The significant result of this unprecedented mass raid – despite its connotations of being virtually a confidence trick on Harris's part to demoralise Germany – was to obtain almost immediate governmental approval for a large expansion of Bomber Command. This saved the command from having to disperse its aircraft to those outside the command. Two immediate attempts to repeat the success of Cologne – against Essen on June 1–2 and Bremen on June 25–26 – were not so effective, but Harris had achieved his prime objectives in preserving Bomber Command as a strategic

force and receiving approval for future massive expansion of the force.

In August 1942 a new formation of huge significance came into being when the Path Finder Force was inaugurated on the 15th under the command of Group Captain (later Air Vice-Marshal) Donald Bennett. Its purpose was succinct – to spearhead main bombing sorties and locate and mark the target accurately before the main bomber stream arrived. Comprised initially of four units – 7, 35, 83 and 156 Squadrons, plus 109 Squadron 'attached' – this nucleus of specially selected volunteer crews was required to sharpen Bomber Command's precision in navigation, target location, and eventual efficiency in destruction of its specific objectives. Un-

der the aegis of Harris – whose personal objections to the new force being a separate formation had been overridden by the Air Staff – the PFF made little impact on the command's results during its early months of existence, with its mixed bag of aircraft types – Stirlings, Halifaxes, Lancasters, Wellingtons, and Mosquitos – and still lacking sophisticated navigational aids except for the semi-efficient *GEE* sets. Nevertheless the PFF crews showed a steadily improving register of successful marking raids. By January 1943, with the introduction of a new aid, *OBOE*, and fresh target-indicating bombs and pyrotechnics such as the 250lb T.I. bomb, Bomber Command, led by units of the PFF, was almost in a position to mount the long-envisaged offensive against Germany. In that same month a conference of the Allies' leaders at Casablanca resulted in a directive to Harris which enjoined him to pursue '. . . the progressive destruction and dislocation of the German military, industrial, and economic system, and the undermining of the morale of the German people to a point where their capacity for armed resistance is fatally weakened.' This call for a virtually unrestricted bombing assault on Hitler's empire could have found no more sympathetic ear than that of Harris. It coincided almost precisely with his personal attitude to the use and war-winning potential of the strategic bomber. By March 1943 Harris had at his disposal a total of 62 squadrons – nearly 1200 aircraft – of which 36 were 'heavy' bomber units equipped with Lancasters (18 squadrons), Halifaxes (11), and Stirlings (7). The latter included a complete Group of the Royal Canadian Air Force, 6 Group, equipped mainly with Wellingtons but converting to Halifaxes, which came into being on January 1. With a steady flow of fresh crews trained in the Commonwealth, and ever-increasing production of Lancasters and Mosquitos, and mounting efficiency in the PFF's target marking and location methods, Harris began his offensive against Germany in accordance with the Casablanca directive by opening the 'Battle of the Ruhr' on March 5–6 with an effective attack on Essen with more than 400 bombers.

Two further raids on Essen, the very heart of the sprawling Krupps industrial complex, created havoc, razed some 600 acres and seriously damaged more than half of the buildings within the area. Of the 1099 bombers which actually bombed on these three occasions, 58 were lost to enemy action. Continuing the battle, Harris despatched his crews to Duisburg and Düsseldorf in force, and made subsidiary attacks on Berlin, Wilhelmshaven, Hamburg, Nuremberg, Stuttgart and other population centres – a total of 43 major raids between March and June 1943. However, precision targets were not entirely ignored. On the night of May 16–17, nineteen specially modified Lancasters of the recently formed 617 Squadron led by the veteran bomber captain, Wing Commander Guy Gibson, DSO, DFC, attacked the Mohne, Eder, and Sorpe dams, which between them controlled the rivers Weser and Ruhr, providing over 130 million tons of water for power stations in the Ruhr zone. Using precise attack methods and specially-constructed explosive canisters, they shattered the dams at Mohne and Eder and damaged the Sorpe. Eight Lancasters were lost, while 34 surviving crew members were decorated for gallantry, including the supreme award of a Victoria Cross to Gibson. Formed in March 1943 specifically for this raid, 617 Squadron was thereafter 'reserved' for specific precision bomb raids for the remainder of the war. The success which crowned the 617 Squadron's crews' efforts against the dams had been achieved by a specially-formed unit, which was given no other commitment until the dams sortie – a luxury in equipment and time not available to Harris's other squadrons in the heat of almost nightly operations.

By mid-1943 the bomber crews' normal tour of operations was about 30 sorties, after which they usually 'rested' by individual postings to non-operational units. They could still be recalled for a second tour later, and indeed a vast number of crew members quickly volunteered for a continuation of 'ops' rather than linger on at flying training school as instructors and the like. Thirty operational sorties, if achieved, could be flown in less than three months on most frontline bomber squadrons – an indication of the pace of the bomber assault by this time. With the loss rate averaging nearly 250 aircraft each month for the period March to August 1943, completion of the required 30 operations was a feat of survival. Let it never be forgotten that every man in the air crews was a volunteer.

By the summer of 1943 Bomber Command had been joined in its offensive by the B–17s and B–24s of the USAAFs Eighth Air Force, whose concentration on daylight sorties forced them to suffer a high casualty rate initially, and com-

SOME 26,000 ACRES IN 43 GERMAN CITIES HAD BEEN VIRTUALLY DEVASTATED, BUT THE OVERALL EFFECT ON GERMAN FIGHTER PRODUCTION WAS SMALL.

Left: HM Queen and Princess Elizabeth (now HM Queen Elizabeth II) visiting bomber crews at Mildenhall on Jul 5, 1944.
Below: Heaviest 'conventional' bomb ever to be dropped in wartime was the 22,000lb 'Grand Slam' HE store, seen here chained into the bomb bay of a 15 Sqn Lancaster, 1945.
Bottom: Lancaster ED905, BQ-F of 550 Sqn, Killingholme begins its take-off for its 100th operation (against Bochum) on Nov 4, 1944, piloted by Flt Lt D A Shaw.
Bottom left: Fg Off Boxsell and the air and ground crews of Lancaster PA187, O-Orange, 467 Sqn RAAF in Apr 1945.

'. . . a catastrophe, the extent of which simply staggers the imagination'.
Goebbels.

plemented Harris's nightly onslaught. This combined bomber offensive was authorised by a fresh directive from the Combined Chiefs of Staff, named *Pointblank*, dated June 10, 1943. Expressing concern at the mounting casualties caused by the enlarging and increasingly efficient Luftwaffe fighter defences, *Pointblank* called for a switch in concentration of bombing to targets directly related to these fighters and their supporting industry. This task was allotted to the American bombers, whose apparently inflexible policy of daylight bombing of precision targets, despite the tragic object lessons of the RAF, continued to be pursued vigorously. Harris's bombers were expected to complement such precision raids by night bombing of related targets, a move which displeased Harris, who considered it to be a return to the impossible chore of hitting specific targets rather than areas. Interpreting the general directive to suit his more practical ideas, Harris next selected Hamburg for devastation, giving the plan the grisly code-name *Gomorrah*. As the second most important city of Germany, Hamburg offered great possibilities as a target for area destruction, and on the night of July 24–25, using the tinfoil strips named *Window* for the first time to blanket German radar screens, 740 bombers dropped 2396 tons of high explosive and incendiary bombs into the vitals of the city and port. The carefully planned German air raid precautionary systems proved useless, and the city's main services were wiped out. The next two days saw US bombers adding to the damage. Then on the night of 27–28 Bomber Command struck again. Some 739 bombers released a further 2417 tons of bombs. Two further night raids, ending on August 2–3 completed the fearful destruction of the ancient city. In just four nights Bomber Command aircraft totaling 2630 had delivered 8621 tons of bombs, half of which were pure incendiary stores. Overall losses to the RAF were 87 bombers. The results were horrific, caused mainly by a phenomenon hitherto unseen – the firestorm which, with temperatures reaching 1000 degrees Centigrade, gouged the heart out of the city. At least 42,000 Germans died in the holocaust, while a further 37,000 were seriously injured. Sixty-one per cent of all habitable accommodation was razed or rendered uninhabitable, and the city's industrial buildings suffered similar damage. Doctor Josef Goebbels, the Nazi propaganda chief, referred to the Hamburg raids in his private diary as, '. . . a catastrophe, the extent of which simply staggers the imagination'.

Between such devastating raids, Bomber Command continued to be called

upon for precise bombing of specific targets. An example was that undertaken on the night of August 17–18 when nearly 600 bombers were despatched to wreck the research station at Peenemünde, home of the giant V2 'retaliation' rocket weapons. This raid, led by an ex-Halton aircraft apprentice, John Searby of 83 Squadron, was air-supervised by a 'Master of Ceremonies' (Searby) – a technique later developed as the role of a Master Bomber on nearly all heavy raids in 1944–45. Apart from a host of other normal targets within Germany, Bomber Command also stepped up its activities in support of the Admiralty and Coastal Command by undertaking a high proportion of 'Gardening' sorties – the code-name for laying acoustic and magnetic sea mines in main rivers, harbour mouths and shipping lanes utilised by the German mercantile fleets. In 1943 13,776 such mines were 'sown' by Bomber Command aircraft in northwestern European waters. In the first half of 1944, a further 11,415 were laid preparatory to the eventual Allied landings in Europe in June. Equally testing of the bomber crews' skill and courage was a series of long hauls across the Alps to raid principal targets in Italy. During 1942–43 many such sorties aimed at Turin, Genoa and other vital objectives were flown by crews of Stirlings – aircraft already suffering because of their lack of safe ceiling. Terrible conditions of tracking both ways across the towering, snow-covered peaks of Europe's natural 'roof' barrier were imposed. When Lancasters were introduced to the 'Ice-cream Run' over Mussolini's empire, an innovation in routing undoubtedly saved many lives when the bombers, instead of threading their return journey through the Alps, continued across Italy and the Mediterranean to land in North Africa. Theoretically this 'shuttle service' permitted the bombers to execute a further raid on the leg back to Britain, but difficulties in maintaining the heavy bombers in North Africa nullified this intention to a large degree.

Harris's next objective was Berlin – the 'Big City', as it was termed by the bomber crews. Beginning on November 18–19, 1943, a total of 16 major raids (400 or more aircraft despatched) were sent against the German capital, ending temporarily on March 24–25, 1944. Despite atrocious weather which usually forced the Path Finder elements to skymark above cloud, these raids devastated over 2000 acres of Berlin, killed nearly 6000 inhabitants, and rendered 1½ million Germans homeless. The cost to Bomber Command was not light – 492 bombers and their crews were 'missing'. The *Pointblank* plan, which had begun in early 1943 culminated in late

February 1944, when for six days and nights, starting on February 23, Bomber Command and the US Eighth Air Force combined in the 'Big Week' to drop 16,506 tons of bombs on Germany – mostly in daylight by the Americans. With the invasion of Europe being planned, and the consequent need for bombers to provide tactical and strategic support to the land and sea forces, the *Pointblank* offensive tailed off. However, two specific raids soon after provide examples of the extremes of success and semi-failure obtained at this period. On the night of March 30–31 a force totalling 999 British and ten American aircraft took off in conjunction with a heavy raid directed against Nuremberg. Eighty of these turned back early, but at least 832 bombed the target. That night the Luftwaffe's fighters were controlled accurately in mass, and 79 of the bombers fell victim to the marauding Messerschmitt Bf 110s, Junkers 88s and others. By the night's end 95 bombers were lost beyond England's shores, while ten more crashed on return and became total write-offs, a loss rate of 13.6 per cent of the heavies despatched. It was the highest single loss figure of the war. At the other end of the scale was an attack on Munich on April 24–25, when Wing Commander Leonard Cheshire, DSO, DFC, flying a Mosquito, marked the aiming point from only 700 feet, and remained over the target at 1000 feet to direct the subsequent bombing. This experiment in low-level marking precision proved highly successful. For Cheshire, already a veteran of four tours of bombing operations, this raid resulted in his being awarded the Victoria Cross on September 8, 1944.

The year-long *Pointblank* assault on Germany had seen Bomber Command's crews fly a total of nearly 75,000 individual sorties, from which 2864 aircraft had been lost; in terms of human beings, a total of more than 20,000 aircrew members were killed or missing. In the stark light of postwar research, the results achieved were not as high as thought at the time. Some 26,000 acres in 43 German cities had been virtually devastated, but the overall effect on German fighter production was small. Due to a prodigious summoning of its economic reserves, German war production in virtually every sphere actually rose appreciably by the end of 1944. If anything, Bomber Command's greatest effect was on the morale of the German people. From early 1944, Germany was on the defensive. The resources necessary for the massive anti-aircraft defence system drained away possible reinforcements and supplies to both the Eastern and, after June 1944, Western Fronts. Widespread ruin of the chief industrial centres, such as the Essen

Above: Air traffic control room: at the 'Patrol Handling Board' is Corp. V Carter; nearest camera is Gp Capt Bonham-Carter.

Krupps complex, had made a huge impact on Germany's war production initially, but was soon rectified by a masterly dispersion of vital production centres.

On June 6, 1944, the greatest invasion force in history crossed the English Channel and clawed footholds on the beaches of Normandy. Bomber Command's contribution to this awesome venture was a dense carpet of bombs – over 5000 tons – dropped on ten of the principal German coastal batteries threatening the landing, apart from numerous individual sorties in other forms of direct support. As night approached, the bombers probed further inland, blasting every known main railway line to the battle zone. The ubiquitous Mosquitos of 2 Group ranged far and wide behind German coastal defences, shattering road and rail links and effectively preventing swift reinforcement of the German defenders. By late June the heavy bombers were brought into direct tactical support of the Allied armies, laying a thick carpet of bombs up to 4000 yards in front of the infantry as it punched its way into France through the

stiff German resistance. Throughout July the British and American bombers unloaded up to 4000 tons of high explosive daily in this manner, gutting German resistance points and demoralising the ground opposition. By virtue of the vast air supremacy attained by the Allied air forces by then, little or no interference was met from the Luftwaffe, a factor which gave unrestricted freedom to the bomber crews in delivering their accurate daylight attacks.

By late August 1944, with the Allied armies flooding across Europe towards Germany, Chief of the Air Staff requested that Bomber Command be released from Eisenhower's direct control, in order to recommence the purely strategic bombing offensive. Priority targets were now defined as Germany's oil refineries and the remaining war industries. During October and November, Bomber Command despatched a series of both day and night attacks on these targets. The shrinking Luftwaffe's night defences gave relatively little opposition, while by day the RAF and USAAF commanded the skies. On

Above: DH Mosquito MM401 of 464 Sqn, with much of one wing missing, and one engine 'out'.

October 14, for example, 1063 aircraft attacked Duisburg in broad daylight and lost just 15 aircraft. That same night 1005 bombers dropped 4547 tons of bombs on Duisburg, with a loss of only six aircraft. Aiding the bomber streams that night were 141 Mosquitos and other diversionary machines – creating almost total confusion among the Luftwaffe night fighter controllers. In December the bomber armada continued to increase its striking power, despatching a total of 15,333 aircraft in all, and suffering the loss of 135 – less than one per cent. By early 1945 German oil and fuel production had already diminished to a relative trickle, starving the aircraft, tanks and other transports still desperately fighting on all fronts. Harris continued to adhere to his personal creed of area bombing of large, conglomerate objectives. No greater example existed in the European bombing campaign than the results of two raids on the night of February 13–14, 1945, when the designated target was the ancient and beautiful city of Dresden. Two waves, comprising a total of 773 bombers, dropped 2660 tons of bombs and in-

cendiaries and decimated the city. Two more raids, by American B–17s on the 14 and 15, completed the destruction. German figures for the horrific number of casualties resulting from this mammoth disaster state that 18,375 were killed, and a further 35,000 were listed as 'missing' – all but about 100 of this grim total being civilians. In fact, an exact figure can never be known because the city at that period was overcrowded with a host of refugees and non-German civilians not normally resident in Dresden.

On April 6 a fresh directive of policy for Bomber Command called for a halt in area bombing, and thereafter raids were confined to crippling oil refineries, shipyards, railway marshalling yards, and other vital communications targets. Nevertheless, on April 25, 318 Lancasters attacked Hitler's private 'castle', the 'Eagle's Nest' at Berchtesgaden. It seemed an appropriate gesture to finalise the many years of the bomber campaign. A gentler and perhaps more satisfying series of 'operations' undertaken by Harris's crews were Operation 'Manna', in which, between April 29 and VE-Day, May 8, 1945, 3156 Lancasters and 145 Mosquitos dropped 6700 tons of food and supplies to the starving Dutch population. And then Operation 'Exodus', the retrieval by air of many thousands of

Allied prisoners of war, many of whom were former comrades of Bomber Command, was launched.

From the very first hours of the war until the final flights above a totally ruined Nazi Germany, the men of Bomber Command had never flinched from their given tasks, which required a unique form of courage and determination, returning night after night in the deadly skies over Europe. Of the overall RAF losses of 70,253 men and women killed or 'missing' in action throughout the war, 47,268 men were from the Bomber Command. In addition 4200 were wounded on operations. Nor should it be forgotten that an additional 8305 men of the bombers died in non-operational spheres, such as flying accidents during training. In terms of operations flown and machines, the command had undertaken 364,514 individual sorties by day and night. Some 8325 aircraft were lost in action. They were astonishingly young men – any man in his late 'twenties' was considered 'old' by his comrades. Yet they bore a mature responsibility upon their shoulders. Bomber captains, so many still below the age of majority, coolly, cheerfully, and skilfully led their crews into the heavens, knowing too well that their chances of survival were slim. They seldom faltered.

By Air, By Sea

With its obvious vulnerability as an island, dependent to a great degree on shipped imports of nearly every vital commodity, Britain's sea defences have always been vital. Naval power and dominance of the oceans necessarily pre-occupied British defence chiefs for many centuries prior to 1939. The introduction of the aeroplane to the Navy prior to World War I provided the possibility of an extended 'arm' for naval reconnaissance; while various trials, experiments, and isolated operations during 1914–18 experimented with torpedo-strike sorties, aircraft carrier-borne fighters and bombers, and general extended reconnaissance for the heavy guns on capital ships. The fierce partisan battles in Whitehall between the wars for 'ownership' of a Fleet air arm controlled by the Admiralty led eventually to such an arm becoming purely naval in character prior to World War II. In the same period the RAF used a wide variety of flying boat designs – over 100 different designs were made or mooted between 1918 and 1939 – and gained slow experience in operating long range oversea cruises and patrols. With the re-organisation of the RAF in 1936, the flying boat squadrons became an integral formation, Coastal Command. Its role was mainly one of watch and ward around Britain's coastal waters and sea approaches, with an extended burden of air communication throughout the British Empire. Despite the importance of guarding Britain's sea life-lines, Coastal Command's priority for modern aircraft and equipment lagged well behind the bomber and fighter programme of the RAF's hasty rearmament in the late 1930s. This was inevitable and, at the time, warranted. Sea protection was a matter for the Royal Navy, while the urgency for a vast expansion of Britain's bomber and defensive fighter squadrons was paramount.

Contrary to perpetuated legends, co-operation between the Navy and the relatively small Coastal Command was excellent from the beginning of World War II. With a common purpose both organisations were partly integrated at the operational control level, though each retained its own responsibilities. Split among three Groups – 15 (Plymouth HQ), 16 (Chatham), and 18 (Rosyth) – on the outbreak of hostilities with Germany, Coastal Command's equipment was a varied mixture of aircraft types. Of the 20 squadrons immediately available, eleven were flying Avro Anson general reconnaissance machines, one was equipped with Lockheed Hudsons, two had the new Short Sunderland four-engined flying boats, two 'strike' units were still soldiering on with obsolete Vickers Vildebeeste torpedo biplanes and the others were still flying biplane flying boats, Saro Londons and Stranraers, with a few Short Singapores. With the exception of the handful of Sunderlands and Hudsons, none had the range, performance or war-load capacity for any operations outside coastal waters. The primary function of the command in the opening months of the war was constant

Above: Short Sunderland 'Weary Willie' of 201 Sqn on Oct 28, 1941 displaying radar antennae and two dorsal gun hatches for additional defence.
Below: Lockheed Hudson, N7303 of 269 Sqn gets a thorough 'going over' in the open. In background, Avro Anson, K6244.

patrol over the northern exits of the North Sea, seeking signs of any German capital ships or surface raiders which might pass out into the Atlantic to prey on merchant shipping. Ironically, even if any such raider was spotted, it was not within Coastal Command's capability to seriously hinder its progress. Any attack would be carried out by Bomber Command aircraft. Improvised versions of the Blenheim IV bomber were added to the command, and in early 1940 a few modified Wellington bombers were brought into use. All suffered from a great disadvantage, in that Coastal Command at this time possessed no effective anti-ship or anti-submarine weapon. Its existing bomb dumps were stocked with standard general purpose high-explosive bombs, weapons which had no effect on either a surface or underwater vessel.

The menace of the submarine was fully appreciated, but little was available within Coastal Command to deal with the underwater killer. On September 3, 1939 eight German U-boats were already stationed in the eastern Atlantic, and within three weeks they sent nearly 150,000 tons of merchant shipping to the ocean floor. From November Coastal Command placed anti-submarine duties on a par with the existing commitment of reconnoitring the North Sea. Yet they were still without an effective attacking

Right: Wellington XIV's of 458 Sqn RAAF based at Gibraltar in 1944 to cover the western entry waters of the Mediterranean.

Right: Flt Lt Turley-George (l) and Flg Off C Fenwick with their catapult-Hurricane aboard the Empire Tide.

Left: Consolidated Catalina amphibian, FP-529. 'Cats' first saw RAF service in 1941 and were used extensively by Coastal Command. Two Catalina pilots were awarded VCs. With its range of 4000 miles, the 'Cat' proved a boon to convoy protection in the east Atlantic.
Below left: Catalina crew leave their Nissen hut at the start of a patrol.

problems. German occupation of the western coastal areas of France permitted open access to the Atlantic for air and sea raiders intent on throttling Britain's merchant shipping routes. In occupied Norway, bounded eastwards by a thousand inlets and harbours, lay an equally serious threat to North Sea shipping. From French airfields the Luftwaffe could now despatch very long-range Focke-Wulf Fw 200 Condor bombers – capable of a 2000-mile range – to harrass the trans-Atlantic lifelines. The Bay of Biscay became a happy hunting ground for U-boats along the southern shipping lanes. Bomber Command was diverted to attacking submarine pens, harbours and other purely naval targets, such as surface raiders in harbour – raids flown with great determination and no little gallantry – but this hastily-mounted air offensive produced little effective result. The main need in Coastal Command was for its own VLR (Very Long Range) aircraft, machines with a four-figure operational range, extended endurance, and effective search, detection and attack equipment. Only then might it be possible to provide a constant umbrella of air guards to the convoys steaming back and forth to the New World. The very presence of an aircraft in the vicinity of any convoy was more than often sufficient to deter a U-boat commander from attacking shipping. Of the 500 aircraft available to Coastal Command in June 1940, just 34 – all Sunderlands – were able to fly and operate beyond 500 miles from shore. From that month until the end of the year, more than three million tons of Allied and neutral shipping was sunk by German U-boats, aircraft, sea-mines and surface raiders. Coastal Command's only tangible results in the same period were two U-boats claimed as damaged. A re-routing of trans-Atlantic shipping to the passage around Scotland produced a slight improvement in loss figures from U-boat predators, who soon reacted to combat this ploy. As a countermove Coastal Command sent two squadrons – Hudsons and Sunderlands – to Iceland in January 1941, and a third unit, 330 (Norway) Squadron, equipped with Northrop float-planes, was sent shortly after.

The U-boat offensive intensified, sinking over half a million tons of merchant shipping monthly during the first half

weapon against any U-boat sighted, and had to rely on calling up naval vessels to actually deal with the target. Radio Direction Finding (RDF) airborne equipment in crude form had been tested in an Anson as far back as early 1937. Yet, despite successful results in locating surface vessels, forerunner of the ASV (Air-to-Surface Vessel) equipment, little was done by the Air Ministry to pursue the progress of such an aid for aircraft of Coastal Command. Until well into 1940 the command had to be content with low-level surveillance of coastal waters and the North Sea, hunting for sight of any U-boat and then relying on other forces to attack and destroy. For the steady volume of merchant shipping bringing vital material to Britain through the Atlantic routes the air crews could provide little protection at this stage of the war. Aircraft operational ranges precluded air coverage of shipping much beyond 450 miles from Britain's shores, and then only rarely by the few Sunderlands. The convoy system had yet to be inaugurated, as Royal Navy surface protection was limited. If the lion's share of Coastal's operations during 1939–40 were spent in monotonous hour upon hour of simply 'watching water', a number of isolated operations at least gave some crews opportunity for more direct offensive work. The first partial success in the anti-submarine campaign came on January 30, 1940, when the *U-55*, already crippled by the Navy, was further attacked by Sunderland 'Y' of 228 Squadron, causing the U-boat commander to scuttle his ship. It was to be six months before the next Coastal success was registered. On July 1 *U-26* was sunk by Sunderland 'H' of 10 Squadron, RAAF in conjunction with the Royal Navy. The ill-fated Norwegian campaign of April-June 1940 saw Coastal aircraft mainly employed in reconnaissance and mine-laying roles. Actual offensive air sorties were undertaken by bombers, fighters, and dive-bombers of the Fleet Air Arm.

With the collapse of France and the Low Countries in mid-1940, Coastal Command faced a multitude of fresh

Right: An early version of the Consolidated Liberator (AM910) with ASV radar masts, four 20mm cannon belly pack, and five additional .303 machine guns. Jun 1941 saw 120 Sqn receive the first Coastal Command Liberators, and subsequently a variety of improved and modified versions gave splendid service in most operational areas.

of 1941. At this point the Admiralty decided to press again for naval control of the RAF's maritime air formations. Backed by Lord Beaverbrook, Minister of Aircraft Production, the Admiralty demanded that the RAF hand over all shore-based Coastal Command aircraft in addition to control of the flying boat units. The custody of the shore-based units was quickly realised to be too much of a responsibility for naval administration, and the Admiralty demurred from accepting it. Nevertheless, it was insisted that Coastal squadrons were not to be used for 'non-maritime' work without consent of the Admiralty, a compromise forced on the RAF commander from April 1941. At purely operational levels this paper reorganisation had little effect, inasmuch as the previous system of integrated operational work continued as before. This satisfied the paper

Below: l-r: AVM G B A Baker, CB, MC; A. Cdre A H Primrose, CBE, DFC; AVM J M Robb, CB, DSO, DFC, AFC; AVM A Durston, AFC; A. Cdre S P Simpson, CBE, MC; ACM Sir Philip Joubert de la Ferté, KCB, CMG, DSO (AOC-in-C); AVM G R Bromet, CBE, DSO; A. Cdre I T Lloyd, CBE; A. Cdre H G Smart, CBE, DFC, AFC.

tigers in Whitehall, but did not interfere with actual operational needs at the 'sharp end'. The traditionally dogged persistence of the British Navy was exemplified in this latest attempt by the Admiralty in its decades-old battle to dismember the RAF.

Though still awaiting re-equipment with long-range aircraft to combat the U-boats in deep waters, Coastal Command had already begun receiving fresh aircraft types designed for a maritime role. As early as November 1939 the first examples of the Bristol Beaufort twin-engined monoplane torpedo-bomber were issued to 22 Squadron, based at Thorney Island, for service trials and crew familiarisation. Early problems with engines and inexperienced crews delayed operational use of the new strike aircraft until the night of April 15–16,

1940. Nine Beauforts of 22 Squadron undertook a mining sortie just north of Wilhelmshaven and lost one aircraft. The design's intended role as a torpedo attack aircraft was not put to operational use until September 11, 1940, when five Beauforts of 22 Squadron left North Coates and, without fighter escort, attacked three merchant ships near Ostend and claimed a hit on one of these vessels. Though Beauforts of 22 and 42 Squadrons completed 38 torpedo sorties by the end of 1940, the crews flew a large proportion of their operations purely as bombers, attacking shipping, ports, harbours, and particularly German capital ships harboured around the French coast. The difficulties of mounting a torpedo strike were exemplified in the early hours of April 6, 1941. Six Beauforts

from 22 Squadron, temporarily based at St Eval, Cornwall, were detailed to torpedo the *Gneisenau* harboured in Brest. Three of the aircraft were bogged down by the weight of their torpedoes and fuel load and never got airborne. One of the other three located the designated target. The pilot of the lone Beaufort, Flying Officer Ken Campbell, made a perilous run-in over the masts of defending flak-ships into a murderous cross-fire of anti-aircraft shells, launched his 'fish' at 500 yards range (which damaged the *Gneisenau* below the water-line), and then crashed and exploded into the harbour. His sheer courage in the face of certain death was recognised by the posthumous award of a Victoria Cross.

The nearest equivalent to a long-range, shore-based aircraft within the command in 1941 was the ageing Whit-ley bomber, three squadrons (58, 502 and 612) of which had been transferred or re-equipped by the spring of that year. By the close of 1941 Whitley GR VII versions were serving with 502 Squadron, equipped with an improved ASV radar, and on November 30, Whitley 'B' of that unit made the first Coastal Command ASV 'kill' when it sank the submarine *U-206*. However, in June 1941 the promise of greater operational 'elbow-room' for Coastal crews came when the first American-built Consolidated Liberator I bombers entered Coastal service, with 120 Squadron based at Nutts Corner, Belfast. These were the vanguard of the command's true VLR types, able to spread Coastal's protecting wings to an operational range in excess of 2000 miles out over the ocean. Though neutral Eire had refused Britain permission to set up airfields within her borders to protect the Atlantic seaboard, Coastal and Fighter Commands were operating from various stations in Northern Ireland – advanced platforms for the Battle of the Atlantic. By June 1941, when the Coastal AOC-in-C, 'Ginger' Bowhill was finally succeeded in his appointment by Philip Joubert, the command had been improved greatly from its eve-of-war state. There were now a total of 40 squadrons, half of which were ASV-equipped. U-boat killing had risen to significant figures during the preceding half-year, while shipping losses were easing considerably. Later that year neutral America had begun providing its own air cover for convoys to ranges well out from her shores, thus assisting in closing the mid-Atlantic gaps in air cover. Equally significant was the introduction of airborne depth charges as Coastal Command's main underwater weapons, replacing the useless high explosive bombs which had previously been the only war load available. A

Below: German submarine U-625 after an attack by Flt Lt S W Butler's Sunderland III, 'U' of 422 Sqn RCAF on Mar 10, 1944. The action took place 400 miles west of Ireland, during a routine convoy cover patrol.

powerful new fighter was introduced in 1941 – the Bristol Beaufighter – a twin-engined lethal destroyer packing a punch of four 20-mm cannons and six .303 machine guns. Early arrivals were those of 143 Squadron at Aldergrove, Northern Ireland in the first months of spring. The command was to use Beaufighters, in increasing numbers and improved versions, until the end of the war, employing Beaufighter squadrons and, later Wings as strike units for attacking every imaginable type of target.

Yet another innovation in 1941 for Coastal Command was the receipt of a number of Consolidated Catalina I flying boats, the first examples going to 209 and 240 Squadrons in Northern Ireland, then based at Castle Archdale. Offering massive range (at maximum, 4000 miles) and an endurance of almost 18 hours, these stalwart aircraft eventually equipped a total of 22 squadrons both in Britain and overseas commands.

Right: The rubberised wading suit worn by 'ground' crews on flying boat units, 'modelled' here by a WAAF mechanic. Below: Bristol Beaufighter NE831, PL-O, of 144 Sqn setting out for a strike on the Norwegian coast, 1944. With four 20mm cannon, six .303 machine guns, and either eight 3in rockets or a torpedo, the Beaufighter was the RAF's most heavily-armed fighter of the war.

Though the vast bulk of Coastal crews flew many hundreds of hours operationally on non-eventful patrols, gazing at boundless miles of featureless ocean, with only the rare sight of an enemy, the inherent hazards of flying over deep waters, hundreds of miles from the nearest shore, were by no means small. Engine failure due to any one of a thousand variables meant ditching in ocean waters. Even if an aircraft 'skipper' managed to ditch successfully – a rare achievement among the giant roller

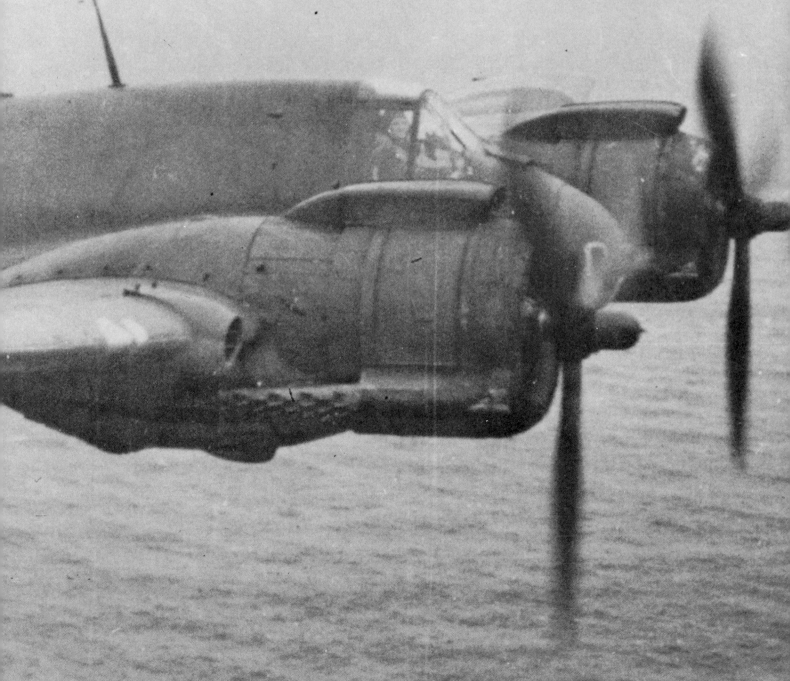

144

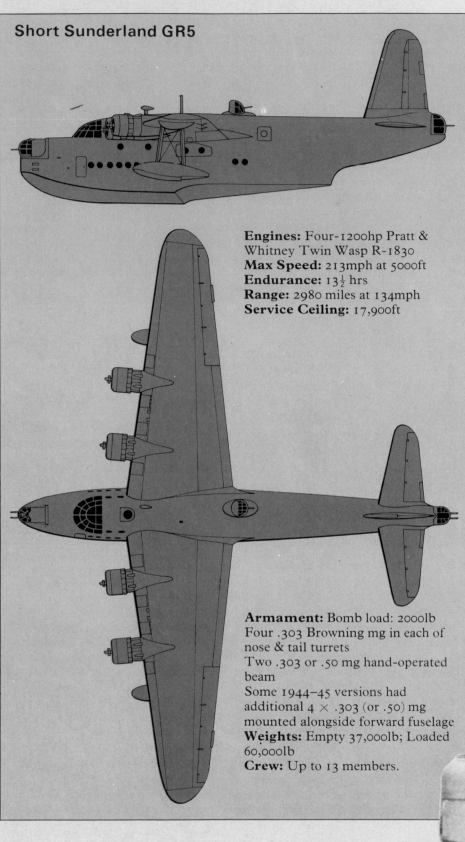

Short Sunderland GR5

Engines: Four-1200hp Pratt & Whitney Twin Wasp R-1830
Max Speed: 213mph at 5000ft
Endurance: 13½ hrs
Range: 2980 miles at 134mph
Service Ceiling: 17,900ft

Armament: Bomb load: 2000lb
Four .303 Browning mg in each of nose & tail turrets
Two .303 or .50 mg hand-operated beam
Some 1944–45 versions had additional 4 × .303 (or .50) mg mounted alongside forward fuselage
Weights: Empty 37,000lb; Loaded 60,000lb
Crew: Up to 13 members.

waves of a pounding ocean – the risk of injury to his crew was high. And if any crew survived such an initial impact with the concrete-hard surface of the sea, ultimate survival was still slim. Once a crew had abandoned their sinking machine, their only hope was the fragile gum elastic dinghy, prey to unpredictable currents and winds. The survivors were subjected to blistering heat or cruel sub-zero temperatures. Such conditions swiftly exhausted ditched crews, whose only faint hope of survival then depended on retrieval by their fellow crews at base. Once any aircraft was reported ditched or simply overdue, the rescue procedure swung into action immediately. But even here the chances of locating a dull yellow micro-dot upon the surface of thousands of square miles of grey-green shifting ocean were incalculable. It is a tragic fact that the combination of such elements, always at the mercy of raw nature in its cruellest form, was responsible for killing more Coastal Command crews than anything perpetrated by the enemy.

From August 1941 Coastal Command became officially responsible for control of all RAF air-sea rescue organisation and co-ordination between all commands. The need for such a unified direction might be emphasised by statistics for the period February to August 1941, during which an overall total of some 1200 air crew members had crashed or ditched in open waters. Only a third (444) of these were rescued.

Below: A Short Sunderland III, EK591, '2-U', of 422 Sqn RCAF settles at Castle Archdale, Northern Ireland on Jul 15, 1944.

The anti-shipping role of the Beauforts and Beaufighters continued in 1942. Over the Atlantic long-range Catalinas, Liberators and Sunderlands maintained their constant patrols above the convoy routes to the limits of their ranges. The entry of America into the war prompted Admiral Doenitz, head of Germany's naval forces, to detach strong elements of his U-boats to the western regions of the Atlantic to prey on shipping near American coastal waters. In terms of merchant tonnage sunk this ploy proved highly rewarding to U-boat commanders, but relieved the mid-Atlantic battle considerably for much of the first half of the year. In a five months' period only nine merchant ships were lost in areas covered by Coastal Command aircraft west of Britain. This temporary 'relief' of pressure enabled Coastal to concentrate more heavily on scouring two main areas – the Bay of Biscay and the northern 'transit' stretch of water of the North Sea through which most new submarines made their breakout into the Atlantic. By July the Biscay zone began to produce good results. Among the reasons for these successes were the use of improved, Torpex-filled depth charges and the introduction of the Leigh Light for night operations. Invented by (then) Squadron Leader H de V Leigh, it was introduced in 1940 and developed over the next 18 months. It was an ASV detection radar set combined with a clear searchlight-type beam of light battery-operated within the aircraft. Once the ASV picked up a submarine contact, this was tracked to the point of the radar 'blip' disappearing from the set's screen, at which point the Leigh Light was switched on, revealing the contacted ves-

sel in a brilliant shaft of light. Immediate attacks which followed were usually successful. On June 4, 1942 four of the only five available Leigh Light-equipped Wellingtons were sent to Biscay to inaugurate these operations. Three of the four successfully contacted fishing vessels in the dark, while the fourth homed on to and illuminated a pair of submarines. One of these, an Italian, was damaged by the Wellington's depth charges and was finished off three days later by a Sunderland of 10 Squadron, RAAF. On July 6 the first positive Leigh Light kill was accomplished by night when a Wellington ('N') of 172 Squadron sank the *U-502*. By May 1945 Leigh Light Wellingtons accounted for 27 U-boats confirmed as destroyed, and a further 23 seriously damaged. Yet another addition to Coastal Command's armoury was the introduction of the VLR Boeing Fortress II – equivalent of the USAAF's Boeing B-17 'Flying Fortress' – which entered maritime operational service with 59 Squadron in August 1942. Its very long range (maximum 2700 miles) gave extra 'reach' to Coastal Command in the urgent race to close the mid-Atlantic gaps in air protection for merchant shipping.

Coastal Command's Beaufighters were gaining experience in the strike role and a measure of success, so much so that

the AOC-in-C, Joubert, asked for a torpedo-Beaufighter version to be produced, and then decided to form all-Beaufighter Wings comprised (initially) of three Beau squadrons of mixed types. The first such Wing consisting of 143, 236 and 254 Squadrons was assembled in November 1942 at North Coates, but it made a poor start. By the spring of 1943, however, the North Coates Wing was fit for operations and began a series of successful devastating assaults on enemy convoys and other surface vessels. These and other depredations on German mercantile strength soon led Admiral Doenitz to demand extra Luftwaffe help in combating the increasingly successful RAF maritime air crews. The Luftwaffe's response was to detach 24 Junkers 88s to western France for work over the Biscay area. Noting the increased air opposition now being met, Joubert detailed two Beaufighter units, 235 and 248 Squadrons, for 'anti-Luftwaffe' activities. The result was an effective defeat of the Junkers, and by November 1943 Luftwaffe air interference was virtually nil.

In August 1942, due to the escalating successes in U-boat destruction along the eastern American coastal waters, Doenitz was forced to concentrate his main U-boat activity in the central Atlantic out of reach of shore-based air-

146

craft. In the same month he reorganised the tactical deployment of his force by commencing the notorious 'Wolf-pack' system of patrols and attacks. These were mainly directed in the mid-Atlantic air 'gaps', beyond retribution from the skies, and resulted in a sharp increase in shipping losses to the Allies. Some half million tons per month were lost during the latter half of 1942 in some of the fiercest naval clashes of the whole struggle at sea. During the same period those U-boats coming under air attack began to fight back, staying on the surface and defending themselves with batteries of light and medium flak guns mounted

Left: Coastal Command Beaufighters attacking enemy shipping in the Borkum Heligoland area on Aug 25, 1944.
Below: The fury of a cannon and rocket barrage are amply illustrated by this view of a 404 Sqn RCAF Beaufighter strike against a German flak ship in the Skagerrak, Oct 15, 1944.

(mainly) on conning towers. This deliberate policy of counter-attack added a further deadly hazard for any attacking aircraft, which was given no option but to plunge deliberately into a hail of usually accurate flak shells during its necessarily steady, low-level attack run over a U-boat. Yet no Coastal crew baulked at this fresh challenge, and U-boat losses continued to rise. Nevertheless, the underwater 'wolves' continued to add to their grisly tally, and in November 1942 they sank a total of 814,700 tons – the heaviest mercantile loss figure of the war. Thus, at the Casablanca Conference of January 1943, one priority decided and immediately implemented was to employ every measure to defeat the U-boat menace. This decision, however, added little to Coastal Command's available strength in aircraft. Instead RAF Bomber Command, already devoting a large proportion of its war effort to attacking purely naval targets and ancillary objectives, was directed to increase

its weight of attacks on such targets. The bombers proceeded to do this by heavy assaults against ports, harbour towns and cities, industries concerned with production of naval material, and U-boat building shipyards. Therefore when Joubert handed over his command in February 1943 to John Slessor, Coastal Command was geared to its peak of activity, and at last was receiving a steady flow of the machines, material and support necessary to undertake its vital tasks. Though two more years of constant, bloody struggle were to ensue before the final triumph, the command had, unknowingly, reached its turning point on the graph of success and worthy achievement.

Before the end of 1942 Coastal Command had been called upon to undertake a responsibility of vast importance: cover and support operations in connection with the Anglo-American invasion of North Africa – Operation Torch. Centre of preparations for this sea-borne invasion was Gibraltar, where two Coastal Command-controlled units, 202 and 233 Squadrons, were based. Three more squadrons were flown in to join them, 210, 500 and 608, while on the eve of the operation Joubert was 'loaned' a Halifax bomber unit, 405 Squadron RCAF, for extra convoy protection duties. At Gibraltar the existing runway of 980 yards length and 75 yards width was extended and resurfaced to a fully tarmacked runway of 1400 yards length and 100 yards width – the final 400 yards projecting out into the harbour waters. Virtually every other foot of available flat surface adjoining was converted to dispersal areas and maintenance accommodation. From November 5 intensive air patrols scoured the entrance to the Mediterranean seeking U-boats or surface vessels of the German and Italian fleets. On November 8 the seaborne invasion convoy began disembarking its troops in Algeria, and for the following four weeks the Gibraltar-based Hudsons and Catalinas of Coastal Command continued their unceasing watch over the back-up supply convoys heading for the

Above: DH Mosquito, RS625 of 143 Sqn, Coastal Command, fitted here with 100 gal drop tanks, under-wing rockets, and an F24 camera in the nose.

invasion beach-heads. They flew more than 8000 hours on operations directly supporting Torch, sinking three U-boats (*U-595, U-259, U-98*) and sharing with a Fleet Air Arm Albacore in sinking *U-331*. In all the crews made 142 U-boat 'sighting' reports, 83 'attack' signals, but 17 aircraft were lost within the same period – some of these falling victim to 'friendly' guns and fighters due to faulty aircraft recognition or simply 'trigger-happy' gunners.

On February 15, 1943 Coastal Command headquarters at Northwood, Middlesex controlled a total of 65 squadrons and five special duties Flights. Several of these units were on loan from the Fleet Air Arm, Bomber Command, and American air services – a practical example of the joint effort now being made to finally defeat the U-boat threat. Yet, despite the agreement reached in principle at Casablanca, full co-ordination of effort and resources in the maritime air war over the Atlantic between American and RAF units was never fully achieved in practice. Understandably, American chiefs of naval-air staff tended to pay more regard to the war against Japan in the Pacific. Fortunately for Slessor the inter-Service integration of effort between the British Admiralty and Coastal Command was, by early 1943, most harmonious, with eager and selfless co-operation marked at every level of operational control and despatch. The main areas of concern to Slessor now were in the North Atlantic and the notorious Bay of Biscay – both sea exits to the Atlantic for U-boats setting out from 'home' ports. Even with aircraft based in Iceland and the Azores, and with the ever-helpful backing of Canadian authorities, the task remained prodigious. Though Coastal Command had never been stronger in terms of units and aircraft, the numbers of truly long-range aircraft available for operations was still re-

Above: Plt Off Harnett, in Mosquito 'Z' of 143 Sqn, attacking shipping in Edj Fiord, Norway on Jan 25, 1945.

latively small, while new, improved scientific devices, such as ASV Mk III and low-level bombsights, were only being produced in a trickle by mid-1943. Sheer numbers of aircraft were not Slessor's chief concern. Adequate strength of the right type of aircraft was more important. The doughty Sunderland continued to give superb service within its admitted limitations, but the great need was for more advanced versions of the American Liberator, fitted with the very latest detection: 'black boxes', or radar. In February 1943 only four squadrons within the command were Liberator-equipped, two of these being USAAF units on temporary loan in England. Undeterred, the Coastal crews waged their unrelenting war with the material to hand – and with mounting success. In May 1943 enemy losses reached their peak, when at least 41 U-boats were sunk, 19 of these by Coastal aircraft. On May 17 Admiral Doenitz admitted defeat in the North Atlantic zone by signalling all U-boat commanders to transfer their attention to less unprofitable areas.

In the Bay of Biscay – the vital area of which was roughly 300 miles by 120 miles – it was estimated that about five out of six U-boats had to pass through to gain the outer Atlantic hunting grounds. It was a zone well within reach of aircraft based in southern England and at Gibraltar. Accordingly Slessor decided to concentrate his main striking and hunting aircraft on scouring the Bay in a systematic fashion. Such patrolling – some 40 to 50 aircraft over the Bay during the crucial hours – added to the fresh tactics by U-boat crews who 'fought back', placed a heavy burden on the shoulders of the Coastal crews. This 'burden' was cheerfully accepted. In

terms of U-boats actually sunk, the success of the new patrolling tactic was modest, though encouraging. Far greater success was achieved by the deterrent effect such constant air pressure had on the U-boat crews, ever-aware of the consequences of air assault and detection. For every 24 hours at sea, some four to five hours had to be spent surfaced for battery re-charging, a period which left U-boats almost sitting ducks for the sharp-eyed Coastal crews. To counteract U-boat flak installations, many Coastal aircraft had fitted additional nose armament. The lead was taken by 10 Squadron RAAF's Sunderlands, which incorporated four fixed .303 (later, .50) machine guns alongside the nose turrets, and used this extra firepower to keep German gunners' heads down during the run-in attack pattern. Swift to react to any air menace, the U-boat commanders soon began travelling in small groups, thus affording mutual protection and lessening the chances of detection. Luftwaffe support stiffened during the same period and now included numbers of Messerschmitt Bf110s and a few Focke-Wulf Fw 190s to support the Junkers 88s based along the French coastline. Opposing them were Coastal Command's pugnacious Beaufighter squadrons, and air combats over the Bay in the spring and summer of 1943 were frequent and fierce.

By September 1943 the U-boats ceased their 'fightback' tactics and resorted to surfacing only by night for the necessary battery-charging hours. This threw the onus of detection and killing onto Coastal's Leigh Light and ASV-equipped aircraft. Within a few weeks German engineers had produced an even more effective device – the *Schnorkel* tubes. These two 14-inch bore tubes – one for 'breathing' and a shorter tube for exhausting – enabled a U-boat to remain submerged at periscope height while

battery-charging. Though the *Schnorkel* incorporated several teething snags at first, the effect was to leave the U-boat free of the dangerous necessity for remaining surfaced for revitalisation of its internal power systems. A second product of German ingenuity was the acoustic torpedo, able to home with deadly accuracy on the noise of cavitation made by any vessel's propellers. Self-manoeuvring by control of its incorporated 'listening' apparatus, the acoustic torpedo initiated a new phase of underwater threats to shipping. The combination of all these new weapons, devices and tactics enabled Doenitz's men to return to former hunting areas and re-adopt the 'wolf pack' ploy. In early October 1943 one such pack chose to prey in the North Atlantic again – and met disaster. Between October 4 and 17 twelve U-boats were claimed as sunk, ten of which were victims of aircraft based in Iceland and the Azores.

On January 20, 1944 John Slessor was succeeded as AOC-in-C, Coastal Command by Sholto Douglas, and could offer his successor a highly efficient and increasingly successful organisation. In 1943 Coastal Command aircraft (including Gibraltar) had destroyed 90 and seriously damaged a further 51 U-boats. Unrecorded are the possible hundreds of occasions when simply by their presence aircraft had deterred or prevented U-boats undertaking destructive attacks on merchant or naval shipping. German submarine crews were by now ultra-conscious of operating under the wings of any hostile aircraft which, even if it did not attack itself, could quickly bring naval forces to the scene of any sighting. This 'air deterrent' undoubtedly saved uncounted thousands of lives and millions of tons of vital material.

On taking over command Sholto Douglas's main concern was preparation for the part his new command had to play in the imminent Allied invasion of France in mid-1944 – guardianship of the vast invasion fleet which was to be assembled and the English Channel waters and approaches in which the fleet would be vulnerable to submarine attack was vital. In April 1944 Douglas issued his directives. The south-western approaches to the Channel assumed first priority, and this area was to be patrolled night and day. At the eastern end of the Channel similar, though slightly lesser, cover was also to be provided. No. 15 Group, based then at Liverpool, became responsible for overseeing the North Atlantic convoy routes, assisted by 18 Group in Scotland. Conscious of the distinct possibilities of this Allied invasion, Doenitz recalled a large proportion of his U-boat commanders to their bases. If an invasion was launched, his submarines would be needed. Fortuitously, this eas-

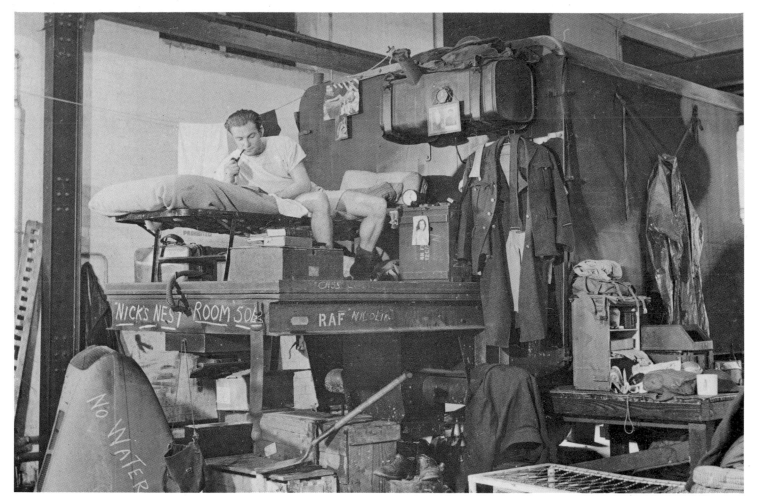

ing of pressure on the Atlantic Battle coincided with Douglas's decision to concentrate the most effective strength of his command in southern England. Always one to search for an offensive outlet, Douglas also stepped up the activities of his strike squadrons in their roving depredations of enemy surface craft. Added muscle to the existing rocket- and cannon-armed Beaufighters came early in the year when fighter versions of the magnificent De Havilland Mosquito came into Coastal Command service. Mainly Mk VIs, armed with rockets, cannons and machine guns, they also included some Mk XVIII versions carrying the huge 57mm Molins shell gun in the nose – the so-termed 'Tse-Tse' Mosquito. One 'Tse-Tse' of 248 Squadron scored an immediate success by sinking *U-976* off the French coast with its shell-gun.

In the weeks preceding the landings in Normandy Coastal Command kept a constant vigilance on all approaches to the English Channel, but it did not neglect the convoy routes. A resurgence of submarine activity in northern waters brought swift reaction from Coastal aircraft in May 1944 and the loss of five U-boats to air action. A sixth U-boat was sunk that month by a Leigh Light Wellington in the Bay of Biscay, a reminder to the now relatively quiet U-boat force that air detection was still effective. On the eve of D-Day Coastal Command

could call on 51 squadrons and three Flights of its own strength, as well as twelve other squadrons on loan from the FAA, US Navy and RCAF and temporarily under Sholto Douglas's direction and control. Thirty of these units were detailed for direct cover of the invasion area and approaches, with twelve squadrons of Beaufighters at 'Readiness' for tackling any German surface vessels which might attempt to interfere. At dawn on D-Day the vast invasion armada was well across the Channel, and the skies were a panorama of Allied air power. As expected a number of U-boats attempted to hack at the fringes of the sea-borne traffic, but these received short shrift from the Coastal crews. In the first four nights of the invasion operations, they sighted and attacked 18 U-boats and destroyed six, while further afield two more submarines were sunk in daylight. The Germans continued their desperate attempts throughout June and July, but by August had tacitly given up trying. Meanwhile, during the same period, Coastal Beaufighters had a heyday of destruction hammering the enemy's surface convoys. In July these made 500 separate attacks and sank at least 22 vessels, apart from creating havoc with the remaining ships with rocket and cannon strafes. Just one example of the concentrated fury engendered by the Beaufighters occurred in late July, when an entire German convoy of ten vessels

Above: LAC 'Jock' Nicol, from Glasgow, relaxes in his 'accommodation' – the Station Armoury at Banff. Below: Flares from Flt Lt L H Baveystock's 201 Sqn Sunderland (DD829, 'Z') illuminate a surfaced U-boat on the night of Jun 7, 1944.

was hammered with rockets and every ship left burning furiously.

Once the Allied armies and air formations were firmly established on French soil and had begun the long thrust towards the heart of Germany, Coastal Command crews settled back into their more accustomed roles. Until the final day of victory in Europe, the long range Sunderlands, Liberators and Catalinas kept up their ceaseless watch over merchant shipping. Nearer home Beaufighter and Mosquito Strike Wings became predators of enemy shipping in coastal waters stretching from France up

Below: Mosquitos of the Banff Strike Wing thread their way through Nissen huts to the main runway, 1945. The wing comprised 143, 235, 248, 404 Sqns and B Flt of 333 Sqn commanded by Gp Capt Max Aitken, DSO, DFC. Mosquitos of 143 Sqn are dispersed at right; in fore-ground is a Percival Proctor IV 'hack' communications aircraft.

to the Norwegian fiords, striking with a swift and terrible destructive power, and almost invariably leaving behind them burning and broken vessels foundering to their watery graves. Once having struck their target, and often in a flak-scarred state, the Beaufighters faced hundreds of miles of open seas to cross before reaching safety, yet many crews – indeed, with very few exceptions – chose to try to return rather than seek safety on nearer shores. The final year of war continued to be fought at a pitch of the highest intensity. The U-boat war never slackened, even though the peak of such activity had long passed. Only when Germany signed unconditional surrender terms in May 1945 were merchant ships finally free to sail the oceans unhindered. From September 1939 to May 8, 1945 Coastal Command aircraft had been responsible for sinking a total of 212 U-boats and seriously damaging a further 120. Of these, Liberator crews were responsible for 71 destroyed and

27 damaged seriously. Throughout the European war Coastal Command crews flew almost 240,000 individual sorties. The cost of this prodigious tally was 1777 aircraft – statistically, almost one aircraft for every single day of the war.

The maritime air war had called for men of unusual skills and rare patience, to spend 20 hours or more encased in an aircraft, plodding to and fro over seemingly endless, limitless grey-green ocean, never relaxing the vigilant search for the hair-thin white spume of a tell-tale periscope trail or a surfaced U-boat. Sorties such as these demanded a combination of physical and mental endurance seldom called upon in other facets of the aerial war. In common with their fellow crews in other commands, Coastal air crews were never deficient in one commodity – sublime courage. To deliberately plunge into a curtain of shells and machine gun bullets, maintaining the rock-steady track necessary to ensure an accurate straddle of any U-

Right: German U-boat being escorted to a designated surrender harbour on May 14, 1945. Coastal Command aircraft were responsible for sinking at least 212 U-boats, and seriously damaging a further 120, throughout the war. Uncounted are the U-boats attacked without visible results, but deterred from harassing merchant shipping.

boat and thereby presenting submarine gun crews with a target they could not miss called for ice-cold control of the inner man. Such heights of human willpower and courage were needed in equal measure by crews of the torpedo squadrons, strike units, photo and meteorological reconnaissance crews. It has been said that without the destructive power of the bombers and fighters the Allies might have not achieved victory. Without the patient, dogged devotion to duty of the Coastal crews, Britain would never have survived to achieve that victory.

THROUGHOUT THE EUROPEAN WAR COASTAL COMMAND CREWS FLEW ALMOST 240,000 INDIVIDUAL SORTIES. THE COST OF THIS PRODIGIOUS TALLY WAS 1777 AIRCRAFT – STATISTICALLY ALMOST ONE AIRCRAFT FOR EVERY SINGLE DAY OF THE WAR.

In African Skies

The northern territories of the African continent bordering the blue Mediterranean Sea are in essence one vast bald desert, devoid of suburban development and hostile in terms of its trackless wastes shimmering in blistering heat by day and near-zero temperatures by night. Only along the rim of the Mediterranean can humanity lead a reasonably comfortable, normal existence. Thus when war came to the Middle East in 1940 the contesting nations could hardly have 'chosen' a more appropriate stage for a bloody conflict of arms. No great cities or dense civil populations were readily involved in the inevitable holocaust of destruction inherent with modern forms of warfare; no massive industrial complexes or centres of 20th-century civilisation available for laying waste. The RAF at this time could look

back on two decades of maintaining an air 'presence' in the area, having spent those years responsibly 'controlling' Iraq, Palestine, Malta, Aden, and Egypt, and closely guarding the nodal point of access to Britain's far eastern empire, the Suez Canal. The service's strength in these areas had never been great; a handful of units equipped mainly with less-than-modern types of aircraft, supplemented by various depots and bases, including the main flying training school, 4 FTS, at Abu Sueir, Egypt. Outside Egypt, along the coastal strips of Libya and Tripolitania and westwards, Italy and France had established parts of their colonial empires, and it was Italy's hasty declaration of war against Britain on June 10, 1940 which extended the war zones to include North Africa and the east Mediterranean countries.

Middle East Command was a somewhat misleading title for an area of responsibility encompassing all RAF units located in Egypt, Sudan, Palestine, Trans-Jordan, East Africa, Aden, Somaliland, Iraq, the Balkans, and countries around the Persian Gulf – an overall area larger than the United States of America in geographical terms. To 'control' this vast zone the AOC-in-C, Air Chief Marshal Sir Arthur Longmore, had just 29 squadrons on the day the Italian dictator, Mussolini, threw down his gauntlet. Of these 300 aircraft, half were in Egypt and the remainder spread in tiny formations around the command. Of the 14 bomber squadrons, nine were equipped with twin-engined Blenheims, while the five fighter units were still equipped with biplane Gloster Gladiators. The other units – apart from two flying boat squadrons flying Short Sunderlands – presented a melancholy picture of out-dated biplanes hardly worthy of description as operational machines. That many of these rendered valuable service during the early months of the conflict was a tribute to the skill and courage of their crews. Nevertheless, at dawn on June 11, a force of 26 Blenheims from 45, 55 and 113 Squadrons bombed the Italian air base at El Adem, damaging it greatly but losing only two aircraft to the fighter and anti-aircraft defences. In the following two weeks air activity gradually increased, including combats with Italian fighters, but on June 24 the Italo-French armistice was signed, leaving Britain to fight alone against the combined might of Italy and Germany in the Middle

East. This event also meant that the sea route from Britain to Egypt via the Mediterranean now ran the risk of assault from the Italian Navy, an important factor in the vital question of reinforcements and replacements for Longmore's relatively weak force. An alternative route of supply was eventually established via West African ports, but this meant long delays in provision of urgent material simply by virtue of the enormous distances involved, particularly by sea routes around the Cape of Good Hope.

Longmore's problems in fulfilling his command's responsibilities in June 1940 included the immediate threat of Italian forces in Italian Somaliland, Abyssinia and Eritrea – menacing the southern supply route via the Cape, and areas in the Gulf of Aden and the Red Sea. With splendid support from South African forces and others from Kenya, the British

Above right: Pilots of 80 Sqn, 1940. Second from right is Fg Off Peter Wykeham-Barnes, ex-Halton Apprentice and Cranwell Cadet, who eventually rose to become AM Sir Peter Wykeham.
Right: Sqn Ldr Ernest Michelson Mason, DFC – known to all as 'Imshi' – who served with 45, 80, 274, 261, 260 and 94 Sqns, 1938–42. He was credited with 18 victories before his death on Feb 15, 1942 during a strafing sortie against Maturba airfield.
Below: Hurricanes of 274 Sqn at Amriya in Nov 1940 – the first squadron in the Middle East theatre to be Hurricane-equipped.

Left: Servicing a Hurricane in primitive conditions typical of the desert scene.
Below: Sqn Ldr Patrick Hunter Dunn, DFC, seated in a Gloster Gladiator of 80 Sqn, 1940. Serving in Egypt, Greece, and the Western Desert, Dunn was credited with at least nine combat victories. Promoted to A Cdre by 1943, Dunn retired from the RAF as an AVM.

forces withstood the early Italian advances and, only after months of prolonged fighting, eventually nullified the threat by virtue of the RAF's and SAAF's air supremacy. Almost simultaneously Italian forces were launched eastwards along the North African coastal strip, intent on invading Egypt, beginning in September. Within a week Graziani's infantry had invaded Sidi Barrani, but ground to a halt a few miles beyond in order to build-up strength for the next big thrust. This respite lasted until the end of October, during which period Longmore continued desperately to reinforce his air units supporting General Wavell's land formations. On October 28, however, a further shock erupted when Italy struck Greece. Though opposed to dispersing further his already inadequate air power, Longmore despatched 30 Squadron (Blenheims) as a token force to defend Athens, but was quickly pressurised by the British government to provide further air aid. Accordingly, two more Blenheim squadrons, 84 and 211, plus a Gladiator unit, 80 Squadron, were sent to Greece and at the end of November, a second Gladiator squadron, 112, was ordered to

hand over its aircraft to the Greek air force. These few units, with little active help from the Greek air force, took a high toll of Italian invaders; 80 Squadron alone claimed 42 Italian aircraft destroyed by the end of the year. Yet another vital task to add weight to Longmore's already heavy responsibility was the defence of Malta – key to naval and air striking power in the Mediterranean.

Although Malta was programmed to receive four fighter squadrons for defence, on June 11, 1940 – the date of Italy's first aerial attack on the island – its actual available air strength was four Fleet Air Arm Gladiators, of which three became the Hal Far Fighter Flight and flew against the Italians for several weeks before additional Hurricanes arrived on the island. Throughout July a total of ten fighters faced odds of ten-to-one in the daily Italian air raids. Additional reconnaissance aircraft from the FAA arrived in ones and twos and became based in Malta, and on August 2, 12 more Hurricanes flew in from the aircraft carrier *Argus*. These provided the nucleus of a new unit, 261 Squadron. More 'teeth' for Malta appeared in the forms of a few

Wellington bombers based there which formed 148 Squadron in December, a few Maryland light bombers, and Sunderland flying boats of 228 and 230 Squadrons. Between them these motley aircraft provided almost constant intelligence about the movements (or rather, lack of movement . . .) of the ostensibly powerful Italian Navy. The result of this reconnaissance was a brilliantly executed attack on their Navy in Taranto harbour. On the night of November 11 Swordfish crews of the Fleet Air Arm effectively crippled the menace of Mussolini's naval power in the Mediterranean. The Wellingtons meanwhile began a series of bombing attacks against ports in southern Italy primarily in an attempt to relieve the pressure on Greece. The trickle of reinforcement aircraft sent to Longmore during these months, though very welcome, hardly affected the overall weakness of the RAF in the Middle East. In Egypt, Wavell's forces were on the brink of a land offensive requiring air support of the highest degree practicable; in Greece, the existing situation could at any moment be exploded by the introduction of German forces to bolster the Italian

Below: Bristol Blenheim I of 211 Sqn, 1940. The saga of the pitifully small RAF contingent of light bombers and fighters in the brief Greek campaign exemplifies the cliche, 'Too little, too late'. . . .

assault; in Malta, the essential base for control of the eastern Mediterranean waters, improved defensive and offensive air power were required. These major factors, apart from lesser vital tasks such as defence over Egypt, presented Longmore with seemingly insuperable problems. Nor were those problems eased by the attitudes of Air Ministry officials and the Prime Minister, Winston Churchill, in England, who preferred to estimate Longmore's effective air strength from theoretical statistics of numerical strength as opposed to Longmore's down-to-earth practical figures of actually serviceable, operationally-ready machines available. With typical Churchillian impetuosity, the recently-installed Prime Minister not only assumed that Longmore already had ample machines and personnel, but expected every fresh pilot and aircraft to be operationally fit virtually upon arrival in the Middle East. Such 'armchair warrior' wisdom did nothing to boost either Longmore's morale or the actual situation.

In early December 1940, Wavell's army began their advance westwards, pushing back the Italians along the northern coast. Air support came from Air Commodore Ray Collishaw's 202 Group which made prolonged bombing raids against Italian air bases, and from fighters making extensive spearhead sweeps ahead of the infantry. From Malta, Wellingtons assisted the 'push'

Right: Spitfire Vb(Trop), EP257, taxies out over the bald rock of Malta, aided by an erk to steady its wing-tips.
Below: Gladiators of 3 Sqn RAAF returning from a desert patrol.

by raiding major enemy bases in Tripoli and Libya, helping to decimate the Italian air force. By early January Bardia was in Allied hands and Wavell was poised to press forward to Tobruk and, eventually, Benghazi. Within the next four weeks, by brilliant strategy and tactics, Wavell's men slashed through all opposition, reached Benghazi, and accepted the surrender of a thoroughly demoralised Italian army. Cyrenaica was now safely in Allied hands, and attention could be given to the continuing conflict in Italian East Africa. It was at this juncture that Churchill and his government intervened yet again, to direct Longmore to provide ten to fifteen squadrons for transfer to Turkey, the object being to intimidate Hitler from intervening in Greece, Bulgaria and Turkey by posing a threat to Rumanian oilfields by air

strikes. Longmore's astonished reaction of dismay to this latest depletion of the air strength he had patiently and carefully nurtured in the face of great difficulties was overridden in Whitehall. Fortuitously Turkey declined to permit an RAF 'presence' within its borders. Accordingly, as an alternative, Longmore was instructed to bolster the existing squadrons in Greece, and three squadrons – 11 (Blenheims), 33 (Hurricanes), and 112 (Gladiators and Hurricanes) – were despatched. In March, 113 Squadron (Blenheims) also arrived in Greece. Notwithstanding the bitter lessons offered by the French debacle of 1940, Churchill and his ministers were once again prepared to set a relatively small, ill-organised force of RAF units against the combined might of the Luftwaffe and its 'partner', the Regia Aeronautica,

in a country ill-equipped for reinforcement or even normal aerial operations. The conviction, in Britain, that Hitler's main drive would be in the Balkans, not Africa, overrode the succinct opinions offered by air commanders 'on the spot', and it speaks volumes for Arthur Longmore's sense of duty and discipline that he complied with such orders from superiors-in rank and status, if not experience.

The subsequent campaign in Greece, following the German assault in March, was brief, tragic, yet commensurate to the highest traditions of the RAF. Tackling superior machines in greater numbers, the Gladiators and Hurricanes waged an unceasing offensive against odds of at least twenty-to-one until late April. Many of its outstanding fighter pilots were lost. Among the dead was

Squadron Leader M 'Pat' Pattle, the South African commander of 33 Squadron's Hurricanes who eventually was established as the RAF's highest-scoring fighter 'ace' of World War II. Finally, on April 24, the last remaining seven fighter aircraft were evacuated to Crete. The RAF ground personnel, in common with other British and Greek troops, were also ordered to quit Greece, and Sunderlands of 228 and 230 Squadrons performed many hazardous rescue operations when retrieving hundreds of isolated parties of men by night and day. In early May a revolt in Iraq, led by the pro-German Raschid Ali, besieged the RAF station and training school at Habbaniyah, but was eventually defeated by a scratch collection of aircraft, flown by trained and partly trained crews. On May 20 even before Raschid Ali's coup

Above: Sqn Ldr M T St J Pattle, DFC, the South African-born commander of 33 Sqn in Greece, 1941.

ON CRETE WERE EXHAUSTED SURVIVORS OF THE GREEK EVACUATION, THE BATTERED REMNANTS OF 30, 80 AND 112 SQUADRONS... TOTALLING JUST 24 AIRCRAFT – TO OPPOSE THE ASSEMBLED AIR INVASION FORCE OF THE LUFTWAFFE NUMBERING 650 BOMBERS AND FIGHTERS AND 700 TRANSPORT AND GLIDER-TUGS.

Above: Short Sunderlands of 230 Sqn engaged in evacuating Army and RAF personnel from Greece, May 1941.

was nullified, German paratroops struck Crete. On Crete were the exhausted survivors of the Greek evacuation, the battered remnants of 30, 80 and 112 Squadrons and an equally weary FAA unit – totalling just 24 aircraft – to oppose the assembled air invasion force of the Luftwaffe numbering 650 operational bombers and fighters and 700 transport and glider-tugs. The preceding weeks had seen unremitting air combat over the island in the course of which the RAF fighter strength had been reduced to seven machines by May 18. These were withdrawn to Egypt the following day to preserve them. Within a week of the initial thrust, Crete was virtually in German hands, and those British and Empire troops still evading capture were in the main evacuated yet again by the Royal Navy and the ever-ready Sunderlands.

The losses in Greece and Crete, in terms of aircraft, were serious but replaceable. What could not be replaced easily were the experienced fighter pilots and bomber crews. In the wider picture of war operations, however, these two tragic episodes had a deep effect on the progress of the land and air war in North Africa. In compliance with his in-

structions from London, Longmore had perforce stripped his air power to support Wavell's brilliant advance and capture of Cyrenaica in order to bolster the Greek resistance to German invasion. If Italy had remained the only opponent there, Libya and the coastal strip would have remained in Allied hands, but in the first week of February 1941, German troops and over 100 Luftwaffe aircraft commanded by Erwin Rommel arrived in Tripoli. With additional Italian reinforcements Rommel began an eastward advance before the end of March, and by late April the Allied troops were back behind the Egyptian border. Only in Italian East Africa could the Allies claim any success during these disastrous months, when British and Empire troops, backed mainly by SAAF air support, concluded the long campaign in triumph. The divergence of air units to Greece had effectively contributed to the loss of Cyrenaica, but the cessation of operations in Somaliland released men and machines to reinforce the Allies now facing Rommel across the borders of Egypt. Reinforcements in aircraft and men were also flowing steadily into Egypt via the West African route; beleaguered Malta was also gradually receiving additional fighters and bombers. The latter, located athwart the main sea routes to Tripoli from Italy, was capable of destroying, or at least hampering

Rommel's lifelines of supplies and reinforcement in North Africa.

Above Malta in the spring and summer of 1941 the skies were constantly filled with Luftwaffe and Italian Air Force massed formations from Sicily. By May the main burden of defence was borne by two Hurricane units, 261 and the newly-formed 185 Squadron. In addition, Malta's offensive was fortified by its Wellington and Blenheim bombers, which continually attacked Sicilian ports and airfields, and harried enemy convoys in open waters. More Hurricanes were convoyed to within air distance of the battered island by aircraft carriers, then flown off to make the final leg of their journey alone. In this manner dozens of fresh aircraft, and pilots, reached Malta and were almost immediately involved in the daily conflict. (The perils of such a method of reinforcement were highlighted on June 14, when 48 Hurricanes flew off *Ark Royal* and *Victorious* but flew too far south of Malta; 37 aircraft were lost in the Mediterranean when they ran out of fuel.) On May 13, however, the German fighters in Sicily were withdrawn in preparation for Hitler's imminent invasion of Russia, thus easing the general pressure on Malta, and permitting its defensive and offensive power to be built up. Attacks on enemy shipping bound for Tripoli were intensified, with some significant effect such as reducing the number of supplies reaching an impatient Rommel, whose eyes were directed eastwards towards the prize of Egypt and the Suez Canal. By the end of May, the RAF in Egypt was recovering quickly from the tragic losses in Greece and Crete. Fresh units were now reaching the country, including the first two Beaufighter squadrons, Nos 252 and 272. These latter units, based near Alexandria, and flying the most heavily-armed fighters to see service with the RAF throughout the war, were the spearheads of other Beaufighter units whose far-ranging depredations of Rommel's armies and air support brought them the fitting title of 'Scourge of the Desert'. In anticipation of Rommel's next move, the Allied armies launched Operation 'Battle-axe' on June 14 in an attempt to regain lost ground. In five days of bloody and costly operations, the attempted advance was halted and thrown back by Rommel's tank formations; the RAF suffered heavy casualties from marauding Messerschmitt Bf 109s now in first-line service in Africa. Part-purpose of 'Battle-axe' had been to relieve the besieged 'fortress' of Tobruk, isolated within German-occupied territory and for many weeks after the operation's failure, much air effort was employed attempting to relieve the Tobruk garrison's pressure, by delivering supplies and relevant local air strikes.

For nearly four months the air war in North Africa became relatively quiet, as each of the main contestants reorganised and increased its strength for the inevitable next 'round'. This, in the case of the Allies, was to be Operation

Above: Flt Lt George Beurling, DSO, DFC, DFM, the highly individual Canadian fighter pilot who achieved lasting fame for his exploits over Malta. He later flew from England with 412 Sqn, but was killed on May 20, 1948 in Rome when he crashed taking off on a ferry flight of a Mitchell bomber.
Below: Hurricane pilots of 80 Sqn at Eleusis, Greece, early 1941. L-r Plt Off 'Keg' Dowding; Plt Off 'Ginger' Still; Sgt C E Casbolt; W.O. 'Mick' Richens; Sgt W E 'Ted' Hewett, DFM; and Fg Off 'Twinstead' Flower. Hewett ended the war as a Sqn Ldr, with 21 accredited victories, while 'Cas' Casbolt was later commissioned and credited with at least 13 victories.

'Crusader' – planned originally for September, but postponed to November 1941. Command of the RAF in the Middle East had passed into the skilled hands of Air Marshal Arthur Tedder, former deputy AOC-in-C to Longmore; the latter, after a long period of coping with crisis after crisis with little material and a total lack of support from his 'masters' in Whitehall had been quietly transferred to England at the end of April. He thus joined a select company of men (Hugh Dowding, Keith Park, Wavell, and others) who, having incurred Churchill's political displeasure by being technically responsible for defeat – or at least insufficiently dramatic victories – were hastily and quietly shuffled into 'backwater' appointments, inadequately thanked or rewarded for what they had achieved in the face of almost insuperable odds. Tedder's main objective in preparing his air command for 'Crusader' hinged on intensive reorganisation of his maintenance back-up, and on an increase in priority for all aspects of tactical support to the army. The first was virtually solved by the dynamic energy of a recent arrival, Air Commodore G G Dawson, whose down-to-earth reappraisal of nearly every facet of the technical and supply organisation trebled the available aircraft strength in six months of hard driving work. On the eve of 'Crusader' – launched finally on November 18, 1941 – the operational air strength available comprised 37 squadrons. Of these, four squadrons were solely for general and photo-reconnaissance; 17 were bombers, light and heavy; and 16 were equipped with

Above: Engine maintenance in the desert – the hard way!

Hurricane, Tomahawk, Beaufighter, and Martlet fighters. It should be well noted that of the overall 37 units, eight were squadrons of the South African Air Force (SAAF). This force did not include the various units based on Malta; Blenheims, Wellingtons, Marylands, and Hurricane II cannon-armed fighter-bombers intensified their forays against Sicilian airfields and, especially, against Axis convoys attempting to supply Rommel. Losses ran relatively high among these bombers but were quickly replaced as fresh convoys continued to run the gauntlet of air attack through the Mediterranean to sustain Malta's defenders. How effective this ceaseless war against Axis convoy shipping was, can be judged by the fact that between June 1 and November 1, 1941, Malta's aircraft alone sunk some 90,000 tons – roughly equivalent to the tonnage sunk by naval submarines and surface craft. This was

BETWEEN JUNE 1 AND NOVEMBER 1, 1941, MALTA'S AIRCRAFT ALONE SUNK 90,000 TONS OF AXIS SHIPPING.

nearly a quarter of all enemy ships operating on the supply routes to North Africa.

For six days previous to the start of 'Crusader' the air units set out to pulverise the enemy's supply and reinforcement lines, flying night-and-day bombing offensives against depots and airfields, and particularly hammering the vital port of Benghazi. By day swarms of Hurricane and Tomahawks challenged the Luftwaffe's Messerschmitts, meeting little opposition initially. Beaufighters swept low across the bald wastes blasting anything which moved, and creating havoc by suddenly striking enemy landing grounds. Once the land offensive swung forward, the Western Desert Air Force – as it was now titled – provided a constant umbrella, warding off bombing attacks and out-manoeuvring the relatively few Messerschmitts which appeared. The

real climax in the air battle came on November 22 when, after a day of prolonged and fierce dog-fighting, the WDAF achieved a moral – if not actual – victory over the marauding Bf 109's. It can be said that this date marked the beginning of the WDAF's aerial supremacy over their opponents, who thereafter rarely attempted to fight on level terms but resorted to a pattern of surprise diving attacks from high altitudes as their main tactic. This ploy, which was to cause heavy casualties in the WDAF in the months to come, was unsuccessful in preventing the WDAF from carrying out its main purpose – direct support of the slogging Eighth Army's infantry and tank formations. Throughout the rest of the North African campaign this gradually increasing dominance over the battlefields was to become the key to final success.

By December 8 Tobruk was in Allied

Top: A WDAF Wellington on its return from bombing Benghasi harbour.
Above: Douglas Boston III, Z2162 of 24 Sqn, SAAF – a unit which fought throughout the Middle East Campaign. The South African (and other Commonwealth countries') contribution to the Mediterranean air war was prodigious.

Above ACM (later, MRAF) Sir Arthur Tedder, who directed the Mediterranean air campaign, and later became Deputy to the supreme Allied Commander, General Eisenhower. Below: Beaufighter VI, 'K', probably from 252 Sqn, setting out from Malta.

hands again, and activity was now centred further west. Daily clashes between WDAF fighters and the Luftwaffe reached heavy proportions, with high casualties on both sides. In the main the German airmen were greatly restricted by an overall lack of fuel – a tribute to the effectiveness of Malta's squadrons against the Mediterranean convoys – and desperate measures were being employed to relieve this situation. The Germans used the trundling Junkers 52 'Iron Annies' as fuel 'tankers' and these braved the ever-alert WDAF fighters in an attempt to bring in fuel by air. On December 22 one such formation was caught over Magrun airfield by Tomahawks and eleven were lost to the wheeling fighters. Evidence of the WDAF's depredations soon became plain as the Eighth Army plodded across Cyrenaica. Each abandoned enemy landing ground was cluttered with shat-

tered aircraft and materials, scarred by cannon and machine gun fire. The shortage of fuel and vital spares had forced the German and Italian air units to abandon hundreds of machines – indeed between Gambut and Benina a total of 458 abandoned or broken aircraft were counted. Hundreds more lay in the open desert, broken-backed or burned-out – mute witness of the heavy fighting of the previous year. The question of supplying Rommel, especially in the light of the roving marauders from Malta's squadrons, led to an additional force of Luftwaffe bombers being brought from the Russian front to Sicily in mid-December; their weight was almost immediately added to the continuing air siege of the battered island. Composed mainly of new Bf 109F fighters and armoured Junkers 88 bombers, the fresh German force was more than a match for the ageing Hurricanes defending

Right: A bomber crew bales out its pup tent after a downpour in Libya – the desert was not all sun and golden sand. . .

Malta, and by February 1942 the island's effective striking power was considerably reduced and Rommel's Afrika Korps once again began to receive supplies.

By Christmas Eve, 1941, the Eighth Army had re-entered Benghazi, while Rommel withdrew to near Agheila, a natural strongpoint, to recoup and prepare for further battle. By now his supply position had greatly improved. In the meantime, *Crusader* forces suffered a serious setback. In the Far East, Japan had struck in Malaya, and orders from London forced Tedder to relinquish some of his carefully husbanded air strength and send four squadrons of Blenheims – Nos. 45, 84, 113 and 211 – to assist the meagre Far East air for-

Above: One of 272 Sqn's early Beaufighters revving up at Edku, near Alexandria, Egypt in Sept 1941. No. 272 was the first to operate Beaufighters in the Mediterranean.

mations. Equally this new factor was to have a depleting effect on Tedder's volume of reinforcement supplies from Britain. With the Eighth Army now standing virtually on the lines held a year before and poised to gain fresh ground westwards, this overall, sudden reduction in air power jeopardised the complete 'Crusader' campaign. Just as Wavell's earlier successful North African campaign had been dislocated by Whitehall's insistence that Longmore send vitally-needed squadrons to the hopeless Greek theatre, so now Tedder's delicate balance of air power covering Malta and the Eighth Army's advance was about to be dangerously weakened by a parallel decision from Churchill's advisers to throw away battle-hardened aircraft and crews into the disastrous Malayan debacle.

The fury of the Luftwaffe was unleashed in escalating strength upon Malta in the opening weeks of 1942. However, it was finally – if tardily – recognised in the corridors of power in London that in Malta lay the key to the eventual defeat of Rommel. Accordingly, efforts were redoubled to supply the gallant island defenders with material and, especially, aircraft and crews.

On the tiny island the bomber and strike squadrons were soon reduced to complete ineffectiveness by the Luftwaffe's intensive assaults (ten to fifteen times a day) aimed specifically at destroying the RAF's airfields at Luqa, Ta Kali, Hal Far, and Safi. The hard-pressed Hurricane pilots – outnumbered and fighting superior machines – continued to rise to meet the endless waves of Junkers and Messerschmitts, in-

flicting great punishment but inevitably losing precious aircraft and, tragically, experienced fighter pilots. Fresh heart was given to Malta when, on March 7, the first batch of Spitfires flew off the carrier *Eagle* and landed at Malta as replacements. Two weeks later on the 21, *Eagle* despatched a second flock of Spitfires for 126 Squadron and this was followed by further Spitfires at the end of the month. Such replacements were often flown in at great peril, sometimes landing in the turmoil of an actual bombing attack, being refuelled and sent immediately into combat within an hour of first touching Maltese soil. Meanwhile, as the combat over Malta reached fresh peaks of intensity, in North Africa Rommel had taken a brilliant gamble and attacked the resting Eighth Army's forward positions. With only three days' supplies and 100 tanks, he swept forward on January 21, catching his opposite

numbers completely unaware. Spearheading this drive, Rommel's Junkers 87 Stukas and fleet Messerschmitt Bf 109s had virtually a free hand for 48 hours in low-level bombing and strafing; their WDAF opponents being bogged down on flooded landing strips at Antelat. As the Afrika Korps advanced rapidly, WDAF units were forced to retreat at minutes' notice to safer strips further east near Msus; but the impetus of Rommel's assault continued to press and, in a purely premature state of near-panic, the first-line infantry formations were ordered to retire eastwards. Air Vice-Marshal 'Maori' Coningham, Tedder's fighting deputy, could do little to prevent this retreat. Without secure landing grounds, his aircraft and personnel were compelled to take up positions too far from the fighting zone to be completely effective. Under cover of a raging sandstorm on January 26, Rommel feinted a move towards Mechili, but pushed his main strength towards Benghazi, which fell into his hands on the 28. Further hasty orders from the front-line army commanders resulted in Coningham's fighters being directed to move further east to Gazala. Meanwhile the Eighth Army fell back to the Gazala-Bir Hacheim line, thus losing the whole of Cyrenaica for a second time. By February 5 Rommel was forced to halt and consolidate. His supply and communication threads were stretched too thinly to permit any further forward movement, at least for the moment. Both

Below: The value of air tactical reconnaissance was learned and superbly embellished during the desert campaigns. Here, a WDAF Hurricane pilot has his camera film developed 'on the spot', immediately after return from a recce.

sides of the battle lines held firm and dug in, and relative quiet now descended on the desert. Throughout *Crusader* and the subsequent scrambling retreat the WDAF had learned and used many significant lessons in tactical support and reconnaissance not the least being the constant need for fluidity and flexibility. On-the-spot ground controllers had been able to bring down air cover and striking power at little notice in the constantly-shifting desert struggles and squadrons were now well-versed in operating from the flat, featureless landing grounds with only the barest necessities to sustain them. Backing the 'sharp end' of the WDAF was the immensely improved maintenance organisation which, between November 1941

and March 1942 had reclaimed over 1000 damaged machines from the desert and reissued over 800 of these as fit again for operations. This reclaiming and repairing of aircraft was now vital as the Malayan and Burmese campaigns continued to drain away the North African's promised supply of fresh aircraft from Britain. In those three months the WDAF had flown more than 16,000 individual sorties of all types, and accounted for the loss of more than 600 Axis aircraft in combat.

The renewed assault on Malta by Sicilian-based Luftwaffe bombers and fighters in early 1942 continued unabated throughout the spring and early summer with individual raids mounting at times to more than 200 bombers,

heavily escorted by fighters. In March alone German aircraft released 2174 tons of high explosive on the island, but lost 60 aircraft to the Allied guns and fighters. The pace increased to a peak during the following month, in which the Luftwaffe dropped 6728 tons of bombs. Spasmodic though determined attempts to replenish the constantly dwindling fighter strength on the island now included batches of Spitfires, but the tempo of the fighting never slackened. As one veteran pilot put it, 'One lives here only to destroy the Hun and hold him at bay; everything else, living conditions, sleep, food, and all the ordinary standards of life have gone by the board. It all makes the Battle of Britain and fighter-sweeps seem child's play in comparison . . .'. By May the German intention of 'taking out' Malta was still unsuccessful, but had at least prevented the RAF based there from striking Rommel's sea-borne supply lines to North Africa. On May 26, now well nourished with fresh fuel, material and personnel, Rommel launched yet another offensive eastwards through Cyrenaica, led by his armoured formations. During the following three weeks of furious attack and counter-attack, the Eighth Army's tanks and Rommel's panzers clashed in open combat while Coningham's fighters – now adapted to carry bombs – bore in at low level, blasting and raking the advancing enemy. At Bir Hacheim a Free French force became besieged but held out for nine days with close air support, before honourably retiring – a delay in Rommel's planned drive eastwards which drained his troops of vital fuel and ammunition. Despite this temporary set-back, Rommel continued to press forward, and on June 24 his advanced panzer squadrons crossed the Egyptian border, intent on no less than the eventual capture of Egypt. The Eighth Army, which had already lost 60,000 men, retired again, to a line stretching from El Alamein to the Qattara Depression – sixty miles west of Alexandria – where it dug in. Its retreat – 400 miles in two weeks – had cost grievous casualties, but not from the air. The WDAF had continued to dominate the skies. Its experience in total mobility enabled its bombers and fighters to keep up a continual bombardment of the Luftwaffe's airfields and depots, forcing Rommel's air support on to the defensive and effectively barring any interference with the Allied retreat along the sole coastal

Below: Curtiss P-40, Kittyhawk of 112 Sqn, adorned with the unit marking, bounces its way to dispersal, guided by a bearded erk on its port wing.

road to Egypt. Only at Tobruk which was at that time beyond WDAF fighter range, were Rommel's Stukas given free range – an illustration of the necessity of air supremacy above any battle zone.

As Rommel probed, unsuccessfully, to pierce the Allied defensive line at El Alamein, Malta once more suffered a blitz of intensified air attacks starting on October 11. By then Malta possessed five Spitfire squadrons and the air during the following week became an arena of relentless combat. By the close of the week – destined to be the final phase in Malta's prolonged agony – the Luftwaffe's losses of almost 100 bombers and fighters became insupportable and the 'mini-blitz' faded away. Desultory attacks continued for some weeks thereafter, but in very diminished strength; Hitler had ordered the transfer of the bomber force elsewhere. Malta immediately reopened its depredations of the Axis sea routes to Africa constantly preventing the re-supply of Rommel's Afrika Korps. On October 19 the WDAF, in preparation for the planned offensive at El Alamein by a rejuvenated Eighth Army, commenced a series of day and night attacks against the German airfields, ports, and supply depots. By then the WDAF had built up its strength to 96 operational squadrons (of which a third were non-British; a total of some 1500 first-line aircraft most of which were in Africa. These faced less than 700 Axis aircraft in the desert itself, not all of which were any match for the WDAF's Kittyhawks, Spitfires, Beaufighters and Hurricanes. The night of October 23, 1942 witnessed an Allied artillery barrage unprecedented in the long campaign, and as dawn filtered through the desert air the Eighth Army attacked unhampered by air opposition due to the WDAF's complete mastery of the skies. By the end of the month Rommel's demoralised troops were in full retreat, leaving 30,000 prisoners of war and large material losses. The subsequent flight westwards along the choked and overcrowded solitary coastal road provided the eager Allied pilots with a surplus of unprotected targets. By November 13

Tobruk was reoccupied, and six days later Coningham's 'dogs of war' were occupying Maturba as General Montgomery's forward troops arrived in Benghazi. Only at El Agheila did Rommel make a stand, delaying the Eighth Army. In mid-December the Eighth Army moved into Tripolitania. Rommel offered further resistance for several weeks until the 'Desert Rats' (Eighth Army) finally occupied Tripoli on January 23, 1943 and the WDAF took up residence at Castel Benito (now, Castel Idris).

The fighting retreat of the Afrika Korps immediately following its defeat at El Alamein was not only in danger from a pursuing army supported by a battle-hardened air force. On November 8, 1942 as Rommel sped westwards, a fresh element of the desert war was introduced when an Allied force beached at Algiers – Operation 'Torch' (originally titled 'Gymnast') had begun. Meeting resistance from Vichy French defenders at first, the combined American and British forces quickly established control of various airfields and key positions but were soon aware of German reinforcements in Tunis. Taking a leaf from Rommel's previous tactics, the Allied troops struck east along the coast, racing forward at such speed that the spearhead elements eventually outstripped the air services' ability to provide immediate tactical help. The result was the temporary local air supremacy of the Luftwaffe. As the advance ground to a halt in December, wintry storms reduced the landscape to a quagmire and effectively halted air operations from most improvised landing grounds. A further 'obstacle' at this time was the lack of unified direction of the American and British air offensive; this problem was solved at the Casablanca Conference in January 1943, when Tedder was appointed air 'supremo' of all air services in Tunisia, Mediterranean, and North Africa. In mid-February Rommel, now in south Tunisia, attacked American troops attempting to split him from his counterpart in Tunis, and initially drove the fresh American forces back. However, he was beaten back again by unified Allied troops and next turned to assault the Eighth Army hard on his heels near Medenine. The offensive failed in the face of prepared defences and the Afrika Korps retired to Mareth. It was Rommel's final battle. In mid-March, a sick, tired man, the legendary 'Desert Fox' flew home to Germany and was replaced by von Arnim. Days later Allied forces in Tunisia commenced the final offensive needed to eradicate the Axis presence in Tunisia. Three days later Montgomery's Eighth Army also pushed forward, outflanking the German Mareth Line and pressing north.

'One lives here only to destroy the Hun and hold him at bay; everything else, living conditions, sleep, food and all the ordinary standards of life have gone by the board. It all makes the Battle of Britain and fighter sweeps seem child's play in comparison . . .'

Right: Wg Cdr Ian Gleed, DSO, DFC in Spitfire Vb, AB502, 'Figaro', leading two Spitfires of 601 Sqn along the North African coastline in Feb 1943. Below: The Repair and Salvage Sections of the WDAF. This convoy of 'Queen Mary' low-load lorries, with its 'booty' of recovered Hurricanes, stops for the traditional 'brew-up'.

The WDAF now came into its own, low-bombing enemy positions and constantly feeding Kittyhawk-bombers into the firing lines every quarter of an hour to bomb and strafe German resistance while Hurricane IID's, armed with 'can-opener' 40mm cannons, ripped open any concentration of armour confronting the Allied infantry.

As German-occupied Tunisian territory shrank in size, the combined WDAF and USAAF aircraft found fatter and juicier targets. On April 18 a mass of 100 fighter-escorted Junkers 52 transports were intercepted by American Warhawks and RAF Spitfires. After a brief but crowded engagement, 52 of the Junkers lay wrecked and burning. Four days later another massacre in the air blasted 16 giant Messerschmitt 323s out of the sky. Nor were such successes confined to the day fighters. On the night of April 30–May 1, Flight Sergeant A B Downing of 600 Squadron in a radar-equipped Beaufighter destroyed five Junkers 52s in rapid succession. Finally on May 13, 1943, the last remaining Axis troops in Tunisia surrendered – the desert war was over. Even during the final weeks of the Tunisian battles, the air forces were probing further afield – bombing Lampedusa, Pantelleria, northern Sardinia, and Sicily and other bases for the retreating Luftwaffe. These were preliminaries to the next great venture by the Allies – the invasion of Italy via Sicily. As the triumphant crews of the Desert Air Force rejoiced in the African victory, Arthur Tedder, whose quiet, yet precise handling of their fortunes throughout the years had provided ideal leadership, sent a message to all members of the Allied air services which read in part, '. . . You have shown the world the unity and strength of air power. A grand job well finished . . .'. The unity of which Tedder spoke existed not only among Allied air services, but was also reflected in the strong common bond forged between all ranks and manner of men of the Desert Air Forces. Air and ground crews had shared equally in the nomadic, near-primitive conditions of living, flying and fighting in the empty wastes of Cyrenaica, Libya, Tripolitania. Life in the desert had a curious appeal to its denizens; an existence reduced to the barest necessities, but a remarkably healthy life despite the grinding monotony of a bully beef menu, lack of water, flies, sand, sand, and sand.

Left: The never-ending necessity of aircraft maintenance – exemplified here by ground crew fitters and mechanics giving Hurricane V7795, 'Alma Baker' a major overhaul. On the near wing, three of the fighter's .303 Browning machine guns await installation.

Final victory had come from the true application of air power over a battlefield – something the Luftwaffe and Regia Aeronautica had failed to appreciate or apply.

Once victory in Tunisia had brought the North African territories under Allied control, plans were immediately completed for the invasion of the European mainland via Sicily and Italy. To this end all Allied air services were combined in one tactical air force, comprised (initially) of 267 squadrons of which 146 were American and 121 British. The USAAF provided the bulk of heavy and medium bombers; the RAF provided fighters and fighter-bombers. Though administered separately, both the RAF and the USAAF units involved came under one common tactical control. On July 10, 1943 the first Allied troops touched down on Sicilian soil, under an air umbrella of Spitfires, Warhawks and other aircraft based on Malta, Tunisia and Pantelleria. Luftwaffe opposition was negligible – command of the air belonged to the Allies. By July 13 the first Spitfire Wing arrived from Malta and commenced operations and was soon followed by a dozen more British and American fighter squadrons. At night, RAF Beaufighters and Mosquitos took heavy tolls of the German bombers' attempts to raid Allied strongpoints – the only relatively safe time at which the Luftwaffe could now operate. Only on the ground was stiff opposition met, thereby restricting air support from the fighters to direct tactical raiding. The heavy bombers meanwhile probed further afield, hammering ports and main towns, including Rome. Prime targets were communication routes, rail marshalling yards and depots. By August 16 Sicily had been successfully evacuated by the Axis troops and the island was completely in Allied hands – a firm stepping stone to invasion of the mainland. The Sicilian campaign had cost less than 400 Allied aircraft, but the German and Italian air services had lost 1850 aircraft destroyed or captured – a crippling toll which could not be replaced easily.

With the imminent invasion of their country accepted as inevitable, the weary and disillusioned Italian population finally deposed its strutting dictator Mussolini on July 25, but made no immediate peace overtures for fear of the strong German forces still occupying a large part of Italy. Though offering Italy honourable terms of surrender, the Allied commanders continued to apply pressure by long-range bombing of major cities such as Milan, raids in which RAF Bomber Command in England participated. An armistice was finally signed in secret on September 3, but was not announced to the world until the evening of September 8. Not only

Left: A scene repeated thousands of times throughout the desert campaigns. Here, Sqn Ldr R Slade-Betts, OC 6 Sqn holds his daily briefing session.
Below: Capt Colin Gray, DSO, DFC, the highest-scoring and most decorated New Zealand fighter pilot of the war. Seen here on Aug 7, 1943 when, as a Wg Cdr, he was the leader of 322 Wg, RAF in the Western Desert.
Bottom: DH Mosquito II, DZ230, YP-A of 23 Sqn, piloted by Wg Cdr P Wykeham-Barnes, DSO, DFC; the first Mosquito arrived in Malta, on Dec 27, 1942.

'*Army plus Air Force equals victory*'.

had Italy capitulated but was now, technically, an ally of Britain and America! If the men of the Eighth Army and the Desert Air Force found it difficult to accept such a complete *volte-face* in political strategy, it could hardly be wondered. Having thoroughly defeated the Italian forces in Africa and Somaliland, at no little cost to themselves, they were now, overnight, expected to accept their enemy of yesterday as today's fighting ally. The eventual invasion of the Italian mainland, and the grim, prolonged struggle northwards by the Fifth and Eighth Armies and their American and Allied counterparts was an extenuated clash of brute strength and dogged resistance. Air supremacy remained the prerogative of the Allied air forces throughout yet could only assist the final victory, not guarantee it. The bloody contest of arms in Italy during the winter of 1943 and into the summer of 1944 was primarily a battle of the foot soldier, supported by heavy artillery, and protected by the strong arm of air forces.

On June 4, 1944, preceding the Allied invasion of France, Rome fell to the Allies. Still pressing northwards, the Allied armies were soon to be checked in their advance. The Italian winter turned the land into one vast mud quagmire and literally bogged down all hopes of speedy transport or communications. In such conditions the only real offensive power lay with the air forces, whose long-range

bombers could now wage unceasing war against Axis targets in Austria, Rumania and Hungary assisted in their efforts by RAF Bomber Command. Enemy oil production centres and depots became the priority, but heavy attention was paid to mining all rivers and major waterways to disrupt communication and supply access. As the Spring of 1945 brought firmer conditions the final Allied offensive in Italy was mounted. Then on April 9, preceded by 825 heavy bombers, 234 medium bombers, and 740 fighter-bombers, the Allies struck, crossing the Senio and forging ahead on a broad front. This aerial battle-fleet devastated the immediate opposition with a carpet of bombs, then paused to let the hundreds of low-level fighters loose on ground targets which threatened the advancing infantry. The aerial bombardment did not let up by day or night until the Allied troops had broken through, fanned across the width of northern Italy, and begun racing forward. Town after town fell to the advancing infantry until inevitably the German commander signed an unconditional surrender on April 24. The actual cease-fire order became effective on May 2, 1945.

The contribution of air power to the struggle was an essential element of the equation 'Army plus Air Force equals victory'. Through its ability to destroy enemy communications and supply routes, its ability to fulfil battle in-

structions instantly and its unceasing support for the earth-bound fighting soldier, air power had ensured final victory. The long path to such a state of complete co-operation and inter-Service understanding had begun in the deserts of North Africa, where age-old dictums of waging war had been drastically revised in the light of brutal experience. Communality of purpose had been engendered between soldier, sailor and airman at every level. Such a lesson had not been learned by the German Luftwaffe and the Italian Regia Aeronautica, and these suffered accordingly. Having lost the reins of air control over the battlefields, the Axis air services never recovered. The damning result of such a loss of air supremacy was to leave their armies unprotected and unsupported in their hour of need, with disastrous consequence. The desert breeding ground for an Allied air-ground partnership gave birth to a fighting combination which was to prove unconquerable in the jungles of Burma or in the plains of Normandy – a combination and partnership-in-arms which only ceased when Hitler's vaunted '1000-years Reich' lay in shattered ruin in May 1945.

Jungle Triumph

In contrast to the war zones fringing the Mediterranean where the RAF had maintained operational units and bases for two decades prior to the outbreak of World War II, the Far East theatre (a misleading title for an area encompassing the vast reaches of the Pacific Ocean, and land masses stretching from Hong Kong to India) was a relatively unequipped area in terms of air power. Indeed, only in the sub-continent of India had the RAF any real presence, and this was composed of eight squadrons of outdated aircraft in September 1939. Hong Kong, long regarded by naval and military authorities as the key centrepoint of Pacific defences for the Empire, was replaced in importance and priority by the tiny island of Singapore, at the tip of Malaya. Here, despite the vehement protestations of Hugh Trenchard, a vast naval base and 'impregnable fortress' of giant entrenched 15-inch guns began to be constructed in the late 1920s. Trenchard's contention that a strong air striking force of torpedo-carriers and long range flying boats would be more effective in the event of any aggressor attempting to capture Singapore was overridden by the military and naval hierarchy. By the autumn of 1939, the £60-million project was virtually completed and Singapore became 'the Gibraltar of the Far East' with only two torpedo-bomber, two bomber, and two flying boat squadrons available for 'immediate' reconnaissance and air striking capability. All six units were equipped with obsolescent biplanes plus a handful of modern aircraft. Only in July 1940

when France unpredictably collapsed, did the Chiefs of Staff meet to amend their previous attitude regarding the role of air power in the Far East; it was recommended that RAF strength by the end of 1941 must total 336 aircraft. In October 1940, the commanders in Singapore urged that the minimum number of aircraft should be 566 and that a series of new airfields should be built. By December 1941, only 362 aircraft – a motley mixture of varying designs – were actually available of which a third were not operationally fit for service. Apart from pure aircraft strength, the RAF in the Far East at the close of 1941 lacked virtually every other facility with which to carry out its proposed role. Few of the hastily commissioned airfields in Malaya – clearings hacked out of the jungle – had reasonable accommodation, maintenance facilities, or defence control systems. An overall lack of co-operation between the Services *in situ* merely exacerbated an already perilously weak situation, because, despite the official history's comment that naval co-operation with the RAF was good, the commander of 27 Squadron, the only designated 'night fighter' defence unit in Malaya, was refused permission to overfly the naval base at Seletar for any reason whatsoever by the base's naval commander.

The total inadequacy of Singapore and Malaya's air defences was a direct result of the locust years of peace; the air service was starved of funds, continually undermined by inter-Service jealousies,

Above left: Vickers Vildebeeste bombers of 100 Sqn at Kuala Lumpur in 1938.
Left: Bristol Blenheim I, L4827, of 60 Sqn flying over the Punjab, India on Jul 11, 1940, an example of the only relatively 'new' designs available in India and Malaya.

and misunderstood by political and service chiefs whose knowledge and views of modern warfare were still chained to a pre-1918 concept. When, in 1940, the dawn of understanding began to infiltrate the blinkered minds in Whitehall, the immediate necessities of the crumbling French campaign precluded any hope of quickly reversing the policies for the protection of Singapore and Malaya, even had the material resources been available. In November 1940, command of the RAF and Army forces in the Far East was given to Air Chief Marshal Sir Robert Brooke-Popham, whose overriding policy dictated by the British government was to avoid provoking Japan in any way, a policy which rigidly hampered Popham's operational needs until the morning the Japanese troops made their first landings on Malayan soil. When, on December 8, 1941, the Japanese struck on the northeastern coast of Malaya – 15 minutes *before* the attack on Pearl Harbour commenced over the international date line – Brooke-Popham's overall air command was composed of seven RAF, five RAAF, and one RNZAF squadrons. Of these, Nos. 27, 34, 60 and 62 Squadrons RAF were equipped with Blenheim I bombers; 36 and 100 Squadrons RAF with Vildebeeste torpedo biplanes; 205 Squadron RAF with only three Catalina flying boats. Two RAAF units, Nos. 1 and 8 Squadrons, flew Lockheed Hudsons; three RAAF squadrons had Brewster Buffalo fighters; and 488 Squadron, RNZAF was also equipped with Buffaloes. Total strength was well below 200 first-line machines and none of the aircraft was any match for the Japanese 'Zero' fighter which spearheaded their onslaught. Within 48 hours of the first Japanese setting foot in Malaya, the battleship *Prince of Wales* and battlecruiser *Repulse* had been sent to the bottom of the ocean, mortally hit by waves of torpedo aircraft from the Japanese 22nd Air Flotilla – a savagely abrupt close to centuries of naval thinking in the Nelson tradition. The blunt prophecies of Hugh Trenchard and the American Billy Mitchell during the 1920s had been vindicated in one swift stroke.

The subsequent dismal campaign in Malaya saw the air defence units ruthlessly and inexorably hacked to pieces, as the superbly courageous crews attempted to halt the Japanese flood. In January 1942, reinforcements, including two squadrons of Hawker Hurricane fighters, were piecemeal, too few and too

Top: Wearing the contemporary SEAC livery of white flashes across tail and wings, Beaufighter RD367 of 27 Sqn beats low across the Burmese plains.
Left: Westland Lysander, N1273, BF-J of 28 Sqn on a supply-drop sortie in India 1942.
Bottom: Curtiss Mohawk of 5 Sqn escorting a supply aircraft across Indian border hills, 1942.

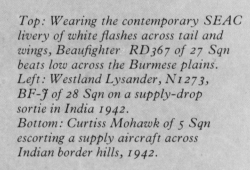

Above: Capt Frank Carey, the London-born ex-Halton apprentice who became the 'soul' of Burma's fighter pilots. His long fighting career in France, England and Burma culminated in inculcating fresh pilots to the Far East theatre with his own brand of tactics and attitudes, resulting in far superior fighting successes in SEAC.

Far right: Plt Off J H 'Jimmy' Whalen, DFC, seen here at Ratmanala, Ceylon in Aug 1942 walking away from his Hurricane IIb, BG827, RS-W of 30 Sqn.

Below: The Douglas Dakota – known to all as the DC – which became the backbone of air support and supply for the jungle armies in Burma.

chief. A substantial number of RAF personnel, air and ground crews, managed to escape the ultimate defeat, and by a wide variety of improvised means and modes eventually reached Burma or India.

The Japanese had invaded Burma too, fighting northwards from Thailand with overwhelming strength, aiming for the vital port of Rangoon. Burma, a natural barrier between India and Japan's existing enemy, China, was a logical objective. Its occupation would not only plug the slender supply lines to China, but would also provide a springboard for the invasion of India. Impenetrable from the north by virtue of the Himalayan mountain range, the 'Roof of the World', Burma is a country roughly the size of Germany (before its modern division), serrated from north to south by tenuous rivers and stark hill ranges, and mantled by some of the densest jungle terrain in the world. Within the dark confines of the jungle lurked every known pest and pestilence harmful, and often fatal, to human existence. Its climate supported humid equatorial temperatures relieved seasonally by roaring monsoon downpours of rain. Meteorological conditions for pilots in Burma varied from bearable tropical climes to terrifying demonstrations of the unbridled power of nature within which no man-made machine could hope to survive. Defending the gates to India in such terrain was a pathetically small Allied force when Japan first launched its drive north from conquered Malaya and Thailand. The British air commander, AVM D F Stevenson, initially, possessed only 37 aircraft, 21 of which were Curtiss P-40s of

late to have any decisive effect on the inevitable outcome. As the Japanese poured southwards through the Malaya Peninsula and finally reached Singapore, moves to continue the fight from Sumatra were already in hand, and on February 10 the last RAF aircraft left the doomed city. Five days later beleaguered Singapore's remaining 70,000 troops surrendered to the invaders. In Sumatra, and within days, in Java, the tattered remnants of the decimated squadrons fought on in ever-dwindling numbers, until the eventual surrender of the islands by their Dutch commander-in-the American Volunteer Group. Strung along the Salween river was a slender chain of airfields recently built. Against this puny force, the Japanese despatched some 400 bombers and fighters. Their first bombing raid on Rangoon was made on December 23, 1941 by 80 bombers escorted by 30 fighters. A second similar raid on Christmas Day killed 5000 civilians. Against superior aircraft and odds, the defending Tomahawks and Buffaloes claimed 36 victories during the two attacks, forcing the Japanese Air Service to retreat and lick its wounds. During the next four weeks no further raids were made, and in the interim Stevenson received reinforcements, a squadron of Blenheim bombers and 30 Hurricanes.

Stevenson used these fresh aircraft to 'lean forward' on the offensive to support the retreating ground forces in Burma, and to attempt to stop further air attacks against Rangoon, he despatched the Blenheims of 113 Squadron on bombing raids against Japanese-held forward airstrips within hours of their arrival in his command. The Blenheim crews destroyed 58 Japanese machines on the ground thereby buying time before the next expected enemy raids which came in the last week in January 1942; but in six days of fighting Rangoon's defenders claimed 50 of their tormentors. The third and final attempt to bomb Rangoon came on February 24 and 25. The 166 Japanese bombers and fighters yet again bore heavy casualties from the unrelenting Hurricanes and Tomahawks losing at least 37 on the first day and 24 on the second. This miniature, yet epic defence of Rangoon achieved its primary purpose – to gain precious time for the Allies, to give the all-conquering Japanese pause. Rangoon

was not raided again until its eventual occupation by the invaders. But the plight of the remaining RAF fighter force was pitiful. Reduced to just six flyable Hurricanes, these aircraft were operating with improvised bamboo tail skids in place of their damaged tail wheels. Facing a Japanese air strength of 250 aircraft, the exhausted Hurricane pilots spent the following few weeks on air cover patrols over the army formations retreating from Rangoon to India offering combat to any intruder marked with the Rising Sun of Japan. On March 21 there were only 10 operational weary Hurricanes and American Tomahawks. All ten gallantly plunged into the battle against 230 aircraft which on that day blasted Magwe airfield – the

RAF's latest centre. Within 24 hours of continuous bombing and fighting, the remaining RAF fighters were obliterated. Throughout April the Allied retreat continued to stumble northward towards the Indian frontier aided and succoured by a rag-bag of aircraft hastily flown in from the Middle East. Flying Lysanders, Blenheims, a few Wellington bombers, and a few fresh Hurricanes, the remaining RAF pilots and crews harried and slashed at the forward elements of the remorselessly advancing Japanese jungle army but the main task of the airmen now was to drop supplies to the ground forces, and evacuate the wounded and civilians. In the latter task the Dakotas and ancient Valentias of 31 Squadron took a lion's share – the begin-

ning of an unsurpassed unit effort in the supply role in Burma during the following three years. On May 20 the last survivors of the Allied retreat, utterly exhausted, sick, and in rags, reached India just before the seasonal monsoon rains burst and halted further pursuit by the Japanese.

During April a Japanese naval force including five aircraft carriers headed towards the key British naval base at Colombo, Ceylon. On April 5 the first air attacks on Ceylon were made by 50 carrier-borne bombers with a strong Zero escort. From the island rose 36 Hurricanes from 30 and 258 Squadrons with six Fleet Air Arm Fulmar fighters which destroyed 18 Japanese machines; they lost 15 Hurricanes and four Fulmars. Further light raids culminated in another heavy attack, this time against the Trincomalee naval base, on April 9. One hundred and twenty Japanese aircraft were met by 17 Hurricanes of 261 Squadron and six Fulmars from 873 Squadron, FAA, and in the ensuing battles 15 Japanese were shot down, and a further 17 probably destroyed. Eight Hurricanes and three Fulmars paid the price for this victory. As the sky

over Ceylon filled with gunfire and manoeuvring aircraft, 60 miles to sea the aircraft carrier *Hermes*, bereft of air cover, was systematically and clinically shattered by other Japanese navy bombers, and sank in 20 minutes. This prime target was thus added to a total of five battleships, two cruisers, seven destroyers and a number of merchant ships sunk by Admiral Nagumo's force, and the Japanese formation withdrew. Nevertheless, the victorious admiral's aeroplane strength had been seriously crippled by losses over Ceylon, and three of his five aircraft carriers were sent back to Japan to replace their lost airmen and aircraft. This depletion in air strength, occasioned by the stalwart defenders of Ceylon, was to be significant in the imminent battle of the Coral Sea, and may have tipped the fine balance between victory and defeat.

The year 1942 was a period of recuperation and strengthening for the RAF in east India as it prepared itself for the grim task ahead of recapturing Burma, Malaya and the Dutch East Indies. In terms of aircraft and fresh maintenance supplies the immediate prospect was bleak. In Europe the RAF was only

just beginning its escalating day-and-night offensive against Germany and the tide of war along the North African coast was pressing heavily against the Allies. Such aircraft as could be spared for the 'Forgotten War' in Burma were, in the main, second-line types – Wellington and Blenheim bombers, and Hurricane II fighters. Based near Calcutta, the RAF slowly built up its muscle for the expected Japanese onslaught – yet waited in vain for many months. Hurricane pilots stood by at immediate readiness each day, their aircraft 'dispersed' along the macadam road known from its colour as 'Red Road', which ran through Calcutta's centre; but air clashes with the enemy were spasmodic and relatively light. Meanwhile, with

Right: Canadian pilots on the Arakan front, Burma on Jun 5, 1943. l–r: Sgts W D Gosling; R A Cramer; C B Smith; and F E McDonald seated on the wing of Hurricane IIc, HW228, 'Pommy'.
Below: Vultee Vengeance III, FB922 getting airborne in Burma, 1944. Vengeances equipped five squadrons in the Far East theatre, and operated with distinction on the Arakan front.

Left: Dakota of 31 Sqn taxies in after yet another vital supply drop. Among the unit's pilots then was Flt Lt David Lord, DFC who, in 1944, earned one of the most deserved VCs of all time when flying a supply sortie to the trapped paratroopers at Arnhem.
Below: Hurricane IIc fighter, adapted to carry 250lb GP/HE bombs for low-level attacks, being loaded at Arakan, 1943.

Lashio and Rangoon in Japanese hands, the former supply link with southern China was cut. In order to re-establish this vital pipeline of war material, a new 'Burma Road' was established – in the air. From small beginnings, an aerial highway across the awe-inspiring Patkai mountain range was inaugurated by Dakotas and C-47s of the USAAF, joined by the doughty crews of 31 and 194 Squadrons RAF. Braving deadly cumulonimbus cloud masses (entry into which would mean instant death as there were internal currents capable of tearing any small aircraft to shreds) the transport crews initiated the 'Hump Crossing' route to China, a lifeline which soon increased in volume to the eventual point where an aircraft was taking off from India every 10 minutes. This massive, dependable use of the air to replace the traditional land supply and com-

munications route for armies was to be the heart of the eventual victory in the Far East theatre.

The tragic lessons of Singapore's fatal weakness in air defence was uppermost in the Allied air commanders' minds as they strove to increase the capability of the aerial units. By June 1942 the RAF in India had managed to increase its striking power from five to 26 squadrons. In addition the tiny Indian Air Force had added a further eight squadrons, though with untried crews. By November the first Spitfires in the Far East – photo reconnaissance machines – had arrived but fighter versions were too precious in England to be spared for another year. The promise of a long-range bombing strike force was realised at the end of the year when a few Liberators arrived, though these proved difficult to service and operate for several months. By the

Above: Sqn Ldr G A Butler, DFC who commanded 11 Sqn (Hurricanes) during the final months of the war in Burma.

turn of the year, the RAF could count a total of 1443 aircraft overall but many were not considered fit for operational tasks. Nevertheless, it was sufficient for the commander-in-chief, Field Marshal Wavell, to launch his first tentative offensive campaign in the Arakan coastal strip, a lunge intended to capture Akyab, in December 1942. Spearheading this relatively modest campaign, the RAF forward units were highly successful in attacking Japanese supply and communications routes and centres by tree-top level surprise ground-strafing. By April 1943, however, the jungle-bound infantry was forced to retreat, and as the monsoon arrived in June, returned to base. While this campaign raged along the coastal area, a unique form of warfare had been instigated inland. Orde Wingate's first Chindit expedition plunged deep into enemy territory supplied and succoured entirely from the air by the transport crews of 31 and 194 Squadrons. Seven columns of Commando-trained Chindits set out from Imphal in February 1943 and slashed their way through a thousand miles of fetid jungle and precipitous mountains creating panic and havoc along their route. Each day their progress was made possible by the indefatigable Dakota and C-47 crews, who provided their only link with base: parachuting guns, ammunition,

Far left: Vera Lynn, 'Sweetheart of the Forces' visiting the crews of 31 Sqn at Agartala, May 1944.
Left: Flt Lt Clyde Simpson of 67 Sqn RNZAF at Akyab, where he destroyed two of five Japanese aircraft which attacked the port in early 1945.
Below: Republic P-47 Thunderbolt II, HD298 of 30 Sqn at Arakan. The 'T-Bolt's' long range made them ideal strafers for attacking Japanese ground troops and installations.

food and medical supplies, and evacuating some of the wounded and sick. When, in June, the surviving two-thirds of the pioneer Chindits reached safety, they were unanimous in their high praise for the RAF crews who, in unarmed, slow transport aircraft had never failed them. It was a microcosm of the tactics which were to provide the rock foundation of later victorious land campaigns in 1944–45. No longer would troops on the ground be dependent on land lines of supply. Now, they could be supplied 'down the chimney'. Such a ploy required air supremacy above the battle zone, and the existing shortage of Japanese aircraft in Burma (precipitated by the ever-increasing American pressure upon Japanese forces strung across the vast Pacific Ocean) in no small measure helped the RAF to achieve this end.

By the end of June 1943 the RAF in India and Burma had been increased to 53 squadrons of which 38 were considered first-line operational units; half of these were equipped with fighters and fighter-bombers for direct tactical support of any jungle campaign. New types of aircraft were now arriving to replace the battle-weary and obsolete Curtiss Mohawk and Hurricane I fighters. Among the newcomers were the mighty Bristol Beaufighters and, in October 1943, the first Spitfire Vs. The first Beaufighters in the theatre were received by 27 Squadron in September 1942, and this unit flew its first offensive operations at Christmas. Further Beaufighters, equipped with night fighting radar sets, arrived with 176 Squadron in January 1943, specifically to defend Calcutta. Two pilots of this squadron, Flight Sergeant A M O Pring and Flying Officer Crombie, an Australian, claimed immediate successes against the few Japanese attempts to bomb the city. The first Spitfire fighter units, Nos. 136, 607 and 615 Squadrons, proved to be a great morale-booster to the veteran airmen waiting patiently for modern weapons. Equally, the ground and air crews of the various Blenheim units (who had performed near-miracles of maintenance on their rapidly ageing machines) welcomed the replacement Vultee Vengeance dive-bombers which now began to arrive. While this reconversion and rebuilding process progressed throughout mid-1943, the Dakotas of 31 Squadron and Lockheed Hudsons of 194 Squadron maintained their supply-dropping to the many outlying and isolated ground formations which were in direct contact with the Japanese jungle armies. The eventual silk-smooth organisation of air supply operations achieved in Burma was a long way off in the future; yet these early supply-drops were responsible for the testing of every technique which was later to become the foundation of airborne lifelines to the armies. These operations continued even through the appalling monsoon during which the weather conditions included everything from cyclone winds capable of tearing a massive Liberator bomber loose from its ground pegging and tossing it into the air like a toy, to dense, soaking rainstorms which blotted out the earth and sky leaving the transport crews to grope blindly.

As the massive ground organisation of air power burgeoned during the year, hundreds of air strips were cleared in the jungle and a chain of radar and wireless units were established throughout the Arakan Yomas and Chin Hills for control and warning duties. At this time, November 1943, the whole British and American forces were integrated in a new command, South East Asia Command (SEAC) led by a fresh Supreme Commander, Admiral Lord Louis Mountbatten. This meant that all RAF operational units in northeast India were amalgamated with the American Tenth Army Air Force and, significantly, all transport and air supply units became a single organisation titled Troop Carrier Command, commanded by Brigadier General D Old, USAAF. Similar integration placed both air services' photo recce units under a single commander, Wing Commander S G Wise, RAF. The prime tasks of the new organisation were to pursue a strategic air offensive against the Japanese, to render direct tactical support for any ground operations, and to maintain a constant air supply. To these ends, the new organisation possessed 48 RAF and 17 USAAF squadrons by the autumn of 1943, a figure which was rapidly increased to 64 and 28 respectively by May 1944. Though many differences in opinion were evident among the higher commanders of both air services during the following year – and were eventually resolved amicably – integration of actual operational efforts at the frontline levels was accomplished readily. Unification of purpose and co-operation produced a fighting spirit among the air crews and local commanders second to none. In the words of Major-General George Stratemeyer, USAAF, deputy commander of the combined air command, 'We must merge into one unified force in thought and deed, neither English nor American, with the faults of neither and the virtues of both. We must establish in Asia a record of Allied air victory of which we can all be proud in the years to come. Let us write it now in the skies over Burma.'

The advent of the new Spitfire fighter squadrons made an immediate impact on the aerial war; on the last day of 1943, 136 Squadron destroyed 12 Japanese aircraft which were part of a force trying to attack Allied shipping off the Arakan coast. In January 1944, 81 and 152 Squadrons, equipped with Spitfire VIII's, arrived to swell their ranks. If the Spitfire pilots had the edge on their Japanese opponents in performance, they still had to face a ruthless enemy. Any Allied pilot forced to take to his parachute was a helpless target on which the Japanese pounced without pity. Small wonder that many RAF and American fighter pilots, their aircraft crippled in combat, preferred to ride their damaged machines down and take their chance on landing safely in the jungle or plain below. The choice between jungle or Jap was a slim one in terms of ultimate survival in Burma. To force-land in the matted green hell of the Burmese jungle was seldom possible to achieve safely, but those few who did accomplish it still faced an implacable enemy – raw nature at its most antagonistic. In the permanently grey, dank underworld of the tropical foliage lurked a hundred natural enemies: fever, fatal malaria, wild beasts, impassable rivers, and if behind Japanese lines, a foe who considered any prisoner of war as something to be cruelly tortured or simply executed. While hundreds of air crews in Europe were shot down in enemy territories and eventually evaded captivity to return, only a relative handful of crews ever left the jungle in Burma after force-landing. A majority were simply never seen or heard of again. The influx into the command of so many fresh pilots required a pre-operational training house to ensure that the unacclimatised fighter pilots could be carefully prepared for the unique combat conditions existing in Burma's skies. Chief architect of the Gunnery and Tactics 'finishing' school at Calcutta was Group Captain Frank Carey, a bantam Cockney-born ex-aircraft apprentice, who had risen from the ranks to NCO pilot and eventually to commissioned rank. He had fought through the 1940 French campaign and the Battle of Britain before coming to Burma and further combat experience against the Japanese. Of Carey's teachings, it was said that the eventual fighter supremacy was gained by pilots '... with the lessons of "Chota" Carey echoing in their ears ...'

As 1943 drew to a close, the continuing build-up of air power throughout the year was having an increasingly destructive effect on the Japanese land forces stretched along the 700-mile Burma front. Beaufighter and Hurricane squadrons swept over the jungle battle lines daily, seeking out enemy transport by road and river, and shattering targets with concentrated cannon and bomb onslaughts. Yet another fresh design from Europe arrived – the ubiquitous De Havilland Mosquito, all-wood fighter-bomber. The first examples were delivered to 27 Squadron, the pioneer Beaufighter unit, in April and in December one Flight of Mosquitos was formed within the squadron. Led by their commander, Wing Commander J B Nicolson, VC, the 27 Squadron's Mosquito pilots flew a series of low-level 'Rhubarbs' in conjunction with the Beaufighters, starting on Christmas Day, 1943. In March, however, the Mosquitos were replaced by more Beaufighters; despite its superlative record in most operational theatres, it had not been a popular aircraft in Burma's humid temperatures. Other units later were Mosquito-equipped but its main contribution to the 'Forgotten War' was in the role of photo-reconnaissance in 1944–45. In mid-1944, the Beaufighter VI's gave way to the more powerful Beaufighter TF.X version which was fitted for carrying eight 3inch rocket projectiles under its wings in addition to the four 20mm cannon and wing machine guns and which was able to give crews an even heavier punch for their individual forays deep into Japanese-held country. Their depredations had a resounding impact on Japanese lines of supply and communication forcing the enemy to resort to riverborne craft to move troops and material. Once this was realised by Allied crews, they added river patrols to their jungle-ranging sorties; blasting everything of possible use to the Japanese from river barges to paddle steamers. Though initial Beaufighter sorties were flown by small formations of four or six aircraft, it quickly became the practice for single aircraft, or often pairs, to operate alone, thereby achieving maximum surprise and a slightly better margin of safety from occasional roving Zero fighters. It was a backwoods war, little publicised, but one which constantly prevented the Japanese from reinforcing their troops and had a devastating effect on morale in the enemy's rank and file. Sorties were normally started before dawn taking advantage of the misty half-light to approach their patrol areas undetected, and flown at tree-clipping heights to stay below any Japanese radar detection devices. It called for a high degree of navigation and concentration to 'jink' between hills and valleys, along snaking rivers bordered by towering

trees, or across the teak-stumped flat lands. Just one second's lack of alertness invited disaster.

Following Wavell's policy that attack is always the primary objective, Mountbatten decided to mount a four-pronged offensive at the close of 1943: to capture Akyab; to push across the Chindwin River; to bring the Chinese troops commanded by the American general, 'Vinegar Joe' Stilwell, south from Ledo; and finally to support more penetrations by Orde Wingate's Chindit columns. These operations, particularly the latter, depended almost entirely on the capability of the air transport crews in providing a constant supply-drop operation. As the infantry moved forward, Troop Carrier Command's Dakotas swung into action plunging low over thickly carpeted hills and into valleys, through eddying currents of terrifying proportions, keeping faith with the jungle-bound soldiers. Deep in Japanese-held territory the fighters and bombers wreaked destruction on Japanese air strips, rail, road, and river routes, and supply bases. Gradually the offensive gained ground until, on February 4, 1944, the unexpected happened; the enemy high command put into operation its 'Operation C' – the invasion of India. Relying on tactics which had been highly successful to date, the Japanese planned a two-pronged assault designed to outflank and divide the Allied armies, and then penetrate into India. Until now such tactics, pursued with fanatical determination irrespective of losses, had invariably meant that opposing troops would retreat. On this occasion two new

elements had been overlooked by the Japanese commanders: Mountbatten's general order that in future the army was to stand and fight, and secondly his absolute reliance on the air forces to provide all supplies and services on the spot. Determined never to retreat again, the beleaguered Allied troops in various hard-pressed locations stubbornly held their positions as massive waves of Japanese troops and aircraft battered against their defences. Supplies from the air came as promised in a constant flow, parachuted into the foxholes and bunkers often only yards from Japanese trenches. In addition, nearly 50 unarmed Auster light aircraft, piloted mainly by American airmen, ran the gauntlet to land and evacuate wounded and sick troops from crude strips often less than 200 yards long within the besieged boxes. This overall demonstration of air control demoralised many Japanese, as one rare prisoner reported, 'It broke our hearts to see the stuff dropping on British troops day after day, while we got nothing.' Another ingenious use for air control came into practice. RAF officers were sent into frontline positions as ground controllers establishing radio communication with various squadrons of fighters and dive-bombers, and thus

Below: Though the submarine menance was small in the Far East, air control over the Indian Ocean and the Pacific, remained a priority. For the various Sunderland and Catalina squadrons operating in these areas, a central base was established at Ceylon. Here three Short Sunderlands are serviced.

were able to describe immediate targets facing the British advances. This 'taxi rank' system, already used to great effect in the North African campaigns, was later employed in Europe after the June 1944 landings in Normandy. It also illustrated the complete inter-Service co-operation which existed throughout the Burma advances in 1944–45, and contributed largely to final victory.

By mid-March the initial phase of the Japanese offensive had patently failed in its intention, yet the planned second phase, a drive to capture the key Imphal plain area, was still launched on March 8. To hold Imphal was crucial to the Allies, and Mountbatten accordingly rushed in reinforcements to its defenders, including an additional 30 supply aircraft which he diverted from the vital 'Hump' supply route to China; this move was taken in the light of the immediate emergency for which Mountbatten then had no 'legal' power to authorise. Twenty Curtiss Commando aircraft and the Dakotas of 194 Squadron were switched to the Imphal battle, flying in the Fifth Indian Division; other troop aircraft carried in fresh troops and nearly 100,000 lb of supplies and guns. Thirty miles north of Imphal, the Allied armies occupying Kohima also became besieged by advancing Japanese, and battles raged around these two tiny but vital defence positions. At Kohima, on a high ridge surrounded by higher hills, some 2000 Allied soldiers fought Japanese soldiers who were entrenched less than the length of a tennis court away. The Allies were sustained by unceasing air supply drops from Dakotas lumbering at 200 feet through a hail of gunfire. Outside the perimeter of the Kohima 'box' – which measured perhaps 400 by 500 yards – Hurricane fighter-bombers and Vultee Vengeance dive-bombers flew 2200 sorties in 16 days, continuously hammering the Japanese with bombs and gunfire.

Meanwhile at Imphal, 150,000 men of the Fourteenth Army were encircled by the Japanese by the end of March. Within the ring the fighters of 221 Group RAF, commanded by Air Commodore Stanley Vincent, were spread thinly over six airstrips in the plains. Ground crews and administrative personnel set up self-supporting 'boxes' – 'pimples' was the local title – in which they were prepared to fight and defend their positions till the last. Air and ground crews undertook all guard duties in each 'pimple' throughout each night, and by day the fighters made a series of strike sorties against enemy positions in the surrounding hill ranges. With the nearest rail head some 140 miles away, all supplies, both of men and material, could only be brought in by air. Throughout May and June the faithful

transport crews, flying incredible hours, delivered an average supply of 275 tons (in May) and 400 tons (in June) on every single day of the siege.

Throughout all these land operations, little interference was experienced from the Japanese air forces, a fact due in no small measure to the operations flown by long-range USAAF Lightning and Mustang fighters who kept up a series of strafing sweeps against the enemy's forward air strips, pinning down many units which might have added strength to the Japanese besiegers of Imphal. Within the defensive 'ring' 221 Group's fighters maintained patrols over the entrances to the Imphal valley, and on one occasion destroyed half of a 20-strong enemy bombing formation attempting to break through. By June, both Imphal and Kohima were lost causes to the Japanese, who started to withdraw their ailing army though it still fought fiercely as it drew back. By June 22 the Kohima-Imphal road was re-opened to the Allies, and the rout of the Japanese 15th Army was in full swing. The seasonal monsoon broke but 221 Group continued to harass the retreating army without significant pause; its Hurricane fighter-bombers in particular took a lion's share of the strikes against troop columns, bridges, road transport and river craft. It can be said truly that at Kohima and Imphal the tide of battle against the Japanese Imperial forces had at last turned. The key to that victory had been an unprecedented massive employment of air power on a scale hitherto thought impossible. Nor was this air feat solely a victory for the air crews but was as much due to the efforts of thousands of ground personnel who had worked to the point of exhaustion in conditions which defy description.

By the end of 1944 the Allied armies were across the Chindwin at Sittaung, Mawlaik and Kalewa in strength and pressing southwards, concentrating the Fourteenth Army in the Shwebo plain ready for the final road to Mandalay and Rangoon. The air services by then had undergone considerable reorganisation and strengthening. The stalwart Wellington bombers had been largely replaced by long range Liberators, capable of hitting strategic targets in the far reaches of Burma; the fighter squadrons had been reinforced by the introduction of American Thunderbolt II seven-ton fighters in many RAF squadrons. The former Troop Carrier Command, disbanded as such in June, had been succeeded by a combined British and American Combat Cargo Task Force, comprised at its peak of 17 squadrons. These relatively few units of transport Dakotas and C-47s were responsible for supplying over 300,000 men during the final offensives of the Burma campaign. That

they were permitted such freedom of movement in the Burma skies was a measure of the aerial supremacy now held by the RAF and USAAF fighters. Spitfires, Thunderbolts, far-ranging Mustangs – and the ubiquitous Hurricane fighter-bombers – had won command of the air by repeated strikes against Japanese airfields; in one sortie at Don Muang, they destroyed 31 enemy aircraft on the ground, 780 miles from the closest Allied air base. Overall numerical weakness in the Japanese air forces in Burma (by October 1944 they had only 125 aircraft of all types) meant the cessation of any significant opposition from the Japanese. In contrast, the enemy land forces, tough, fanatically determined, and on occasion led by brilliant tacticians, fought on to the bitter end. Their supply lines became the chief concern of SEAC's heavy bombers which, by early 1945, were capable of attacking targets between 2000 and 3000 miles away, and on arrival over their objectives, destroying even small rail bridges with Azon bombs which were radio-controlled from the parent bomber. Elsewhere the Liberators and Mitchell bombers had developed a technique of saturation bombing of areas known to contain Japanese troops and centres, drenching the areas with a rain of highly explosive bombs which effectively crippled any build-up of enemy strength. To the west of the main Allied land thrusts, along the Burmese coastline, a series of amphibious landings were made, tactically covered and supported by the fighters which, after bloody fighting, resulted in the recapture of Akyab and, in January 1945, Ramree Island. These quickly became springboards for aerial supply and fighter-bomber operations in the continuing inland drive to Rangoon. In February, an assault across the Irrawady river against Pagan saw Thunderbolts of the RAF using a new form of aerial destruction – Napalm liquid fire.

During all these operations the patient Dakotas continued to plod over mountain and valley, delivering, in February 1945 alone, more than 60,000 tons of food and ammunition to the forward elements of the Allied armies. Their task was no sinecure in terms of combat flying, and a large proportion of the cargos were delivered to forward airstrips, such as Meiktila, under heavy ground fire from Japanese located around the perimeters of the landing grounds; seven Dakotas were lost in this way on March 20. Even more susceptible to enemy fire were the tiny Sentinel L.5 light aircraft – nicknamed by jungle troops, 'Angels' – which flew in and out in any conditions in the forward areas; their sole task of evacuation of sick and wounded men overrode any considerations of safety for the crews aboard.

Above: A scene which epitomises the chief air 'ingredient' in the final victory in Burma as a Dakota faithfully releases needed supplies to a 14th Army unit.

By the beginning of April 1945 the main armies began a 'race' to reach Rangoon – about 300 miles south – before the May monsoons commenced. The already heavy commitments of the tactical air units and the Combat Cargo Task Force were redoubled, as all possible strength was thrown into the offensive. The heavy bombers promptly subjected Rangoon to an intensive bombardment which continued throughout the month. Its effect can be judged from the fact that the Japanese made no attempt to defend the city from the subsequent advanced formations of troops who arrived by parachute or landed from the sea on May 2 – the city was empty of enemy forces. Next day the 26th Division entered the city from the north, just hours before the first torrential monsoon downpours fell. Now only one more battle of serious proportions was to be fought before the final freeing of Burma: the Battle of Sittang Bend. Here, some 20,000 Japanese, bypassed in the drive to Rangoon, were sandwiched between the main Fourteenth Army formations and the British formations in the Pegu Yomas bordering Siam (Thailand). Captured enemy documents indicated that these troops intended to break out of the 'sandwich' eastwards across the Pegu Yomas into Siam; accordingly Mountbatten prepared to ambush and counter this proposed move. In some of the bitterest fighting of the whole Burmese war, the Japanese were finally driven back, losing over 6000 as casualties and 740 who became prisoners of war, between July 20 and August 4. Air support for the Allied troops followed a now-familiar pattern; Spitfires, Hurricanes and Thunderbolts were employed on 'cabbie' patrols directed by frontline RAF and Army ground controllers. The pilots were later estimated to have killed about 2000 Japanese. It was the last fling by a defeated army. Behind them the ragged survivors had left 100,000 dead in the jungles of Burma, plus an untold number whose deaths were impossible to verify or record.

With the recapture of Burma, the RAF prepared to implement 'Operation Zipper', the planned reconquest of Malaya while in England 'Operation Tiger Force' was being prepared, to escalate the final stages of the defeat of Japan. Neither operation was needed. On August 6 and August 9, 1945, American Superfortresses dropped the world's first atomic bombs on Hiroshima and Nagasaki respectively. The horrific devastation and losses of civilians gave Japanese leaders little alternative but to accept unconditional terms of surrender. The greatest global war in the history of mankind was over. In Burma the Japanese army commanders, steeped in traditional strategy, though brilliant in imaginative tactical ploys, had badly underestimated the new factor of air power. Even at the peak of strength, the combined British and American air services in the Far East theatre amounted to just 48 fighter squadrons, 18 bomber, and 24 transport units. Each, individually and collectively, had made a vital contribution to the eventual triumph. By their sacrifices and utter determination the air and ground crews in South East Asia Command had added a new doctrine to warfare – air power would supply, support and succour a land army completely independent of ground routes and lines of communications. Probably the simplest symbol of that doctrine as practised in the humid air over Burma was the lumbering Douglas Dakota, or 'DC' as it was affectionately called. Its importance to the land campaign was summed succinctly by one ragged, weary Chindit as he stepped from a Dakota after being retrieved from a spot 500 miles behind Japanese lines. Turning to the Dakota's skipper, the soldier patted the aircraft fuselage and remarked with heartfelt sincerity, 'You can keep your VCs and MCs, sir – give me the DC's anytime . . .'

Jet Age

When, on May 8 1945, VE-Day ('Victory in Europe') was officially declared, the RAF's overall strength comprised 1,079,835 men and women. The bulk of these were engaged in Europe and the Middle East, but in Burma and the Pacific theatres the struggle to subdue Japan continued. In England plans for a British long-range bombing force to be sent to the Pacific to aid the USAAF's offensive against Japan were mooted

as far back as 1943. The original conception was a force of 40 Lancaster squadrons, to be based on various Pacific islands. Development of very long-range versions of the basic Lancaster was quickly undertaken, resulting in the Lancaster Mk IV and V – retitled Lincoln Mk I and II respectively. After more than a year of wide changes in the proposed composition of this force, methods of achieving the required ultra-range cap-

ability, and indeed even the aircraft types to be used, the official title 'Tiger Force' was designated on February 24, 1945. By then its main elements were Nos 5 and 6 Groups RAF Bomber Command, equipped with Lancasters, to become strengthened by Lincoln bombers. Vast planning in the minutest detail had been accomplished by VE-Day, but when Tiger Force was on the brink of moving eastwards, the need for it was abruptly annulled, when USAAF B-29 Superfortresses dropped two atomic bombs – on Hiroshima on August 6 and another on Nagasaki on August 9. Japan agreed to surrender, and on August 15, 1945 the free world celebrated VJ-Day ('Victory over Japan'). The greatest war in human history was over.

In terms of human sacrifice the RAF had suffered grievously. Between September 3, 1939 and August 15, 1945 air crew casualties alone had amounted to 70,253 killed in action and 22,924 wounded. In addition 13,115 had become prisoners of war, some 2000 of those shot down escaping or evading capture. It must be remembered that a high proportion of members serving under the all-embracing title 'Royal Air Force'

Above: HM King George VI inspects Cranwell cadets in Jun 1945.
Below: Marshal of the RAF, Hugh Trenchard inspecting aircraft apprentices at Halton, 1945 – his 'Brats': Behind him a distinguished entourage includes the contemporary CAS, Lord Portal, and AVM Arthur Barratt.

were in fact non-British in nationality. Of the 340,000 men who saw aircrew service, at least 134,000 had come from the Dominions and Commonwealth countries. Many thousands of others wearing RAF blue were refugees from Nazi-conquered or occupied countries. All had borne their proportion of losses, the very flower of their generation and irreplaceable youth. The largest single group of casualties within the RAF were from Bomber Command, which had flown a grand total of 364,514 sorties and lost 8325 aircraft on actual operations. Casualty figures numbered 47,268 aircrew members killed and a further 4200 seriously wounded among the bomber crews. On the ground, the indefatigable 'erks' – the rock foundation for the operational squadrons – also suffered heavily. Airmen and airwomen killed on active service amounted overall to 9671; a further 6561 were wounded or injured; and 4490 had become prisoners of war (3253 of these in the Far East theatre of operations). In all, the RAF had suffered almost 100,000 men and women killed – some two-thirds of its comparative total

strength in September 1939; and perhaps 75–80 per cent of the RAF's equivalent manning strength in the 1970s.

No survey of the RAF during the years 1939–45 can fail to emphasize the part played by the RAF's 'gentler sex' – the Women's Auxiliary Air Force. In sheer numerical strength the WAAF represented 22 per cent of RAF 'manning' in Home Command when it was at its peak; and 16 per cent overall at that period circa 1943. The origins of full-time serving female members of Britain's air services are traceable to December 1916. The Women's Royal Air Force was created alongside the infant Royal Air Force on April 1, 1918. This new branch of the service was formally disbanded on April 1, 1920, some 32,000 women having served in its ranks. It was not until June 28, 1939 that the Women's Auxiliary Air Force came into being. When war with Germany was declared the WAAF mustered totals of 234 officers and 1500 airwomen in non-commissioned ranks.

190

Throughout the war a steady influx of new recruits swelled the ranks of the WAAF to a peak strength of 181,835 (all ranks) on July 1, 1943. By the end of the war airwomen were serving in virtually every facet of RAF activity except operational aircrew, and were mustered in more than 80 different ground trades. The overall intention behind formation of the WAAF was to substitute women in certain tasks, thereby releasing airmen for more operational priority duties. However, by mid-1943, WAAFs were employed in a variety of purely mechanical trades, working alongside the normal male ground crews, and were integrated into dozens of other semi-technical working formations. Few Bomber Command and Fighter Command crews will forget

the comforting sound of a precise but distinctly female voice on their R/T earphones, guiding them back to a base airfield after the hell of an operational sortie over France or Germany. Other direct evidence of the many female trades recruited included the large number of transport drivers who conveyed air crews to and from dispersals; parachute packers; flight mechanics; even to the humble WAAF serving a crew's operational egg in the Mess. To a great degree life as an airwoman, particularly on flying stations, was no sinecure. Working and domestic accommodation and the appurtenances of 'normal' civilised living conditions were on a par with those of the men; yet the 'feminine touch' was always apparent. For the first

two years of its existence the WAAF, though working alongside the RAF, was legally not subject to the laid-down RAF codes of discipline and punishment. Indeed, throughout the war interchange of salutes between members of the male and female formations was virtually left to individual standards of courtesy. This changed to a certain degree when, from April 25, 1941, the Defence (Women's Forces) Regulations declared that all personnel in the WAAF were now legally members of the Armed Forces of the Crown, thereby subject to some (though by no means all) sections of the Air Force Act with effect from June 12, 1941. As purely one example of the pre-June 1941 situation, no member of the WAAF could be charged with desertion or ab-

sence without leave; and refusal by any airwoman so charged to accept any form of punishment meant that she could simply leave the WAAF without prior notice. No legal charge could be brought against her for so doing! Yet, knowing this, many young WAAFs working on various fighter stations and sector control units in 1940 stayed at their posts during the devastating Luftwaffe raids and refused to be sent to safer berths.

Right: Avro Lincoln B.2, a derivative of the Lancaster. Many saw operational service in the Malayan and Kenya campaigns of 'peacetime'.
Below: Gloster Meteors of 66 Sqn at Duxford being re-armed, circa 1948–49.

Right: Armourers of 33 Sqn loading a De Havilland Hornet with 3in rocket projectiles. In addition to its four 20mm cannon in the fuselage belly, Hornets could carry 500lb HE bombs under their wings. With its top speed in the region of 470mph, the sleek Hornet saw service from 1946 to 1955.
Below: The Boeing Washington – 'anglicised' version of the wartime USAF B-29 Superfortress. Most Washingtons had been replaced by 1955 with Canberras. Seen here, is a Washington of 15 Sqn, a heavy bomber, used by the RAF.
Bottom: Short Sunderland GR5, VB889 of 201 Sqn unloading its cargo on the Havel Lake, Berlin, during Operation Plainfare, 1948.

Inevitably, once peace broke out, the RAF began to demobilise its wartime personnel and decrease its aircraft stocks. Though with little resemblance to the post-1918 Armistice chaos in demobilisation procedure, this rapid depletion of manning and material had its depressing effect on those members of the service already serving on a regular engagement. In particular, the vast surplus of wartime trained or part-trained air and ground crews provided numerous problems of employment during the interim period of awaiting demobilisation. Even in 1946 it was no uncommon sight to see Flight Sergeants and Warrant Officers, ex-operational crews with chests bearing campaign and gallantry medals, utilised as AC2 Drivers, Mechanical Transport (MT). For the young regular airman or officer it became a period of frustration. No firm policy was issued until late 1946 on postwar permanent commissions. Many war-recruited airmen in ground trades, rapidly promoted to meet wartime exigencies, suddenly formed a block in promotion to the junior-ranked regular airman, already contracted to a career in the RAF. The prolonged vacillation in Whitehall on outlining a definite policy for manning in the peacetime service was

responsible for many worthy airmen and junior officers opting to leave the RAF for civilian careers. Many of these men would have enhanced the quality of personnel on whom the future RAF would depend. Instead moves were made to create an RAF Reserve Command, and the prewar Auxiliary Air Force territorial force was re-formed.

The years 1945–46, if dismal to the serving individual in terms of worries over his future, provided several examples of practical experiments in facing the future jet age prospects of the RAF. On November 7, 1945, Group Captain H J Wilson, flying a Gloster Meteor F4, set up a new world speed record of 606.25 mph. This figure was raised by some 10 mph nearly a year later by Group Captain E M Donaldson. Both feats were admittedly one-off special flights under semi-ideal conditions, but the advent of jet fighters in RAF front-line service was imminent, and the complex problems of converting from piston engines to jets required a bank of experience and information on operating fighters near to the sound barrier. The war-created Royal Air Force Regiment, with its proud battle honours of every operational campaign from 1942, was officially announced as a permanent in-

tegral part of the RAF on July 10, 1946 – a tribute to the khaki-clad airmen, renowned for their physical toughness and rugged prowess on the battlefields of the world. In the same year the first jet fighter squadrons of the postwar RAF were formed into all-jet Wings. The first, comprised of 56, 74 and 245 Squadrons, was formed at RAF Bentwaters, Suffolk. A second Wing was soon to follow, comprised of 222, 234 and 263 Squadrons, based at Boxted. All were flying the Meteor F3 version. The second jet fighter design to enter RAF operational service was a radically-different shape – the twin tail-boom De Havilland Vampire. First to be equipped with this new jet was 247 Squadron in early 1946; and in September 247 was joined by 54 and 72 Squadrons to form the first Vampire Wing, based at Odiham, Hampshire. For the rest of Fighter Command squadrons continued to operate advanced marks of Spitfire and Mosquito fighters.

In Bomber Command the jet age was yet to dawn. Though mainly still equipped with the doughty Lancaster, some units had at least progressed to the larger variant, the Avro Lincoln, which first came into first-line service with 57 Squadron in 1945, too late to see oper-

*Left: 45 Sqn DH Hornet at full bore, Tengah, Singapore, circa 1954.
Right: North American Sabre (nearest) and Hawker Hunter of 112 Sqn; both are marked with the unit's WWII insignia of sharks' teeth. Sabres served in the RAF from 1953–56.
Below right: The three V-bomber designs which eventually formed Britain's 'nuclear deterrent' force in the 1950s and early 1960s. An Avro Vulcan delta-wing leads a Vickers Valiant (nearest) and the crescent-wing Handley Page Victor.*

ational service during World War II. Equally, RAF Transport Command – in peacetime no less hard-pressed to fulfil all the duties requested – was still using a motley mixture of wartime aircraft, including 'cleaned-up' ex-bombers. One stalwart type in use was the elephantine Avro York – yet another derivant of the Lancaster – which had been in service since March 1943 in small numbers.

In 1948 the RAF was again placed on an operational war footing in two distinctly different spheres. Near to home, the Russian occupation of east Germany meant that Berlin was dependent on road, rail, and air communication and supply routes passing through or over Russian-occupied zones. By suddenly denying all access by land, the Russian authorities effectively isolated the German capital – virtually a direct challenge to the Allied occupation forces in western Germany. It was then decided to link with Berlin solely by air supply, and on June 28, 1948 the RAF flew its first

Below: Bristol Brigand delivering a rocket broadside during anti-Communist 'bandit' operations in Malaya, 1951; 84 Sqn revived its 1920s custom of distinguishing Flights by painting playing cards on the Brigand's fins. Alongside the nose, the unit motif – a scorpion – was added.

sorties to the besieged city. Initially, No. 46 Group RAF received a directive calling for an effort of 400 tons of food and essential supplies daily. Using only Dakotas at first, the air effort was quickly backed up by Avro Yorks at Wunsdorf. In July the Dakotas moved base to Fassburg, where they were soon replaced by Douglas C-54 Skymasters of the USAF. Soon these were joined by Sunderland flying boats, which alighted on the Havel See, and a variety of British civil airliners pressed into service. From June 28 to October 31 nearly half a million tons of supplies were flown into Berlin by air, roughly 30 per cent of which was delivered by RAF-controlled crews, and the remainder by the vaster transport fleet of the USAF. Though no interference came from the Russian air force, the airlift fleet was severely restricted in movement by being confined to three narrow air corridors. To stray from them would have invited retaliation from Russian jet fighters. This remarkable airlift sustained Berlin until May 1949, when the Russians finally lifted their blockade of land routes, a tacit admission of defeat for their challenge to the Allies. Operations continued for some five months after this lifting of the blockade in order to build up Berlin's stocks. But during the official Operation 'Plainfare' a total of 94 RAF aircraft had

flown the impressive tally of almost 50,000 individual flights of mercy, an equivalent of just over 18 million miles. It was during 'Plainfare' that the RAF's first postwar transport design came into operational service, the Handley Page Hastings, which equipped 47 Squadron initially in October 1948, and which with a sister squadron, 297, participated in the Berlin airlift. The final 'Plainfare' flight was undertaken by a Hastings on October 6, 1949.

The second commitment for the RAF in 1948 took place in Malaya. After centuries of European domination many of the Far East countries emerged from the 1939–45 war determined to reshape the future of their governments – the beginning of a world-wide rush to national self-determination. In Malaya one predominant 'liberation' movement was Communist-inspired, led by a Chinese Communist section of the guerrilla armies formed during the war to fight Japanese occupation forces. Ironically, the leader of this anti-European force in postwar years was Chin Peng, a Chinese Communist who had been awarded an OBE by the British government for his resistance work against the Japanese. The spark which set Malaya ablaze came on June 16, 1948, when three rubber planters were murdered by Communist terrorists. Two days later a national state of emergency was officially declared – an 'emergency' which was to last for twelve years. The RAF in the Far East was spread thinly from Singapore to Hong Kong at this time, but Kuala Lumpur in Malaya was selected as the most convenient air strip from which to provide air strikes against the jungle army of terrorists – an 'army' comprised of perhaps 6000 dedicated men, but with the potential of half a million local 'recruits' among the native population. In July 1948 elements of 28 and 60 Squadrons (Spitfire FR 18s) were detached to 'K.L.', and on July 21 the first official sorties of 'Operation Firedog' (the cover title for the whole Malayan Emergency campaign) were flown by two Spitfires of 60 Squadron. In the following month 45 Squadron's Beaufighters flew into Kuala Lumpur and, on the 19 flew the first

Above: Shepherding an Avro Vulcan at night by use of electric wands.

'Firedog' strike sorties. Dakotas of 110 Squadron joined these squadrons for supply and communication duties.

From the start of 'Firedog', and indeed, throughout the twelve years' operational effort, the main bases for RAF contribution remained on Singapore Island. Here were three established RAF stations – Changi, Seletar and Tengah. Changi became headquarters for administration and transport operations; Seletar remained the chief maintenance unit, and home of the RAF's flying boat units – the 'Kipper Fleet', as it was affectionately termed; while Tengah became the chief purely operational strike base for bombers and fighters. The vital photo-reconnaissance units operated from Seletar. This task was initially in the capable hands of 81 Squadron, which flew Mosquito PR 34s and Spitfire PR 19s. In support of the main squadrons, a tiny Air Observation unit (AOP), No. 1914 Flight, equipped with

the fragile Auster AOP 6s, was formed in 1948, and gradually enlarged to become 656 Squadron. Its duties included target-marking, reconnaissance, casualty evacuation, supply, communication, and even leaflet-dropping. By 1958, when 656 Squadron was transferred to the newly-created Army Air Corps, the unit could claim a massive record of 143,000 individual sorties – more than any other single unit involved in 'Firedog'.

For the first two years RAF operations were mainly in the strike or reconnaissance roles, and gradual building up of air power in the region. Assisted on occasion by Fleet Air Arm carrier-borne aircraft, the Spitfires, Beaufighters, Mosquitos, and Dakotas were even joined by Seletar's Sunderland flying boats in a land-bomber role. In November 1950, however, the jet era entered its operational phase, when six Vampire FB5s set out from England on their 9000-mile ferry flight to Singapore. They arrived in the first few days of December and were allotted to 60 Squadron

on December 4 at Tengah. As full replacement of 60 Squadron's Spitfires was implemented, an intensive conversion training programme to the new jets was instigated, and on April 26, 1951 Vampires flew the first British jet air strike in the Far East. Other fresh designs to join in 'Firedog' operations also arrived at this period. No. 45 Squadron, which had begun exchanging its Beaufighters for Bristol Brigands in late 1949, was joined by 84 Squadron's Brigands in April 1950. A significant addition to the RAF's strike power was the De Havilland Hornet, the RAF's last piston-engined operational fighter. With a top speed close to 470 mph and armament of four 20-mm cannons plus wing rockets, the Hornet began replacing 33 Squadron's obsolescent Hawker Tempests in March 1951. For the next four years Hornets were to bear the brunt of operations in Malaya. The early months of 1950 also saw the introduction of heavy bombers to the Malayan campaign. On March 15 No. 57 Squadron's Lincolns left their UK base at Waddington to fly to Tengah. They undertook several weeks of bombing sorties against the jungle terrorists, the first of many UK-based Lincoln squadrons to be detached to Malaya for two- or three-months' periods of such operations during the following years. On July 16, 1950 No. 1 Squadron RAAF's Lincolns flew into Tengah as a 'permanent' heavy bomber unit for 'Firedog', and in its first year of operations the unit's silver Lincolns flew 744 sorties. The squadron was to remain on these duties for eight years, during which time it flew more than 3000 sorties and released 33 million pounds of high explosive onto terrorist targets.

Supply and the support role increased in 1950 when, on April 1, the first RAF operational helicopter unit was introduced when three Sikorsky Dragonfly HC2s composed the Casualty Evacuation Flight, based at Seletar. Three years later, a shift of base was made to the naval airfield at Sembawang, by which time the Flight was retitled 194 Squadron. Operating over the lush green jungle, these 'choppers' proved invaluable in extracting casualties and sick from otherwise inextricable situations. This role was extended quickly to supplying vital material and personnel to jungle-based infantry units. Together with the ubiquitous Austers, the helicopters also pioneered a new form of warfare by undertaking 'crop-denial' sorties, spraying crops and vegetation being cultivated by the Communist terrorists for food, and thereby instigating a role repeated on wider scale later by the USAF in the Vietnam campaign. On the first day of 1951, 60 Squadron flew its ultimate Spitfire operation, which was immediately hailed in the popular press as 'the last Spitfire operation' with ample eulogies of the type's long and distinguished service. This amused 81 Squadron at Seletar, who continued to fly its Spitfires until April 1, 1954. They accumulated a total of 1029 operational sorties in the interim. No. 81 Squadron also had the 'honour' of continuing operational use of the few remaining Mosquitos until December 15, 1955, when it flew the squadron's 6619th 'Firedog' sortie with Mosquito RG314 – the final RAF Mosquito operational sortie. Meanwhile, 81 began receiving its first Meteor PR 10 jets in November 1953.

While the Malayan campaign mounted in strength and scope, events in Britain brought a variety of changes in equipment and policy for the RAF generally. In January 1951 the British Prime Minister, Clement Attlee, announced plans for enlarging the service in line with his

Right: QRA – Quick Reaction Alert. The duty 'four-minute' crew of a 27 Sqn Vulcan jump to it at Scampton, on receipt of the operational signal to scramble.

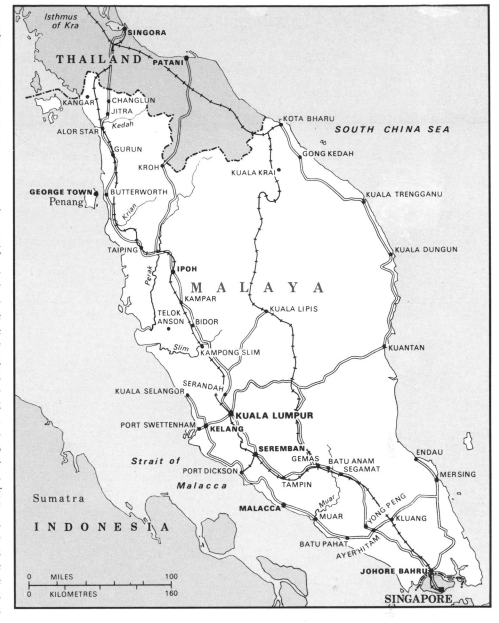

government's overall rearmament intentions. Within the service that same month heralded a new trade and promotion framework; a dual 'ladder' of promotion prospects incorporating the traditional ranks for non-commissioned airmen, and a new scale of 'technician' status levels of rank wherein promotion depended on both time and merit; NCO levels in the latter 'ladder' being outwardly evident by inverted chevrons of rank. This scheme for (eventually) all ground tradesmen was an extension to some degree of the previous attempt to introduce entirely new categories of rank status amongst non-commissioned air crew personnel. With the aim of segregating the flying branch of the service from all non-flying branches, former NCO aircrew were remustered to five new categories of aircrew, and exchanged their traditional rank chevrons for a slightly gaudy laurel wreath badge worn on the tunic sleeve, embellished with various 'stars' in light blue cloth. An extension of this ill-received attempt to separate air and ground personnel was a scheme to create separate 'Aircrew Messes' wherein membership was entirely aircrew, divorced from the traditional Officers' and Sergeants' Messes. The aircrew scheme – subjected to widespread criticism and no little ill-

feeling – was short-lived, and in August 1950 was abandoned, with the former system of ranks reintroduced. The only new rank retained was that of Master Aircrew – equivalent to Warrant Officer. In its original concept, the Technician scheme of promotion for ground tradesmen created untold confusion in simple disciplinary and administration matters, particularly among relatively older officers of junior rank steeped in past customs. From then until the present day fresh schemes, and modifications of this scheme, have continued to disrupt the prospects of ground tradesmen periodically – systems perfectly feasible in theory when outlined on a desk in a Whitehall office, but usually far from perfect in practice and application at hangar-floor level.

In terms of pure equipment, May 1951 saw the introduction of the RAF's first jet bombers when 101 Squadron at Binbrook began receiving its first English Electric Canberra twin-jet aircraft. Superbly conceived and aesthetically beautiful, the Canberra previewed the all-jet Bomber Command, but most units continued to operate the angular Lincoln for several years to come. In Coastal Command a successor to the existing Lancaster MR3s was introduced in early 1951 when the first Avro Shackleton

Is were issued to the command's OCU at Kinloss, Scotland. Essentially yet another derivant of the Lancaster-Lincoln parentage, the Shackleton, in increasingly modified forms, was to serve the RAF faithfully for the next two decades. In Fighter Command most units were by now equipped with advanced marks of Meteor and Vampire jets; fast, manoeuvrable interceptors but armed only with 20mm cannons – weapons of a calibre and performance rejected as obsolescent by the Luftwaffe in the early 1940s. More heavily-armed, superior performance jet fighters for replacement were already coming off the designers' drawing boards. Most significant of these were the swept-wing Hawker Hunter F1, the first of which, WB188, first flew at Boscombe Down on July 20, 1951. Production Hunters did not become available until 1954, when the first examples entered first-line RAF service. Even then a variety of troubles inherent with introduction of a new design, not least of which was the early Hunter's inability to use its full cannon armament without serious loss of engine performance, caused further delays before the Hunter could assume its rightful place as an excellent operational fighter. A second swept-wing design, the Supermarine Swift, also came into first-

Canberra bombers of 12 Sqn lined up at Hal Far airfield, Malta, in 1956, marked and loaded in preparation for the invasion of Egypt's Suez Canal zone.

English Electric Canberra B(I)F

Engines: Two–6500lb thrust Rolls-Royce Avon 101
Max Speed: 570mph at 40,000ft
518mph at sea-level
Range: 2660 miles (normal load)
Service Ceiling: 48,000ft
Armament: Bomb load (internal), 6000lb
Also AS30 air-ground missiles if needed
Weights: Loaded normal 40,500lb
Max. 46,000lb
Crew: Two

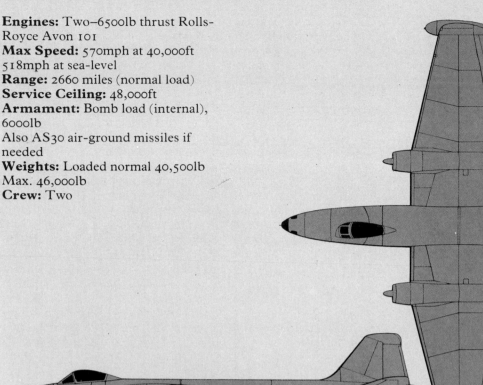

Avro Shackleton MR3

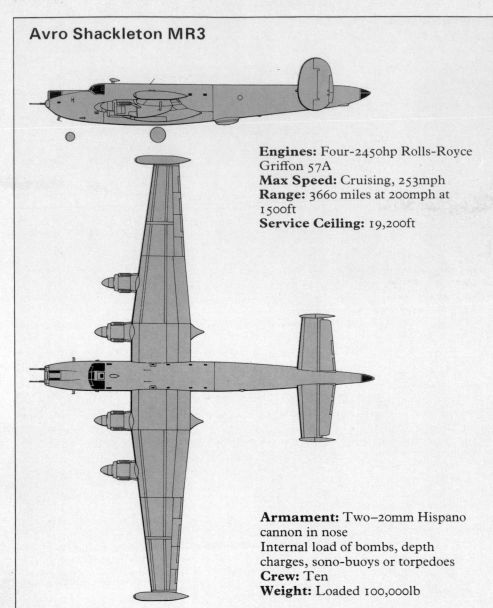

Engines: Four-2450hp Rolls-Royce Griffon 57A
Max Speed: Cruising, 253mph
Range: 3660 miles at 200mph at 1500ft
Service Ceiling: 19,200ft

Armament: Two–20mm Hispano cannon in nose
Internal load of bombs, depth charges, sono-buoys or torpedoes
Crew: Ten
Weight: Loaded 100,000lb

*Above: Result of a bombing sortie by a 27 Sqn Canberra against an Egyptian tank assembly plant at Huckstep, Nov 5, 1956, the 41st anniversary of its formation.
Below: A Handley Page Hastings on Malta during the Suez operations, 1956.*

line use in early 1954, but it soon proved to be inferior in its intended interceptor role and was quickly revamped as a low-level fighter-reconnaissance machine. While waiting for these new fighters, the RAF purchased a stop-gap design from America, the Sabre swept-wing jet. From 1953 to 1956, Sabres equipped a total of twelve squadrons. All but two of these were based in Germany. During this period a Whitehall edict removed all non-commissioned fighter pilots from the Sabre squadrons.

Still heavily committed to operations in the Malayan anti-Communist campaign, and strongly involved in western European defence schemes, the RAF was called upon for yet another operational ploy in 1954 – bombing the rebel Mau-Mau faction in Kenya. For this task several Lincoln bomber units were used to back up the tiny Kenyan air services. The increasing conversion to an all-jet RAF had been exemplified in the previous year when, at the Queen's Coronation Review at Odiham, 640 aircraft had performed a meticulous and highly impressive fly-past and review parade for the Sovereign. Two-thirds of the aircraft present were jet-engined. In January 1955 the RAF entered a fresh era. The first V-bomber, the sleek Vickers Valiant, came into service with Bomber Command. It was the first of three major V-designs. The second was the Avro Vulcan, and the third, Handley Page's Victor, was intended to convert RAF Bomber Command into an awesome deterrent force, capable of instant retaliation in depth against any would-be aggressor. Intended and designed to lift a nuclear or conventional war load, the Valiant remained the only V-bomber in service for two years before it was joined by the Vulcan and Victor in squadron service after the summer of 1957. In August 1955 another major move was the start of the first all-jet training programme using Jet Provost aircraft, in which future pilots commenced their flying instruction from the outset. In June 1956 Transport Command began its 'conversion' to jet age machines when four-jet Comet aircraft entered service with 216 Squadrons at Lyneham – the world's first jet transport squadron.

In the Far East the Malayan campaign still dragged on. A disproportionate effort in material and money was expended on bombing and strafing jungle areas suspected of harbouring terrorist forces. April 1955 saw the disbandment of 33 Squadron (Hornets), while in July two Sunderland units, 205 and 209 Squadrons, at Seletar, were merged into one unit. A third Sunderland squadron, 88, was disbanded the previous year. These moves were due simply to a diminishing ability to keep the Sunderlands serviceable with virtually no stock of replacement items. The Korean War had seen little RAF participation beyond the support role of certain AOP light aircraft, but Sunderlands had been involved to a small degree. They were based at Iwakuni and flew patrols over the adjacent seas. All Hornets still operating in the Far East were replaced in 1955. The only remaining unit, 45 Squadron, re-equipped with Vampire FB9s in May 1955, and then exchanged these for Venom FB1s in October. In June that year the first Malayan General Election took place, which resulted in the recently-formed Alliance Party gaining majority control. This party was based on multi-racial foundations and largely anti-Communist. From this point the terrorist campaign gradually eased in intensity. But in February 1955 101 Squadron, equipped with jet Canberra bombers, joined the Far East Air Force (FEAF) and, on February 23 flew the first jet bomber strike of the campaign. A further addition to FEAF's strength was the arrival of No. 14 Squadron, RNZAF in May 1955. It was equipped with Venom FB1s and was committed to a three-years' operational tour.

The year 1956 proved a fateful one for the RAF in many respects. On February 10 its virtual founder and chief advocate, Lord Trenchard, died at the age of 83. He was given a funeral in keeping with the huge debt owed to him by the nation, while, only six weeks before his death, Trenchard had achieved his personal ambition for the force he had nurtured and defended in its adolescent years when the new Chief of Air Staff, Dermot Boyle was appointed – an ex-cadet of Trenchard's Cranwell scheme. In May the first Avro Vulcan jet bombers joined the RAF at No. 230 OCU, Waddington.

English Electric Lightning F6

Engines: Two–12,690lb thrust Rolls-Royce Avon 301 (16,360lb thrust with re-heat)
Max Speed: 1500mph at 40,000ft (Mach 2.27)
Long-range cruising, 595mph
Range: 800 miles (with ventral tank)
Initial climb: 50,000ft/min. (Time to 40,000ft, $2\frac{1}{2}$ mins)

Service Ceiling: Over 60,000ft (details still restricted)
Weights: Empty 40,000lb; Loaded 50,000lb (approx)
Armament: Various air-air guided missiles (details restricted)

Top: Another delta-wing design was the Gloster Javelin all-weather interceptor. The first twin-jet delta fighter in the world, it entered RAF fighter service in Feb 1956 in small numbers, but eventually equipped 18 squadrons in England and overseas.
Above: Victor fuel tanker undertaking air-to-air refuelling of a pair of 29 Sqn Lightnings.
Left: Vulcans and Lightnings on a trial flight.

And on October 11 the first British atom bomb was dropped from a V-bomber, Vickers Valiant WZ366 of 49 Squadron, during trials at Maralinga, South Australia. Only weeks later the RAF was committed to war operations in the Mediterranean zone. The key to the whole crisis which erupted in October 1956 was the Suez Canal. Its protection had been placed in British hands in a series of agreements and treaties dating back to 1888. After World War II Egyptian anti-British feeling led to the overthrow of King Farouk and a transfer of power to the Egyptian Army, led in fact by Colonel Nasser. In 1954 Britain and Egypt signed a new agreement which permitted Britain to defend the Canal but provided for gradual withdrawal of all other British forces in the country. In the following year Nasser bought Russian arms from Czechoslovakia and the Western powers reacted swiftly by refusing financial assistance to Egypt for construction of the Aswan High Dam project. Nasser's instant reaction was to announce Egyptian nationalisation of the Suez Canal Company on July 26, 1956; 44 per cent of this company's holdings had been British-owned.

Acutely aware of the growing rearmament of Egypt and Syria, the British and French governments had already considered plans for landing troops in Egypt

Below: Venom FB4's of 5 Sqn start up at Wunstorf, Germany, on Oct 12, 1957 for their final flypast before the unit is disbanded.

to protect their joint interest in the Suez Canal. Israel was also seriously disturbed by the growing Arab rearmament programme. Attempts to improve the delicate political situation following Nasser's seizure of the Suez Canal Company met with little success. Nevertheless, while these negotiations were proceeding the French and British fleets put to sea, and troops were moved into Cyprus and Malta. In mid-September the first RAF units, including a Valiant squadron, arrived in Malta. By October the preparation plans were completed, and British forces awaited the final signal to proceed. Then Israel launched an attack on Egyptian positions east of the canal in the evening of October 29. Israel had no friend in Britain's government. Indeed, in that same month, Britain had declared that if her ally, Jordan, were attacked by Israel, British aircraft would bomb Israel.

As Israeli troops and aircraft blasted their way across the Sinai Peninsula and threatened Port Tewfik at the southern end of the Suez Canal, Britain and France issued a joint ultimatum to both Israel and Egypt on October 30. It stated unambiguously that unless both countries ceased all military activity and withdrew to positions at least ten miles either side of the canal, British and French forces would land and occupy all key positions along the canal. Israel, at that date

still east of the canal, agreed, but Egypt refused. This refusal sparked off the British-French intervention expedition. On October 30 the RAF had 18 bomber squadrons based on Malta and Cyprus as well as seven fighter squadrons and ten other units providing paratroop transport, photo-reconnaissance and maritime backing. In addition five aircraft carriers of the British Fleet carried 17 squadrons or air units of the Fleet Air Arm. The RAF's main objectives in the expeditionary plan were to destroy the Egyptian Air Force and other installations such as oil and fuel dumps or armament depots. The Allied ultimatum was rejected by Egypt in the early hours of October 31, but the first RAF strikes were not made until that evening when Canberras of 10 and 12 Squadrons, and Valiants of 148 Squadron – all from Malta bases – dropped 500lb and 1000lb conventional high explosive bombs on twelve Egyptian airfields along the length of the canal zone. These targets continued to be attacked on the two following nights. By day fighters from the RAF and Navy enlarged the strike offensive. Between November 1–6 these assaults destroyed at least 260 Egyptian aircraft on the ground and met no aircraft opposition, though several Allied aircraft suffered damage from anti-aircraft fire and other causes.

Early in the morning of November 5

some 750 British and French paratroops were dropped on key points around Port Said. The British contingent were conveyed and dropped by three Hastings squadrons and three Valetta squadrons from Cyprus. Their objective was Gamil airfield. The overall plan was to secure Port Said, then move southwards to secure the canal, and then west to Cairo. At dawn on November 6 a seaborne invasion force of infantry landed at Port Said and fought steadily through the town, covered constantly by (mainly) FAA strike aircraft attacking pockets of strong resistance in front of the Allied troops. During the afternoon a strong dash southwards brought Allied troops to El Kantara, but rumours were already spreading of a cease-fire order. Such an order came into effect at midnight – the result of widespread international pressure and opposition to the Anglo-French invasion as well as considerable opposition in Britain itself. The subsequent consequences and implications of halting the intended safeguarding of the Suez Canal have no place in this history, but several aspects of the Suez affair offered hard lessons to the British government in the context of air power. Not least was the obvious need to acquire independent control of nuclear deterrent capability. Such a need was accentuated when, at the peak of the invasion, Russia threatened to despatch atomic-

Centre: A Hunter tucks in tightly after leaving Wittering.
Bottom: Hawker Hunters of 20 Sqn, from Tengah, Singapore over local terrain.

Avro (HS) Vulcan B2

Engines: Four–20,000lb thrust Olympus 301
Max Speed: 645mph (estimated)
Range: 4600 miles, high altitude, without flight refuelling (max)
Service Ceiling: 55,000ft (approx)
All-up weight: 200,000lb (approx)
Armament: One *Blue Steel* rocket-propelled AS missile or, conventional HE bomb load internally. No defensive weaponry.

Left: Avro Vulcan of 617 Sqn, based at Scampton, in low-level camouflage livery.

XM572

head rockets onto London and Paris if the Allied forces completed their full occupation of Egypt as intended. Had any such threat been implemented, Britain was in no position to retaliate and could not depend on American goodwill to back any such retaliation. Other immediate lessons learned included the necessity for a strong, highly mobile air transport tactical force, able to switch ground troops to any area at the shortest possible notice – a policy adopted by the RAF in the following few years, when Transport Command was expanded. This led to the formation of No. 38 Group, comprised of transport units with their own fighter tactical support squadrons in January 1960. The Suez 'seven-day war' also emphasised the strategical importance to Britain of retaining Cyprus as a military platform, despite the subsequent years of internal unrest.

The build-up of the RAF as a V-Force for nuclear deterrent received a heavy blow on April 4, 1957, when the Defence White Paper of Duncan Sandys revised the whole future policy for the air defence of Britain. Advocating the demise of manned systems, it proposed 'collective defence' – a dependence on foreign aid in aerial offensive material, and a wider reliance on unmanned guided missiles as Britain's aerial defence. Fighter Command, hitherto with both offensive and defensive roles, was to be restricted simply to protection of the V-bomber bases. Such an overall policy of reliance on push-button warfare had an immediate depressing effect on normal RAF recruiting, and an almost equally depressing effect on morale among air crews. Extra energy was expended on

beefing up the RAF's strategic mobility, despite a background of British political decisions which would soon withdraw military presence from many overseas countries and territories. A year later, in February 1958, another White Paper announced the decision to purchase THOR intercontinental ballistic missiles (ICBMs) from America for Bomber Command; and in July the first Bloodhound surface-to-air missiles went into service with Fighter Command. The whole concept of massive nuclear retaliation – the so-termed 'Tripwire Strategy' – was finally abandoned officially in 1968. It left a legacy of an air force desperately low in pure combat, front-line machines and their necessary technical back-up materials, a legacy only now being overcome gradually, in the face of continuing financial cut-backs.

If the future seemed bleak to the air crews and airmen of the 1957–58 period, it did not affect their day-to-day application to their existing duties. The expanding V-bomber force continued seeking greater mobility and potential, flying several trans-global missions of endurance and thereby gaining experience in airborne refuelling to extend air range and striking power. New aircraft were being proposed, notably the announcement in December 1958 that a future replacement for the Canberra aircraft was to be developed – the TSR-2. In 1959 it was announced that a new strategic freight aircraft, the Britannic (later re-named Belfast), was on order. In June the same year Transport Command received its first example of the Bristol Britannia four-turboprop airliner/freighter. In October 1959 the first major overseas inter-Service com-

mand was established since World War II at British Forces Arabian Peninsula at Aden. In Malaya the prolonged anti-Communist war finally halted officially on July 31, 1960. From its beginning in 1948, Operation 'Firedog' had involved the RAF in a total of 375,849 sorties, flying an estimated $47\frac{1}{2}$ million miles on operations. Fresh blood was injected into Fighter Command the same year when 74 Squadron at Coltishall, Norfolk took delivery of its first English Electric Lightning interceptor. Bomber Command completed the setting up of its Thor ICBM force, and was promised early introduction of the Blue Steel and, later, Skybolt missiles. But the most significant change for the RAF that year came in December, when the Minister of Defence announced that, in accord with the United Kingdom becoming one of four NATO air defence regions, Fighter Command would now operate under the aegis of SACEUR – a decision implemented from May 1, 1961.

Though primarily concerned with defence matters in Europe, the RAF continued to uphold its long traditions of aid and mercy-flights in areas further afield. On July 1, 1961, in response to the request of the ruler of Kuwait, RAF Hunters, Canberras, and V-bombers were sent to the Middle East and mainly concentrated around the Persian Gulf. They proved to be an effective deterrent against the threat to Kuwait sovereignty. In October Operation 'Tana Flood' was quickly mounted in which RAF transport aircraft dropped food and supplies to Africans in Kenya cut off by widespread floods; an operation extended over four months to include similar mercy flights in Somaliland. In November fur-

Below: Avro Shackleton MR3 of 201 Sqn in 1970. The first Shackleton versions joined RAF Coastal Command in 1951 and was originally designed as a development of the Avro Lincoln.

ther help was given to citizens of British Honduras who had suffered from the devastation of a hurricane.

By early 1962 the false philosophies of the 1957 Defence White Paper had been realised, and in February the annual air estimates included a restatement of the overall up-dated responsibilities for the RAF. Emphasis was made on the 'essential need' for manned aircraft in the immediate future, and the need for long-range striking power against submarines and surface vessels was given equal prominance. The statement committed the RAF to much of its former role in support of land forces, air defence of Britain, strategic air mobility, and the major element in nuclear and conventional striking power. In December that year the situation in South-East Asia brought the RAF into action in its tactical ground support role, when helicopters and fighters were involved in quelling a revolt in Brunei, operations which continued until the spring of 1963. Shortly thereafter Indonesia began its 'confrontation' with Singapore and Malaysia, involving the RAF in further extensive operations which were protracted until August 1966.

The greatest change in control of the RAF came when, on April 1, 1964, the Ministry of Defence was created. From this date the RAF, instead of being administered by its own ministry, came under the Air Force Department of the Ministry of Defence. The former Air Council now became the Air Force Board; and the Secretary of State for Air was relabelled the Minister of Defence for the RAF. A more immediate impact on the rank and file of the RAF occurred on March 1, 1964. With effect from that

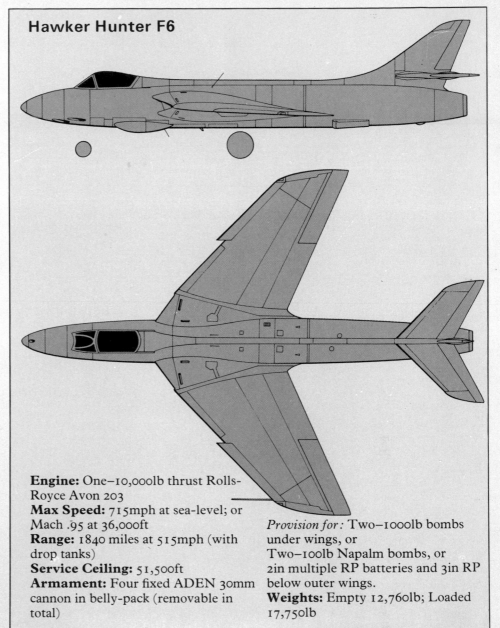

Hawker Hunter F6

Engine: One–10,000lb thrust Rolls-Royce Avon 203
Max Speed: 715mph at sea-level; or Mach .95 at 36,000ft
Range: 1840 miles at 515mph (with drop tanks)
Service Ceiling: 51,500ft
Armament: Four fixed ADEN 30mm cannon in belly-pack (removable in total)

Provision for: Two–1000lb bombs under wings, or
Two–100lb Napalm bombs, or
2in multiple RP batteries and 3in RP below outer wings.
Weights: Empty 12,760lb; Loaded 17,750lb

date all aircraft servicing maintenance within the RAF was transferred to a new Centralised Servicing reorganisation. Ostensibly for purposes of cost-effectiveness and overall smoother provisioning and production, the practical result was to remove all former ground crews from the squadrons and place them in a conglomerate station establishment. It meant an abrupt end to a long tradition of intimate co-operation, loyalty, and relationship between the air and ground crews. The 'family' atmosphere which had prevailed so successfully for some 50 years in Britain's flying services ceased. Thus, on the pretext of 'efficiency', and under the tag of 'progress', a general feeling of objectivity soon crept into the general attitude of technical tradesmen to the crews and, particularly, aircraft. It had no effect on technical standards, but no longer could the fitters and mechanics speak of 'our' aircraft, or 'my' crew. The former positive identification was gone. Whatever sound reasons and supporting statistics might have been propounded by the instigators of this latest change, they entirely overlooked the effect such a bureaucratic innovation might (indeed, *did* . . .) have on morale at hangar floor and crew room level – yet another example of the side effects of long-distance administration far removed from the realities of operational life in the RAF's 'sharp end'.

If the vast organisational changes of 1964 created misgivings within RAF circles, the following year proved to be near-traumatic. On February 2, 1965 the Prime Minster announced the cancellation of the P.1154 V/STOL supersonic interceptor and HS 681 V/STOL transport projects in favour of alternative American Phantom and Hercules aircraft respectively, while on April 6 the Budget Speech included notification that the TSR–2 project was also to be cancelled. The aircraft only made its first

Top: The C-120 Hercules.
Left: McDonnell Douglas Phantom of 6 Sqn – a 'weapons system' with more than Mach 2 capability.
Opposite bottom: SEPECAT Jaguar tactical strike fighter of 54 Sqn.
Below left: Global mobility for the RAF was well provided in the 1960s by the Lockheed C-130K Hercules C1 (l) and the BAC VC10.
Below: A pair of Wittering's Hunters in loose Vic formation ('Finger Four') with two Hawker-Siddeley Harrier VTOL fighters.

flight on the previous September 28. These were the first steps in a decade of financial cut-backs, shifting policies, and sweeping changes in administrative organisation for the RAF. In January 1966 the gradual move of the RAF's Technical College at Henlow to combine with the RAF College at Cranwell was completed. The Airfield Construction Branch was disbanded. And, for reasons best known to Whitehall, the Technical Branch of the RAF became retitled as the Engineering Branch. Abroad, various RAF stations and units were slowly being cut down. In October Gibraltar was stripped of its aircraft resident squadron and reduced to the status of a staging post. Such changes were followed by the February 1967 Defence White Paper announcing the proposed merging of Bomber and Fighter Commands into a single Strike Command by April 1968. In the latter half of 1967 RAF families and eventually all personnel and aircraft were withdrawn from Aden – scene of several years of operational effort against Yemeni-threatened intrusion and, latterly, local unrest and no little terrorist activity against the British presence.

Below: Hawker Siddeley Nimrod four fan jet long-range patrol and maritime reconnaissance aircraft. It replaced the Shackletons which had given the RAF more than 20 years of exceptionally reliable service.

The moves towards general reduction in material and geographical location were reflected in personnel. In July 1967 a redundancy scheme for long-serving ground tradesmen – mostly in the senior NCO and warrant officer brackets – offered generous terms and an immediate release from the service, known to the more senior recipients as the 'Copper Handshake'. The response among many disillusioned airmen was greater than the Air Ministry had perhaps anticipated. Six months later further evidence of sweeping defence cuts came when a previous order for 50 American F–111Ks (swing-wing fighters) was cancelled. The diminution of manning accelerated. At the same moment the intention to withdraw from the Far East and Persian Gulf was announced for completion by December 1971. At the end of April 1968 Bomber and Fighter Command lost their separate identities and were merged into Strike Command. And on June 1 the formerly separate Flying Training and Technical Training Command were also amalgamated to become the single Training Command. In this, the 50th Anniversary year of the RAF's original formation, it seemed ironic that it should be suffering such reductions in men and material – and, indeed, in long-held traditions. By the end of 1968, though theoretically possessing some 2000 aircraft, the service manning was little more than 120,000 (all ranks).

If the service was numerically small, its quality remained high in both men and material. The V-bomber force, operationally experienced and now with a Blue Steel missile capability, stood ready for instant action. Lightning fighters carried Firestreak or Red Top air-air missiles for long-range interception. Coastal Command, though still soldiering on with new marks of the ageing Shackleton, was on the verge of receiving the vastly better Hawker Siddeley Nimrod jet 'hunter'. In Training Command all-through jet instruction was now established. Air Support Command (the latest title for the former Transport Command) ranged the globe in Comets and Britannias, but was soon to include fourteen four-jet VC10s and ten Belfast turbo-prop freighters. Under its aegis, the command's tactical 38 Group had new Andover and Hercules transports, plus Argosies, and Wessex helicopters. The Group's fighter squadrons, still equipped with Hunters, were due to replace these with Phantoms, V/STOL Harrier (P.1127) fighters, and Jaguars. Even the more mundane facets of RAF life were catered for by the introduction in February 1969 of the world's most technically advanced computer at RAF Innsworth to deal with personnel records of the service. During 1969 the first Phantom FGR Mk 2 and FG Mk 1 squadrons – 6 and 43 respectively – were formed. And on October 1 the first RAF Harrier squadron (No. 1) and first Buc-

caneer squadron (No. 12) were officially formed. In November the command merger scheme was completed when Coastal merged into Strike Command, leaving the RAF organised into just four commands – Strike, Air Support, Training, and Maintenance. In the following month the RAF Staff College at Andover, after 47 years, amalgamated with the Staff College at Bracknell.

The RAF entered the 1970s with an increasing commitment of involvement in Europe, meeting this responsibility by an expansion of its strength based in West Germany. Primarily concerned with providing tactical reconnaissance and interception roles, this increase in strength was concerned with fighter aircraft in the widest sense. The first Harrier unit in Germany, 4 Squadron, formed at Wildenrath on June 1, 1970, followed a month later by the first Phantom FGR2 unit, 14 Squadron, at Bruggen. At Honington, Suffolk 15 Squadron became the RAF's first Buccaneer unit, destined for Germany in 1971. The October Defence White Paper announced an order for four additional SEPECAT Jaguar attack squadrons to be sent to Germany in the reasonably near future. Further Phantom and Harrier units were soon to follow.

What appeared to be an annual 'routine' in retitling RAF formations continued to be evident in the early 1970s. On September 1, 1972 Air Support Command merged into Strike Com-

mand, thereby completing the creation of a single UK-based operational Strike Command. A year later Maintenance Command was again re-labelled, as Support Command. The continuing process of 'streamlining' the service – a euphemism for simple reduction in quantity and financial backing – was a steady drain. Its extent might be judged by comparison of pure aircraft strengths over two decades. In July 1952 the RAF reached its post-World War II peak with a total of 6338 aircraft of every type on charge. By 1967 the official figure released was 2004. In 1973 the RAF could only acknowledge a total of little more than 500 aircraft. Its present (1977) figure is necessarily a matter cloaked in secrecy, but with the continuing trend of making defence services a prime target for cuts in government spending it can hardly be large. Though the RAF has always been guided by Hugh Trenchard's original theme of 'quality before quantity', it cannot be denied that once having achieved qualitative standard, quantity is of high priority.

Today the Royal Air Force continues to represent Britain's foremost defence and its offensive spearhead. The maxim 'he who controls the air, controls' remains as true now as it was during the past 60-odd years of military aviation. Methods and means may have changed. The principal truth is unaltered. Of the service itself, the 'ironmongery' has

Above: HRH the Prince of Wales tries his hand as pilot of a Queen's Flight Westland Wessex 'chopper'. In the family tradition of his grandfather, King George VI, Prince Charles is a qualified pilot.

changed out of all comparison with the fragile wood, linen, and wire machines flown by the RAF's founder-members in 1918, but the quality and spirit of the modern airman is not a jot less than his hardy predecessors. Both in the air and on the ground, the present Royal Air Force is a highly skilled, technically professional force, manned by men of necessarily high intelligence, trained to a peak of expert proficiency. Yet despite the modern era of computerised airborne technology, the essential nature of today's airman differs little from that of his father's and grandfather's air generations. The regular airman of yesteryear would find remarkably little change in the 'atmosphere' of a 1977 crew room or Mess ante-room. The slender but unbreakable chain of unwritten RAF traditions provides a tangible link between the leather-clad pilot of a 1918 Sopwith Camel and the pressure-suited 'driver' of a 1977 Mach 1 SEPECAT Jaguar. The classic words of Walter Raleigh in 1922 remain as true today; 'The Royal Air Force is strong in the kind of virtue that propagates itself and attains to a life beyond a life. The tradition is safe.'

'*The Royal Air Force is strong in the kind of virtue that propagates itself and attains to a life beyond a life. The tradition is safe.*'

Appendices

Appendix 1: Aircraft Technical Data

Aeroplane	Engines Number	HP	Manufacturer and model	Max Speed	Endurance/Range	Service Ceiling
Bristol F2b	One	280hp	Rolls-Royce Falcon III	125mph at sea level 108mph at 13,000ft	3hrs	20,000ft
Sopwith F.1 Camel	One	130hp 110hp	Clerget rotary, or Le Rhone rotary	105mph at 10,000ft	2½hrs	18,500ft
Hawker Fury 1	One	525hp	Rolls-Royce Kestrel IIs	207mph at 14,000ft	305 miles	28,000ft
Westland Wapiti IIa	One	550hp	Bristol Jupiter VIII	135mph at 5000ft	360 miles	20,600ft
Fairey Swordfish	One	750hp	Bristol Pegasus XXX	139mph at 4750ft Cruising: 104-129mph at 5000ft	Normal load: 546 miles	10,700ft
Short Sunderland GR5	Four	1200hp	Pratt & Whitney Twin Wasp R-1830	213mph at 5000ft	13½hrs 2980 miles at 134mph	17,900ft
De Havilland Mosquito FB VI	Two	1230hp	Rolls-Royce Merlin XXI	380mph at 13,000ft	1205 miles (1705 with extra tanks)	36,000ft
Avro Lancaster B1	Four	1460hp	Rolls-Royce Merlin 20 or 22	275mph at 15,000ft (fully loaded) Cruising: 200mph at 15,000ft 245mph at sea level	2530 miles (7000lb load) 1730 miles (12,000lb load) 1550 miles (22,000lb load)	19,000ft
Supermarine Spitfire 1XE	One	1710hp	Rolls-Royce Merlin 63 or 63a	408mph at 25,000ft	980 miles (max)	44,000ft
Hawker Hunter F6	One	10,000lb thrust	Rolls-Royce Avon 203	715mph at sea level or Mach .95 at 36,000ft	1840 miles at 515mph (with drop tanks)	51,500ft
English Electric Canberra B(1)F	Two	6500lb thrust	Rolls-Royce Avon 101	570mph at 40,000ft 518mph at sea-level	2660 miles (normal load)	48,000ft
Avro Shackleton MR3	Four	2450hp	Rolls-Royce Griffon 57A	Cruising: 253mph	3660 miles at 200mph at 1500ft	19,200ft
English Electric Lightning F6	Two	12,600lb thrust (16,360lb thrust with re-heat)	Rolls-Royce Avon 301	1500mph at 40,000ft (Mach 2.27) Long-range cruising: 595mph	800 miles (with ventral tank) Initial climb: 50,000ft/min (Time to 40,000ft, 2½mins)	Over 60,000f (details still restricted)
Avro (HS) Vulcan B2	Four	20,000lb thrust	Olympus 301	645mph (estimated)	4600 miles, high altitude, without flight refuelling (max)	55,000ft (approx)

Armament	Weights Empty	Loaded	Page (illust.)
One fixed .303 Vickers mg forward One Scarff Ring-mounted .303 Lewis mg rear (often two) Two 112lb bombs under wings	1745lb	2590lb	10
Two fixed, synchronised .303 Vickers mg forward Could be fitted with four 25lb Hales bombs under fuselage	962lb	1482lb	10
Two fixed, synchronised .303 Vickers mg	2623lb	3490lb	10
Bomb load: 500lb under wings and fuselage One fixed .303 Vickers mg forward One Scarff Ring-mounted .303 Lewis mg rear	3180lb	5400lb	55
One fixed Vickers .303 mg forward One ring-mounted .303 mg rear (Lewis or Vickers G.O.) One 18in, 1610lb torpedo or one 1500lb mine, or, Two 500lb & two 250lb bombs or eight 60lb Rocket Projectiles	5200lb (Land plane versions)	9250lb	45
Bomb load: 2000lbs Four .303 Browning mg in each of nose and tail turrets Two .303 or .50 mg hand-operated beam. Some 1944-45 versions had additional 4 × .303 (or .50) mg mounted alongside forward fuselage	37,000lb	60,000lb	144
Bomb load: 1000lbs in bomb bay. Four to eight 3in RP under wings Four 20mm Hispano cannon forward belly Four .303 Browning mg in nose	14,300lb	22,300lb	104
Bomb load: 8000lbs (initially). Up to 22,000lbs (special modified version) FN5 nose turret with two .303 mg NF50 mid-upper turret with two .303 mg FN20 tail turret with four .303 mg FN64 ventral turret with one .303 mg (early models only) (above was standard on introduction; later, nose turrets were often deleted and faired over, ventral turrets removed, newer-type mid-upper turrets installed – some having twin .50 mg)	Tare 37,000lb	All-up 65,000lb	120
Two 20mm Hispano cannon Two .50 Browning mg	–	7500lb	101
Four fixed ADEN 30mm cannon in belly-pack (removable in total) Provision for: Two 1000lb bombs under wings, or Two 100lb Napalm bombs, or 2in multiple RP batteries & 3in RP below outer wings	12,760lb	17,750lb	209
Bomb load: (internal) 6000lb AS30 air-ground missiles if needed	–	40,500lb normal 46,000lb max	199
Two 20mm Hispano cannon in nose Internal load of bombs, depth charges, sono-buoys or torpedoes	–	100,000lb	200
Various air-air guided missiles (details restricted)	40,000lb	50,000lb (approx)	202
One Blue Steel rocket-propelled AS missile or, conventional HE bomb load internally. No defensive weaponry	–	All-up weight 200,000lb (approx)	207

Appendix 2

The following table lists every man ever awarded a Victoria Cross for aerial operations. Strictly speaking, not all belonged to the Royal Air Force – a fact which has, in the past, led to various forms of inter-Service bureaucratic squabbling in the pursuit of vicarious honours. The complete list is presented here simply to record a full gallery of the 51 men who earned their supreme award in the air. The table is in chronological order of dates for the individual action concerned; or, where the award was made for consistent gallantry over a period, by date of the first announcement in the *London Gazette*. Ranks are contemporary at those dates.

Lieutenant William Barnard Rhodes Moorhouse, RFC, 26 April 1915
Flight Sub-Lieutenant Reginald Alexander Warneford, RNAS, 7 June 1915
Captain Lanoe George Hawker, DSO, RE att'd RFC, 25 July 1915
Captain John Aidan Liddell, MC, RFC, 31 July 1915
Second Lieutenant Gilbert Stuart Martin Insall, RFC, 7 November 1915
Squadron Commander Richard Bell-Davies, DSO, RNAS, 19 November 1915
Major Lionel Brabazon Wilmot Rees, MC, RFC, 1 July 1916
Lieutenant William Leefe Robinson, RFC, 3 September 1916
Flight Sergeant Thomas Mottershead, DCM, RFC, 7 January 1917
Lieutenant Frank Hubert McNamara, RFC, 20 March 1917
Captain William Avery Bishop, DSO, MC, RFC, 2 June 1917
Captain Albert Ball, DSO, MC, RFC, 8 June 1917**
Second Lieutenant Alan Arnett McLeod, RFC, 27 March 1918
Lieutenant Alan Jerrard, RFC, 30 March 1918
Captain James Thomas Byford McCudden, DSO, MC, MM, RAF, 2 April 1918**
Captain Ferdinand Maurice Felix West, MC, RAF, 10 August 1918
Major William George Barker, DSO, MC, RAF, 27 October 1918
Captain Andrew Weatherby Beauchamp Proctor, DSO, MC, DFC, RAF, 30 November 1918**
Major Edward Mannock, DSO, MC, RAF, 18 July 1919**
Flying Officer Donald Edward Garland, RAF, 12 May 1940
Sergeant Thomas Gray, RAF, 12 May 1940
Flight Lieutenant Roderick Alastair Brook Learoyd, RAF, 12 August 1940

Flight Lieutenant James Brindley Nicolson, RAF, 16 August 1940
Sergeant John Hannah, RAF, 15 September 1940
Flying Officer Kenneth Campbell, RAF, 6 April 1941
Squadron Leader Hughie Idwal Edwards, DFC, RAF, 4 July 1941
Sergeant James Allen Ward, RNZAF, 7 July 1941
Squadron Leader Arthur Stewart King Scarf, RAF, 9 December 1941
Lieutenant-Commander Eugene Kingsmill Esmonde, DSO, RN, 12 February 1942
Squadron Leader John Dering Nettleton, RAF, 17 April 1942
Flying Officer Leslie Thomas Manser, RAF, 31 May 1942
Pilot Officer Rawdon Hume Middleton, RAAF, 29 November 1942
Wing Commander Hugh Gordon Malcolm, DFC, RAF, 4 December 1942
Flight Lieutenant William Ellis Newton, RAAF, 16 March 1943
Squadron Leader Leonard Henry Trent, DFC, RAF, 3 May 1943
Wing Commander Guy Penrose Gibson, DSO, DFC, RAF, 17 May 1943
Flying Officer Lloyd Allan Trigg, DFC, RNZAF, 11 August 1943
Flight Sergeant Arthur Louis Aaron, DFM, RAF, 13 August 1943
Flight Lieutenant William Reid, RAF, 4 November 1943
Pilot Officer Cyril Joe Barton, RAF, 30 March 1944
Sergeant Norman Cyril Jackson, RAF, 26 April 1944
Pilot Officer Andrew Charles Mynarski, RCAF, 13 June 1944
Flight Lieutenant David Ernest Hornell, RCAF, 24 June 1944
Flying Officer John Alexander Cruickshank, RAF, 17 July 1944
Squadron Leader Ian Willoughby Bazalgette, DFC, RAF, 4 August 1944
Wing Commander Geoffrey Leonard Cheshire, DSO, DFC, RAF, 8 September 1944**
Flight Lieutenant David Samuel Anthony Lord, DFC, RAF, 19 September 1944
Squadron Leader Robert Anthony Maurice Palmer, DFC, RAF, 23 December 1944
Flight Sergeant George Thompson, RAF, 1 January 1945
Captain Edwin Swales, DFC, SAAF, 24 February 1945
Lieutenant Robert Hampton Gray, DSC, RCNVR, 9 August 1945

NB: ** refers to *London Gazette* announcement date.

Appendix 4: Abbreviations used in History of the RAF

RAF Rank abbreviations
AC2 Aircraftman Second Class
AC1 Aircraftman First Class
LAC Leading Aircraftman
CPL Corporal
SGT Sergeant
F. SGT Flight Sergeant
W.O. Warrant Officer
PLT OFF Pilot Officer

FG OFF Flying Officer
FLT LT Flight Lieutenant
SQN LDR Squadron Leader
WG CDR Wing Commander
GP CAPT Group Captain
A. CDRE Air Commodore
AVM Air Vice-Marshal
AM Air Marshal
ACM Air Chief Marshal

MRAF Marshal of the Royal Air Force

RAF 'Status' abbreviations
SNCO Senior Non-Commissioned Officer
OC Officer Commanding
CO Commanding Officer
AOC Air Officer Commanding

Appendix 3

No single volume can hope to provide a succinct, all-embracing account of 60 years of constant change and operational efforts; to tabulate every book ever published touching on the subject of RAF history would require a separate, very thick tome. Nevertheless, the following select titles are commended to the discerning student who requires a deeper study of the service, its origins, actions, and personnel. It should be apparent that these comprise a personal selection by the author. Many are learned diatribes; some are biographies by, or of, significant figures in RAF history; others are first-hand accounts by individuals exemplifying events, people and contemporary attitudes. Collectively they offer not only reliable historical facts but some insight into the very spirit of the RAF – a spirit which grew rapidly into a solid foundation for the tradition of service loyalty felt by those many airmen to whom the RAF is a vocation and not merely a paid career. One essential ingredient of that tradition is the esoteric form of Service humour peculiar to the RAF, hence the inclusion of *RAF Slang* and *The Airman's Songbook*. The British Serviceman has always retained two unalienable 'rights': to grumble (without malice) at any facet of Service life; and to treat the most serious aspects of life, love – and death – with his own brand of fatalistic humour.

1912-18

History of British Military Aeronautics, P W L Broke-Smith; Cedric Chivers, 1968
War in the Air, Vols 1–6, Maps & Appendices, W Raleigh & H A Jones; Oxford Press, 1922–37
Air Publication 125, 2nd Edition, HMSO, 1936
Birth of the Royal Air Force, J A Chamier; Pitman, 1943
The Third Service, Sir P Joubert; Thames & Hudson, 1955
The Air Weapon, C F Snowden-Gamble; Oxford Press, 1930
Story of a North Sea Air Station, C F Snowden-Gamble; Oxford Press, 1928
Five Years in the Royal Flying Corps, J T B McCudden, VC; Aeroplane Press, 1918
The Clouds Remember, L Bridgman & O Stewart; Gale & Polden, 1936
Trenchard, A Boyle; Collins, 1962
Sagittarius Rising, C Lewis; Peter Davies, 1936
Per Ardua, H St G Saunders; Oxford Press, 1944
Recollections of an Airman, L A Strange; J Hamilton, 1933

1918-39

First in the Field, A E Cowton; Mrs D Cowton, 1963
Pilot's Summer, F Tredrey; Duckworth, 1939
Flying Years, C H Keith; J Hamilton, 1937
The Baghdad Air Mail, R Hill; E Arnold, 1929
Flying and Soldiering, R R Money; Nicholson & Watson, 1936
To the ends of the air, G E Livock; HMSO, 1973
Stand Easy, B J Hurren; J Long, 1934
Empire of the Air, Viscount Templewood; Collins, 1957
Flying between the wars, A Wheeler; G T Foulis, 1973
History of Air Ministry, C G Grey; Allen & Unwin, 1940
CFS, J W R Taylor; Putnam, 1958
Squadrons of the RAF, FLIGHT Publishing; 1935
The RAF Year Book, 1938, L Bridgman; C G Burge, 1938
I Hold my Aim, C H Keith; G Allen & Unwin, 1946
The Mint, 'AC Ross' (T E Lawrence); Jonathan Cape, 1955

1939-45

Royal Air Force, 1939–45, Vols 1–3, D Richards & H St G Saunders; HMSO, 1952–54
Strategic Air Offensive against Germany, 3 Vols, Apps, Sir C Webster & N Frankland; HMSO, 1961
Defence of the United Kingdom, B Collier; HMSO, 1957
Wings of the Phoenix, HMSO, 1949
Bomber Offensive, A T Harris; Collins, 1947
Fighter Command, P Wykeham; Putnam, 1960
The Narrow Margin, D Wood & D Dempster; Hutchinson, 1961
Penguin in the Eyrie, H Bolitho; Hutchinson, 1955
The Desert Air Force, R Owen; Hutchinson, 1948
One Man's Window, D Barnham; William Kimber, 1956
Task for Coastal Command, H Bolitho; Hutchinson, 1945
Forgotten Skies, W W Russell; Hutchinson, 1946
Jungle Pilot, B Sutton; Macmillan, 1946
Enemy Coast Ahead, G P Gibson, VC; Michael Joseph, 1946
The Nuremburg Raid, M Middlebrook; Allen Lane, 1973
The Central Blue, J Slessor; Cassell, 1956
Winged Words, Heinemann, 1941
Slipstream, R Raymond & D Langdon; Eyre & Spottiswoode, 1946
The Forgotten Ones, P Joubert; Hutchinson, 1961
Airman's Songbook, C H Ward-Jackson; Sylvan Press, 1945
Dictionary of RAF Slang, E Partridge; Michael Joseph, 1945
Pathfinders, W Anderson; Jarrolds, 1946
RAF Biggin Hill, G Wallace; Putnam, 1957
Birds and Fishes, P Joubert; Hutchinson, 1960
Wings over Olympus, T Wisdom; G Allen & Unwin, 1942
Briefed to Attack, H P Lloyd; Hodder & Stoughton, 1949
2nd Tactical Air Force, C F Shores; Osprey, 1970
Fighter Pilot, P Richey; Batsford, 1941

AOC-in-C Air Officer Commanding-in-Chief
CAS Chief of the Air Staff

Misc abbreviations used
AASF Advanced Air Striking Force
ADGB Air Defence of Great Britain
A.I. Airborne Interception (radar)
ASV Air-to-Surface Vessel (radar)

CFS Central Flying School
GOC General Officer Commanding (Army)
FAA Fleet Air Arm
HE High Explosive
GP and MC (bombs) General Purpose, and Medium Capacity
RAAF Royal Australian Air Force
RE Royal Engineers

RNZAF Royal New Zealand Air Force
RCAF Royal Canadian Air Force
SAAF South African Air Force
SEAC South-East Asia Command
U-Boat *Unterseeboat* (German) – submarine
USAAF United States Army Air Force
VLR Very Long Range
WDAF Western Desert Air Force

Index

Acknowledgements

The author would like to thank the following people who helped him produce this History of the RAF: Mike Badrocke, who is responsible for the technical drawings and cutaway illustrations; Richard Natkiel, who produced the maps; and David Eldred, who designed this book.

Author's Collection 8–9; 13 top; 16–17; 19; 20–21; 22–23; 24 bottom; 24–25; 28 centre; 29; 30–31; 34 centre; 36 top; 37; 38–39; 39 top; 44 bottom right; 44 bottom left; 44 centre; 46–47; 47 right; 50–51; 51 right; 54; 55 bottom; 57; 59 top; 64–65; 70; 71; 72–73; 81; 84 right; 84 left; 84 bottom; 88; 88–89; 89 right; 89 left; 90 right; 91 right; 92; 92 bottom; 92–93; 95; 97; 98; 98–99; 109; 117; 118; 119; 119 left; 122 top; 125; 127; 132 top right; 140 top; 141 top; 150–151; 153; 154; 157; 160; 161; 165; 175 bottom; 180–181; 183; 188–189; 189; 190–191; 200–201
Imperial War Museum 11 top; 72–73 bottom; 74 centre; 76–77; 77; 78; 80; 80–81; 83 right; 83 left; 86; 90 left; 90–91; 91 left; 94–95; 94–95 bottom; 101; 103; 106–107; 108; 111; 114–115; 120; 121; 122 right; 126; 126–127; 130–131; 132; 136–137; 138–139; 146; 146–147; 153 top; 156; 158; 160–161; 162–163; 166; 167; 167 top; 168–169; 176; 176–177; 178–179; 181; 182–183; 187
Ministry of Defence (Air) 4–5; 14–15; 26 top; 28 bottom; 40; 44 top right; 47 left; 48–49; 49; 49 bottom; 52; 53; 59; 63 top; 65; 66–67; 87; 96 left; 172–173 top; 192 top; 192–193; 194 top; 195; 196; 197

Courtesy XV Squadron RAF 120 top; 132 top left; 192
Late Sir A. Longmore 13 centre right; 22
G. S. Leslie/J. M. Bruce Collection 15; 39 centre
CFS, RAF 17; 18–19
Late Air Cdre A. W. Bigsworth 23 top; 25
Vickers Aviation Ltd 24 top; 47 top
Sqn. Ldr. J. A. Shaw 27; 28 top
Courtesy 27 Squadron RAF 26 centre; 200
Short Brothers & Harland Ltd. 34 top; 56–57
P. Rosie 42 top left; 42–43
C. A. Sims 50: 52–53; bottom
AELR Brussels 74 top right; 78–79
RAAF 101 bottom; 156–157
Graphic Photo Union 102–103; 108–109
Illustrated 110; 149 top
Sqn. Ldr. H. Lees 128; 130 top
via Wg. Cdr. F. E. F. Prince 23 centre left
Lt. Col. T. M. Hawker 24 centre
I. P. R. Napier 36–37 bottom
Courtesy RAF Finningley 31 top;
Courtesy RAF Wyton 32–33;
Wg. Cdr. E. D. Crundall 34–35;
Mrs F. Thornhill 36–37 centre;
via C. C. H. Cole 36 centre
Wg. Cdr. G. H. Lewis 36–37 top;
via Flt. Lt. C. G. Jefford 42 top centre;
via K. M. Molson 41 centre;
via N. L. R. Franks 40–41;

British Official 74–75; 96 right; 98–99 top; 113; 118–119; 139; 141; 143; 152–153; 154 left; 163; 185
R. J. Wilson 6–7; 202; 202–203; 206; 206–207; 207; 210; 210–211; 211 top; 211 bottom right; 211 bottom left; 214–215
Public Archives of Canada 44 bottom; 93 left; 116–117; 142; 144–145; 159 top; 177; 179
Photo News Agencies 82 left; 96 bottom; 106–107 top; 107; 154–155; 164 top
Robert Hunt Library 8; 11 bottom; 80 top; 101 left; 112–113; 123; 124; 124–125
Bippa 81 top; 134–135; 149; 164; 170–171, Front jacket
Grp. Capt. G. I. Carmichael 12–13; 15; 20 top; 21
Courtesy 201 Squadron RAF 32; 137; 151; 208–209
Flight International: 13 centre left; 62–63; 67
Sqn. Ldr. C. P. O. Bartlett 26–27; 28; 31 centre
31 Squadron Association 51 left; 52–53; 182
Courtesy 12 Squadron RAF 63; 74 top left; 198–199
Grp. Capt. C. F. Gray 86–87; 114 left; 170
Planet News Ltd. 100; 116; 162
Central Press 114; 130; 140

via W. O. Duncan 41 top;
Handley Page Ltd. 41 centre right;
Sopwith Aviation Co. 44 top left;
I. Allan 55 right;
Westland Aircraft Ltd. 54 bottom;
A. J. Carew 58;
Boulton Paul Ltd. 61;
Bristol Co. 60;
Late Sqn. Ldr. A. S. K. Scarf, VC 68–69;
Fairey Aviation Co. 69;
Dr. D. L. Gleed 70 top;
M. Ross 82 right;
R. F. Watson 82–83;
Charles E. Brown 86–87 bottom;
Sqn. Ldr. P. G. Leggett 93 right;
Associated Press 106;
RNZAF 111 top;
Sport & General 116;
B. A. Winston 125 left;
V. Auborg 132 bottom left;
D. Marrow 142–143;
N. Carr 148;
Courtesy 80 Squadron RAF 159;
Courtesy 6 Squadron RAF 170 top;
Sqn. Ldr. L. Davies 172–173;
via B. Robertson 174–175;
D. A. F. Jackson 175 top;
A. Pearcy, Jr. 180;
Courtesy 45 Squadron RAF 194;
Flt. Lt. R. A. Brown 195 top;
K. Munson 203 top; back jacket;
Courtesy 5 Squadron RAF 204–205;
Courtesy RAF Gutersloh 213;
Orbis Publishing Ltd. 2–3;